This Book Comes With a Website

Nolo's award-winning website has a page dedicated just to this book, where you can:

KEEP UP TO DATE – When there are important changes to the information in this book, we'll post updates

READ BLOGS – Get the latest info from Nolo authors' blogs

LISTEN TO PODCASTS – Listen to authors discuss timely issues on topics that interest you

WATCH VIDEOS – Get a quick introduction to a legal topic with our short videos

You'll find the link in the introduction.

And that's not all. Nolo.com contains thousands of articles on everyday legal and business issues, plus a plain-English law dictionary, all written by Nolo experts and available for free. You'll also find more useful **books, software, online services,** and **downloadable forms.**

7th Edition

Every Dog's Legal Guide

A Must-Have Book for Your Owner

Mary Randolph, J.D.

NOLO
LAW for ALL

SEVENTH EDITION	JANUARY 2013
Cover Design	SUSAN PUTNEY
Book Design	TERRI HEARSH
Proofreading	ROBERT WELLS
Index	SONGBIRD INDEXING
Printing	BANG PRINTING

Randolph, Mary.
  Every dog's legal guide : a must-have book for your owner / by Mary Randolph. --
7th ed.
     p. cm.
  Includes index.
  ISBN 978-1-4133-1821-0 (pbk) ISBN 978-1-4133-1822-7 (epub ebook)
  1. Dogs--Law and legislation--United States--Popular works. 2. Dog owners--Legal
status, laws, etc.--United States--Popular works. I. Title.
  KF390.5.D6R36 2012
  346.7304'7--dc23
                         2012028764

This book covers only United States law, unless it specifically states otherwise.

Please note

We believe accurate, plain-English legal information should help you solve many
of your own legal problems. But this text is not a substitute for personalized
advice from a knowledgeable lawyer. If you want the help of a trained
professional—and we'll always point out situations in which we think that's a
good idea—consult an attorney licensed to practice in your state.

Acknowledgments

I owe the idea for this book to my friend Steve Elias, who also made many good suggestions on the manuscript. Steve died suddenly in December of 2011, leaving a legacy of friendship and of a deep passion for justice. He is sorely missed.

Editors Jake Warner and Barbara Kate Repa kept me, and the book, going. Without their sharp minds and sharp wits, this book wouldn't be half as good, and writing it wouldn't have been half as fun.

I'm very grateful to the people who reviewed the manuscript or provided expertise: my friend Loren Gerstein, formerly a mediator with Community Boards of San Francisco; Terri McGinnis, practicing veterinarian and author of *The Well Dog Book* and *The Well Cat Book;* Mike Mansel of Insurance Associates; the late Phyllis Wright of the Humane Society of the United States; and two dog-lovers, Robin Leonard and Lulu Cornell. Special thanks to Stanley Jacobsen, a constant source of clippings, good humor, and M&Ms.

Ella Hirst did extensive and very helpful updating for the fourth edition.

Jackie Mancuso and Susan Putney have both created wonderful covers for this book. Toni Ihara and illustrator Linda Allison also helped make the book look so good.

Finally, my thanks to all the people of Nolo, who've kept me supplied with dog cartoons, anecdotes, news stories, and title suggestions (how about "In Pro Pup" or "Dog Do's and Don'ts"?).

About the Author

Mary Randolph gave up the practice of law to write and edit Nolo books and software, and never regretted it for a minute. She received her law degree from Boalt Hall, the law school at the University of California at Berkeley. She is the author of Nolo materials on living trusts, *8 Ways to Avoid Probate, Deeds for California Real Estate*, and *The Executor's Guide: Settling a Loved One's Estate or Trust*.

Table of Contents

Introduction

The law is a dull dog.
        —Charles Dickens

This book is for people who own dogs, live next door to dogs, get bitten by dogs, or otherwise deal with dogs—which, with the American dog population at an estimated 78 million, includes just about everybody.

Back when most Americans lived on farms or in small towns, few legal rules affected dogs and their owners. After all, most dogs were unlikely to run afoul of the law unless they harmed livestock—an offense for which there were universally harsh penalties.

Not so in modern society. Increasing urbanization has meant stepped-up animal regulation. In both crowded cities and sprawling suburbia, there is too much traffic and too little open space to allow dogs to run loose. And to protect ourselves from dogs whose owners we no longer know, vaccinations, licenses, and sometimes even liability insurance are required.

Legal questions come up constantly. What can I do if the dog down the street barks all night? How many dogs can my neighbor keep? What can I do if I buy a dog and find out it's not healthy? Am I legally liable if my dog bites a child who's teasing it? Can my landlord, who told me I could have a dog, evict me for violating the no-pets clause in the form lease I signed?

This book answers many common questions, or shows how to find the answers as quickly and easily as possible.

Most law that governs animals is local: it is controlled by cities and counties. State law is involved to a lesser, but increasing, degree, and federal law hardly at all. So "dog law" varies every time you cross a city boundary. Obviously, no one book can tell you what the law is in every town in the country. But we can tell you what to look for and what to expect, and steer you to the right place or people so you can find it yourself.

In fact, the local nature of dog law is usually an advantage when you're trying to find out the rules in your town. Your legal research may be as simple as searching your city's ordinances online or going to the public library, opening up the big three-ring binder that contains the city ordinances, and reading the entries under "Dogs."

A note on endnotes. At the end of each chapter, there are endnotes, which contain legal citations to important statutes, court decisions, or interesting articles, so that interested people can look them up for themselves.

Get Updates and More Online

When there are important changes to the information in this book, we'll post updates online, on a page dedicated to this book: **www.nolo.com/back-of-book/DOG.html**. You'll find other useful information there, too, including links to related blogs, podcasts, and videos.

Dogs and People

First as scavengers, later as companions, servants, and protectors, dogs have been with us a long, long time. But the fate of dogs in the crowded modern world is uncertain. Dogs fit easily into past human societies based on hunting and gathering, and later on agriculture, but less room is left for them in today's cities. Forty percent of U.S. households have at least one dog, according to the American Pet Products Association. But dogs are now outnumbered by cats. Writer Cullen Murphy summed up, only half-facetiously, the broader implications of this shift:

> *Consider an America congenial to the dog: it was a place of nuclear or extended families, of someone always home, of children (or pets) looked after during the day by a parent (or owner), of open spaces and family farms, of sticks and leftovers, of expansiveness and looking outward and being outside .... Consider an America conducive to the cat: it is a place of working men and women with not much time, of crowded cities, of apartment buildings with restrictive clauses, of day-care and take-out food, of self-absorption and modest horizons.*[1]

Increasing intolerance for dogs is shown in more and more laws, which regulate when dogs must be confined, where their owners may take them, and even how many may live in a house. But before getting into the legal rules, here's a brief look back at the shared history of people and dogs, and how they've come to play such a ubiquitous role in our society.

A Little History

> *Only two animals have entered the human household otherwise than as prisoners and become domesticated by other means than those of enforced servitude: the dog and the cat.*
>
> —Konrad Lorenz, *Man Meets Dog*

Most people think they know how dogs came to be part of the human family: someone living in a cave took in an orphaned wolf puppy and tamed it. Or wolves hung around human encampments looking for scraps and gradually got tame, learning how to interact with people. Or wolves started hunting in cooperation with humans and were rewarded with a share of the kill. Probably none of these theories is accurate. But luckily for all of us who like to speculate, we may never know for sure.

Experts differ on just when dogs were domesticated. Some say the evidence indicates domestication as far back as 14,000 years ago. Almost all agree that the dog was the first—by as much as several thousand years—domesticated animal.

What wild animal metamorphosed into the modern dog—an animal we now know so well that its Latin name is *Canis familiaris?* With the advent of DNA sequencing, there is no longer much doubt that the gray wolf (*Canis lupus*) is the ancestor of the modern dog. Some biologists even consider them the same species, and dogs have almost certainly been crossbred to wolves since domestication.

Dogs are biologically suited to domestication, says one writer, because of their tendencies toward curiosity, a willingness to move, and the ability to learn throughout life. These traits (which are shared by humans, by the way) allowed them to approach human settlements and enter into a symbiotic relationship with people.[2]

After agriculture replaced hunting and gathering, and permanent settlements replaced the nomadic way of life, selective breeding of domestic animals began in earnest. It is that breeding—the human tinkering with canine evolution—that eventually led to today's astonishing variety of domestic dogs. People bred dogs to emphasize certain desired characteristics and, over the years, developed breeds with the traits they needed. Thus the coursing hounds—salukis, greyhounds, and others— got the long legs, good eyesight, and slender build they needed to chase prey long distances over open terrain. (Believe it or not, the original idea was not to have them chase mechanical rabbits around a track.) Other hounds—bassets, beagles, and bloodhounds, for example—got their extraordinarily keen noses, which enable them to trail prey. Herding dogs such as collies and sheepdogs were bred for intelligence and the herding instinct. Toy poodles, Chihuahuas, and other tiny dogs are scaled-down versions of full-sized ancestors. The list goes on.

Dog Art

The American Kennel Club Museum of the Dog, in St. Louis, Missouri, contains paintings, photographs, sculptures, and prints of dogs. Visitors are encouraged to bring their dogs with them—if the dogs are leashed and obedience trained. If they get tired of the art, they'll find doggy treats, water, and a place to exercise.

The museum is located in Queeny Park, at 1721 South Mason Road, St. Louis, MO 63131, 314-821-3647. For more information, see www.themuseumofthedog.org.

The Dog's Place Today

Dogs still herd sheep, sniff out drugs, help owners with disabilities, and guard buildings. But the main contribution of most dogs these days is companionship. Dogs make people smile and laugh, give them uncomplicated and unconditional love, and stick with them when others have gone.

Dogs as Companions

Dachshunds are ideal dogs for small children, as they are already stretched and pulled to such a length that the child cannot do much harm one way or the other.

—Robert Benchley

Studies and surveys of dog owners consistently reach a simple but important conclusion: Pets make their owners happy. Fifty-seven percent of pet owners, if stranded on a desert island, would prefer to be with their pet than another person, according to the American Animal Hospital Association.[3]

Hurry Up, Boy, or We'll Be Late for Work

Almost 20% of American companies let employees bring their pets to work, says the American Pet Products Association. Looking for one of those companies? Try www.SimplyHired.com/DogFriendly. A study at the Virginia Commonwealth University business school—conducted by Professor Randolph Barker—found that dogs in the workplace reduced employees' stress levels. Researchers measured the levels of stress hormone (cortisol) in 76 employees' saliva four times a day. Among the people who had brought their dogs to work, stress levels fell 11% by the end of the day; among others, they went up as much as 70%. The researchers also noted that having dogs around increased interactions among coworkers, as people volunteered to walk the dogs.[4]

Many parents get a dog "for the children," because they believe that growing up with a dog gives a child companionship and teaches responsibility, gentleness, and compassion. They're right, according to several studies. For example, a group of preschoolers allowed to care for a puppy at their school became more cooperative and sharing, according to the researchers who studied them. "They have to put themselves in the pet's position and try to feel how the pet feels," explained one researcher. "And that transfers to how other kids feel."[5]

On a standardized personality test (the Minnesota Multiphasic Personality Inventory), graduate students who had owned dogs as children showed significantly higher self-esteem ("ego strength") than those who had not had pets. The researcher theorizes that having a dog lets a child form attachments without fear, because of the unconditional acceptance the dog gives the child. The dog's trust helps the child trust himself. (They may also be healthier physically. A study of 400 Finnish children found that those raised with dogs were less susceptible to respiratory infections. In their first year, babies with dogs in the home were 44% less likely to get an ear infection, and 29% less likely to need antibiotics, than babies whose households didn't include dogs.)[6]

And perhaps children should consider getting a dog "for the parents." According to one study of 454 new parents, men who are attached to their pet dogs also make better fathers. The dog-owning dads consistently scored higher on tests geared to measure their perceptions of happiness about their relationship with their babies, their marriages, and their role as fathers.

Those Brits and Their Dogs

The French may take their dogs to restaurants, but no people love their dogs more than the British. (Witness all those photos of Queen Elizabeth with her corgis.) The tens of thousands of pet owners who responded to an unscientific survey by the BBC in 2004 reported that:
- 65% of pet owners buy birthday presents for their pets
- 59% of dog owners let pets sleep in their bedroom, and
- 59% of pet owners miss their pets most when they go away, compared to 27% for partners, 11% for children, and 3% for friends.

Dogs as Therapists

A psychotherapist would have much to learn from watching the way a dog listens.

—Dr. Victor Bloom[7]

Four out of five people who responded to a *Psychology Today* survey said that when they were lonely or upset, pets were often their closest companions. One woman in a difficult family situation wrote that without her dog, she "could not tolerate life."[8]

This finding explains why the most striking benefits of an animal's companionship are reaped by people who lack close human relationships: neglected or disturbed children, lonely older people, or prison inmates. For example, a study of fifth-graders found that for children who were emotionally neglected, pets served as confidants and friends—in essence, substitute parents.[9]

Therapists and administrators now routinely use animals to treat or manage such patients. But for the most part, animals entered into the world of psychological therapy serendipitously. One psychiatrist, for example, happened to have his dog in his office when a young patient came early for an appointment; the dog became an integral part of the child's therapy. In the 1970s, an entire course of research was triggered when troubled adolescents in an Ohio State University hospital—many of whom had refused to communicate with the staff—asked to play with dogs used for behavioral research, which they had heard barking in a nearby kennel. Even the most withdrawn patients improved after contact with the dogs.

Get Involved

More and more groups are looking for volunteers to take animals to visit hospitals, nursing homes, adult day care centers, and special children's treatment centers.

For more information, contact a local humane society or check out Therapy Dogs International at www.tdi-dog.org, or www.dogplay.com/Activities/Therapy/index.html.

In one study of children with severe emotional problems, half were given traditional therapy, and the rest were allowed to play with a dog during their therapy sessions. The children who received conventional treatment got worse (as measured by standard tests of ability to control themselves and empathize), but the children who played with dogs got better.

It is not an exaggeration to say that pets can give people a reason to live. Often, people institutionalized in prisons or hospitals, for example, have no goals, no responsibility, no variety in their lives. Animals, either as visitors or residents, make the atmosphere more home-like and can have a wonderful, enlivening effect on morale.

Pets Are Good for You

Pet Partners (formerly the Delta Society) has put together a long list of the health benefits of owning a pet that have been documented by scientific research. Here are just some of them:

- People with borderline hypertension had lower blood pressure on days they took their dogs to work.
- Seniors who own dogs go to the doctor less than those who do not.
- Pet owners have lower blood pressure and lower triglyceride and cholesterol levels than nonowners.
- Contact with pets develops nurturing behavior in children, who may grow to be more nurturing adults.
- Pet owners have a higher one-year survival rate following coronary heart disease.
- Having a pet may decrease heart attack mortality by 3%. This translates into 30,000 lives saved annually.
- Children exposed to pets during the first year of life have a lower frequency of allergic rhinitis and asthma.
- Children who own pets score significantly higher on empathy scales than nonowners.
- Owning a pet can enhance children's cognitive development and self-esteem.

You can see more at www.petpartners.org.

And for more information on the human-animal bond, check out the Research Center for Human-Animal Interaction at the University of Missouri College of Veterinary Medicine (www.rechai.missouri.edu) and the Human-Animal Interaction Research sponsored by the National Institutes of Health (www.nichd.nih.gov/about/org/crmc/cdb/prog_hai).

An institutionalized person who is allowed to care for a pet may become more alert, involved, and sociable. As one prison psychiatric social worker put it, "the therapeutic results are nothing short of miraculous."[10] Take the story of Jed, who had been in a nursing home for 26 years after suffering brain damage in a fall. He was believed deaf and mute. When he saw Whiskey, a German shepherd-husky dog that had just been placed in his nursing home, he spoke his first words in 26 years: "You brought that dog." He began to talk to the staff and other residents, and to draw pictures of the dog.[11]

Dog owners go to the doctor less than people who don't own dogs, concluded another study of 1,000 elderly Californians. Dog owners had 21% fewer contacts with physicians than did participants who didn't own dogs. The researcher, UCLA professor Judith M. Seigel, surmised that the dogs were a "stress buffer," which lessened the need of their owners to seek out physicians in times of psychological stress.[12]

If you do get sick, a pet can help you get better faster. One study compared postcoronary survival of pet owners versus nonowners; among the pet owners, 50 of 53 lived at least a year after hospitalization, compared to 17 of 39 nonowners. Even eliminating patients who owned dogs (whose health might have been improved just from the exercise of walking the dog), the pet owners still did better. In a follow-up study, the same researcher found that pet owners' worry about their animals actually speeded their convalescence by providing "a sense of being needed and an impetus for quick recovery."

Now that scientists in the medical and psychiatric communities have accepted what pet owners have always known—that animals make people feel better—they have set about documenting the physiological effects animals have on people. When people pet dogs, especially ones they have grown attached to, their blood pressure drops. The same happens when people talk to a dog—although talking to another person usually raises blood pressure. Friendly interactions with dogs release the hormone oxytocin in both the person and the dog. Oxytocin is involved in all kinds of human social bonding, including between mothers and infants.[13]

Even the presence of a dog is comforting. In one study, people who took a standardized anxiety-measuring test when the experimenter's dog was in the room scored lower than those who took the test with only the experimenter present. Another experiment showed that women attempting a difficult task felt less stress and fared better when their dogs were nearby than when a human friend was close.[14]

> ### Don't Prescribe a Dog for the Taxpayer's Blues
>
> You may know your dog helps keep you healthy, but don't try to tell the Internal Revenue Service that. The IRS doesn't allow you to deduct the cost of a pet as a medical expense, unless the dog is a guide dog or other specially trained service dog. (See Chapter 2, State and Local Regulation.)
>
> You can't claim your dog as a dependent, either: the IRS said no to a woman who wanted "head of household" rates because she lived with 25 dogs and cats.[15]

Let's let that old dog-lover Freud have the last word on the psychology of dog-people relationships. Here's how he described the "extraordinary intensity" with which he loved his dog, Topsy: "Affection without ambivalence, the simplicity free from the almost unbearable conflicts of civilization, the beauty of an existence complete in itself … that feeling of intimate affinity of an indisputed solidarity."

Dogs in the Law

Dogs occupy their own odd niche in American law and its principal predecessor, the "common law" of England. Common law is what has evolved as judges decide cases, one by one, over hundreds of years. Unlike statutes, the common law is not written down in one place, but instead is deduced from the judges' writings. The English common law came to this country with the colonists, and forms the basis for the law of every state except Louisiana (which took its law from France's Napoleonic Code).

Under English common law, dogs were not considered to have any intrinsic value. They were kept, in the eyes of the law, merely for pleasure. Only "useful" domestic animals (ones you could eat or put to work), such as cows, horses, sheep, and chickens, were considered to have value. This reasoning seems especially odd when you look at how many dogs were kept to catch rats, herd sheep, or guard houses, but that's the way it was.

Because dogs weren't "property," it wasn't illegal to steal them under the common law. It took an act of Parliament (or a state legislature, in this country) to make stealing a dog a crime. And even when a legislature did act, the result wasn't always a paragon of logic: in England at one time, it was a felony to steal a dog's collar but a misdemeanor to steal the dog.[16]

Nowadays, the law in most places and for most purposes treats dogs just like other kinds of property. Because a dog is property, it has no legal rights of its own. So a dog can't inherit property or sue in its own name. Those rights are reserved for its owner.

But cracks are appearing in this doctrine. Sometimes, courts just cannot ignore the fact that dogs aren't items of property in the way that, say, appliances are. One refrigerator is pretty much like all the others that rolled off the same assembly line. But every dog is unique. They are the subject of custody disputes by divorcing couples, and owners sue for emotional distress when their pets are injured.

It's been proposed that dogs be treated more like children than like property, so that instead of owners they would have guardians. (A few places, including Boulder, Colorado, Berkeley, California, and the state of Rhode Island, now refer to pet owners as guardians.) But a radical departure from traditional law—which would, among other things, allow pets to own property—is extremely unlikely to happen anytime soon.

Endnotes

1 "Going to the Cats," by Cullen Murphy, *Atlantic Monthly* (August 1987).

2 "In From the Cold," by Stephen Budiansky, *New York Times,* Jan. 1992, adapted from *The Covenant of the Wild: Why Animals Chose Domestication* (Wm. Morrow).

3 Cited in *Health Magazine*, October 1996.

4 "Bringing your dog to work can ease stress, study finds," *Los Angeles Times*, Mar. 31, 2012.

5 "Loving a Pet Is Good Kid Therapy," *San Francisco Chronicle,* Jan. 11, 1990.

6 "Babies With Pets Not Dogged by Colds: Study," *Philadelphia Inquirer*, Jul. 10, 2012.

7 Quoted in Slovenko, "Rx: A Dog," Journal of Psychiatry and Law, vol. 11, no. 4 (1983).

8 "The Pleasure of Their Company," by Horn and Meer, *Psychology Today* (August 1984).

9 "Loving a Pet Is Good Kid Therapy," *San Francisco Chronicle,* Jan. 11, 1990.

10 "The Pleasure of Their Company," by Horn and Meer, *Psychology Today* (August 1984).

11 *Ethology and Nonverbal Communication in Mental Health,* Corson and Corson, eds. (Pergamon Press 1980), quoted in *Guidelines: Animals in Nursing Homes* (California Veterinary Medical Ass'n).

12 "Pet Owners Go to the Doctor Less," *New York Times,* Aug. 2, 1990.

13 "Made For Each Other," by Meg Daley Olmert, *Psychology Today,* May 5, 2010.

14 *Science News,* Nov. 2, 1991.

15 *Davidson v. Commissioner,* Tax Court Memo. (CCH) Dec. 34, 524, 1977-232.

16 *Law Without Lawyers,* by Two Barristers-at-Law (John Murray, London, 1905).

State and Local Regulation

Owning a dog, which used to be a pretty simple proposition, is becoming more and more complicated as government regulation in this area mushrooms. The crackdown can be traced to urbanization: As dogs and people compete for space, the trend is for cities to put more restrictions on dogs and, sometimes, to limit the number or kind of dogs that city dwellers may have.

This chapter looks at the basic areas of government regulation that affect most dog owners.

Special rules for assistance dogs. Many local laws don't apply to service dogs trained to help owners with disabilities. (See Chapter 8, Assistance Dogs.)

Barking dogs. Local and state laws may specifically require owners to keep barking dogs from being a nuisance. (See Chapter 7, Barking Dogs.)

How to Find Local Laws

Local governments are still in charge of most kinds of basic animal regulations, including limits on the number of dogs per household, license and vaccination requirements, and leash laws. Laws covering these issues tend to be broadly similar everywhere, but their details vary significantly from town to town.

To find out what the law is where you live, you must do some research. That may be as simple as calling the local Animal Control or Health Department and asking your question.

If you want to read the law yourself—always a good idea—you can probably find it in the city or county ordinances, which are often called the "municipal code." Most cities make their ordinances available online, at their official websites.

The code should also be available at your local public library, the law library in the county courthouse, and at city hall, usually in the city clerk's or city attorney's office.

In most towns, even large ones, local ordinances are kept in a big loose-leaf binder. You can probably find what you need simply by looking in the index under "Dogs" or "Animals."

Licenses

Whether you live in the city or the country, you have to get a license for your dog. And it's important to remember that almost all laws require not only that you buy a license every year, but also that you keep the license tag on your dog at all times. There is, of course, a practical reason: the tag is often the only way animal control officials have of identifying a dog they pick up or that someone turns over to the animal shelter.

License Fees

In most places, basic annual license fees are about $10 to $20. Almost everywhere, fees are higher for animals that have not been spayed or neutered. Some places have raised fees for unaltered animals substantially to encourage people to get their pets spayed or neutered. In King County, Washington, for example, licenses for unaltered animals cost $60—but owners also get a $25 voucher, accepted by most local veterinarians, toward the cost of spaying or neutering.

Several factors may reduce the fee you pay:

- Licenses for specially trained or service dogs that help their owners are usually free. (See Chapter 8, Assistance Dogs.)
- Disabled or older people are sometimes given free dog licenses. Free licenses may be limited to dogs that have been spayed or neutered. Some cities also require that household income be below a certain amount.
- You may be able to buy a "lifetime license"—valid for the dog's lifetime, not yours. Pennsylvania makes such licenses available if the dog has some kind of permanent identification such as a tattoo or microchip.[1]
- If you have a lot of dogs, you may be able to (or be required to) get a kennel license that covers all the dogs—a sort of volume discount. (See Chapter 3, Buying and Selling Dogs.)

Where to Get a License

City governments regulate animals within their borders; in unincorporated areas, the county takes responsibility. No matter where you live, you can probably get your license by mail. Some places now make licenses available online. Check the city or county website for a licensing department, or just call a general city hall or animal control number.

To get a license in most places, you must produce a current rabies vaccination certificate. This explains why puppies are usually exempt from the license requirement until they get their adult rabies vaccination, at about four months old. Vaccination records, by the way, are sometimes how a local government keeps dog owners honest; the veterinarian administering the shot must send a record to the county, stating whether or not the dog is licensed.

If your town offers reduced license fees, you'll need proof of whatever makes you eligible: for example, a veterinarian's certificate stating that the animal has been spayed or neutered, or a document from a training institute that says your dog is a trained service dog.

If you move from the city or county that issued the license, you may have to get a new one from your new town. However, in some states (New Jersey, for one), a license is good anywhere in the state. If you move out of state, you almost certainly will need to get a new license, within about 30 days after you arrive in the new state.

If You Don't License Your Dog

What happens if you don't buy a license for your dog? Well, it's sort of like driving a car without bothering to get a driver's license. If you're never stopped by the police or hit by another car, no one will be the wiser. And if your dog never bothers the neighbors, is never lost, stolen, or nabbed by animal control, and never bites anyone, you may get away with not having a dog license. But if any of these things happens, the penalty for not having a dog license is bigger than the price of buying one in the first place.

When a licensed dog is picked up and impounded by animal control personnel, they can check the city's license records to identify—and notify—the owner. Unlicensed dogs are often euthanized (put to sleep) sooner than dogs with license tags. (See "Impounding and Destroying Dogs," below.) If you go away for the weekend, and your dog escapes from the back yard, the two or three extra days a licensed dog is given at the shelter could mean the difference between getting it back and losing it for good.

It's also still fairly common to find legislation that makes stealing only *licensed* dogs a crime—implying that stealing an unlicensed dog is legal.[2]

How Many Dogs Can You Keep?

In rural areas, how many dogs you keep is pretty much your own business, as long as the dogs aren't a nuisance. But many cities restrict residents to two or three dogs per household, not counting puppies less than a certain age, usually eight weeks to four months or so.

The goal is to cut down on the problems that dogs cause in urban areas. Court challenges to such ordinances almost always fail.[3] As one court upholding such an ordinance put it, "Too many dogs in too small a space may produce noise, odor and other conditions adverse to the best interests of the community as a whole."[4] Another court upheld a town's limit of two dogs per household because the town had been reacting to a rash of problems involving dogs, including dogs roaming at large, dog bites, excessive barking, and owners' failure to clean up after their pets. The man who sued owned four dogs when the ordinance was passed; the court ruled that the law could still be applied to him.[5] The Georgia Supreme Court, however, found a county ordinance unconstitutional because it didn't include the criteria that a dog owner had to satisfy in order to get a permit for keeping more than four dogs.[6]

Violating the law will probably earn you a fine and possibly even a jail sentence. A judge in Holland, Michigan—which has a two-dog-per-household maximum—sentenced a man to 90 days in jail for refusing to give up any of his three dogs. The dog owner spent a few days in jail before agreeing to part with one of his animals. (An effort to change the law in Holland, to allow three dogs per household, failed in late 2011.)

Flat limits on the number of dogs per household are increasingly popular but are by no means universal. In Oakland, California, dog owners banded together to defeat a proposed ordinance that would have required people with more than three pets to get a city permit. The pet owners were joined by the Oakland Society for the Prevention of Cruelty to Animals and a local American Civil Liberties Union chapter.

There are variations on this kind of straightforward limit. You may, for example, have to get a special kennel license if you have more than three or four dogs. That means extra fees, rules, and, often, inspections by city officials. (See Chapter 3, Buying and Selling Dogs.)

You may wonder how these rules are enforced. After all, animal control officials don't go door to door taking a dog census. They rely, for the most part, on complaints or chance observation. So as a practical matter, someone who has more dogs than is allowed under the law is likely to get in trouble only if the dogs cause problems and a neighbor complains. The moral: no matter how many dogs you have, don't let them be a neighborhood nuisance. And if there are problems, work them out before the neighbors go to the authorities.

Even if a city doesn't have a set limit on the number of animals, neighbors bothered by too many animals may complain to Animal Control or sue. If a court decides that the animals are a nuisance—that is, that they interfere with neighbors' enjoyment of their property—the owner may be ordered to get rid of some animals. (See Chapter 7, Barking Dogs.)

Vaccinations

Most states require dogs to be vaccinated against rabies, which is rare but not unheard of in domestic animals. It is almost always fatal in humans.

Usually, you must have proof that your dog has an up-to-date rabies vaccination to get a dog license. Vaccines that last for three years are available for dogs more than four months old, making compliance easy. Many cities offer low-cost vaccinations at permanent clinics (such clinics usually offer spaying and neutering for a reduced fee as well), or special one-day clinics where owners merely have to show up to get pets vaccinated.

Don't think your dog is safe from rabies because you live in a city and rarely come into contact with wild animals. Common species of "urban wildlife"—skunks, raccoons, and bats—can spread the disease to pets. Healthy wild animals usually avoid domestic animals, but sick ones may not, and they are also more likely to be out in the daytime. Cats may also spread the disease.

Some cities impose additional vaccination requirements—for example, you may be required to get your dog immunized against distemper, a relatively rare but very contagious and usually fatal disease in dogs.

You may need to have proof of recent vaccinations for your dog before you can take it into another state or country. (See Chapter 6, Traveling With Your Dog.)

Leash Laws

Whatever may be said about the affection which mankind has for a faithful companion, modern city conditions no longer permit dogs to run at large.

—California Court of Appeal[7]

Long gone from most of America are the days when you could answer a longing whine from your dog by opening the back door and letting it roam the neighborhood at will. Besides the fact that many people live in apartment buildings where back doors open onto upper-story balconies, roaming dogs are considered outlaws almost everywhere, either by state law or by city or county ordinance.

"Leash laws" generally require dogs to be on a leash and under control whenever they're off their owners' property, unless a specific area is designated for unleashed dogs. Some laws apply only at night (when dogs may do the most damage to livestock) or allow an owner to have a dog unleashed if it is under "reasonable control."[8]

Walking a Dog Off-Leash

Even dog owners who let their dogs off a leash only because they're confident they have complete control over them are probably in violation of a leash law.

The intensity of enforcement, however, varies from city to city and neighborhood to neighborhood. In many places, an owner is unlikely to be cited if the dog really is under voice control and not bothering anyone, even if in technical violation of a leash law. But in some cities, police enforce leash laws strictly, especially if they have received complaints about unleashed dogs in a certain area. Ask about the custom in your neighborhood. A police department may have adopted an informal policy of not issuing citations in the early morning if a dog is under control, but strictly enforcing the leash law in a crowded park where a surfeit of dogs have made it unpleasant or unusable for others.

Dog parks. Across the country, dog owners' groups, frustrated by strict leash laws, are championing city parks with areas set aside just for dogs. People can turn their pets loose and then, like parents at the edge of a playground, watch, scold, and applaud the results. The idea seems to have originated in Berkeley, California, where a fenced half-acre of Ohlone Park was set aside for dogs in 1979. The Ohlone Park Dog Owners Association, now a nonprofit corporation, still oversees the park. Like other such groups, it encourages owners to clean up after their dogs and provides plastic bags near trash cans.

Law and Order in Suburban Los Angeles

Here's a legal interpretation problem for you: If the law requires a dog to be on a leash, does the owner have to be holding on to the other end?

Jean Bessette of Van Nuys, California, was ticketed for walking his Labrador retriever, Rex, without a leash. Bessette protested that the dog was on a leash. The problem was that Bessette wasn't holding the other end of the leash—Rex was, in his mouth.

Bessette and Rex went to court, where Rex balanced dog biscuits on his nose to show how well trained he was. The pair got off with a warning.

Dogs Running at Large

A dog running loose can be picked up and taken to the animal shelter by municipal or county animal control officers. The owner will be fined and charged for the cost of impounding the dog. (See "Impounding and Destroying Dogs," below.) If the dog is unlicensed, there will be another fine as well.

There are other risks to allowing a dog to run at large. Of course, there's the obvious danger that the dog will be hit by a car. Owners are also letting themselves in for financial liability if the dog causes trouble—bites someone or makes a bicyclist fall, for example. To take an extreme example, in 1983, two men were severely injured when the driver of a truck in which they were riding swerved to avoid hitting a dog that had run into the road. They sued the dog's owner, and a judge awarded them $2.6 million.[9] (Liability is discussed in detail in Chapter 11, Dog Bites.)

Dogs that damage property or injure livestock while running at large may be subject to other laws—including the "shoot first, ask questions later" rule that prevails in most rural areas, allowing a farmer to kill any dog that's threatening livestock. (See Chapter 9, If a Dog Is Injured or Killed.) And if a dog threatens or injures a person, it may be classified as a "vicious dog" and made subject to strict regulations. (See Chapter 12, Dangerous Dogs.)

Off-Limits Areas

Dogs, on or off a leash, are simply not welcome in many places. Usually, taking a dog to a beach, zoo, restaurant, or farm won't make you any friends and may get you a quick and stern request to leave. State and local laws ban dogs, for health reasons, from places food is prepared, served, or sold. Some cities also bar dogs from city parks.

Surely, though, you can let your dog run in wide-open spaces? It depends. On federal land, the rules change from area to area. In officially designated "wilderness" areas, dogs are allowed on a leash, but the leash requirement is rarely enforced where there are few people and even fewer park rangers. Some national parks and national monuments allow dogs on leashes; some don't allow dogs at all. In national forests, dogs are usually allowed in at least some areas.

State and local rules are unpredictable. Most trails and campgrounds of the California State Park system, for example, are closed to dogs. Check the rules before you load your backpack (or your dog's) with kibble and set off.

Assistance dogs. Guide and other specially trained service dogs are allowed places other dogs aren't. (See Chapter 8, Assistance Dogs.)

Impounding and Destroying Dogs

Many dog control ordinances attempt to give animal control authorities the power to pick up, impound, and sometimes even destroy dogs. But the government's authority is limited by the U.S. Constitution. Here's where the dog's legal classification as "property" comes in handy: The Constitution says the government can't deprive you of your property without giving you due process—that is, notice and a chance to have a hearing. There are, however, important exceptions to this rule: If a dog is unlicensed or running at large, you've probably lost your right to be notified before the dog is picked up or, in some cases, destroyed.

Dogs Running at Large

If a dog running at large poses an immediate danger to the public, most courts agree that the government has the power to impound and destroy it, without first notifying the owner. If a dog is in the act of attacking a person or livestock, anyone, including government employees, may lawfully do anything necessary to stop it. (That's discussed more fully in Chapter 9, If a Dog Is Injured or Killed.)

Laws may not, however, give animal control authorities excessive power to act without first trying to notify an animal's owner. For example, an Idaho statute that said that any dog "running at large in territory inhabited by deer" was a nuisance and could be killed by a game warden was ruled unconstitutional by the state supreme court.[10] Similarly, the Michigan

Attorney General issued a legal opinion that in that state, animal control officers were not authorized to kill a dog merely because it was running at large. Only a court could order the dog destroyed.[11]

False Imprisonment?

If your pet is picked up by overzealous animal control officers and locked in the doggie slammer for the weekend, chances are it will come home smelly, frightened, and hungry. Can you recover from the city or county for its "wrongful arrest" of your innocent dog? Probably not. The law acknowledges only injury to you, not your dog. If, though, the dog becomes sick or is injured because of the wrongful stay at the animal shelter, you may be able to sue successfully.

Remember that you have a chance of winning a lawsuit only if the shelter was wrong to pick up your dog or kept it after you tried to bail it out. If your dog just got caught running around unleashed, and the shelter didn't break any of its own rules about notifying you or releasing the dog when you paid your fine, you've got nothing, legally, to complain about.

Dogs in Owners' Possession

Occasionally, animal control authorities seize a dog that isn't running loose. Only dogs that have bitten someone or, even more rarely, proven to be an incorrigible nuisance are taken from their owners this way. (The "vicious dog" laws that allow this are discussed in Chapter 12, Dangerous Dogs.)

Unless a dog is running at large, or an emergency requires immediate action, most courts would agree that an owner who has possession of a dog is entitled to:

- notification before the dog is seized
- notification before the dog is destroyed, and
- a chance to argue, in court, that the dog shouldn't be destroyed.

Most courts, then, would rule unconstitutional any law that allows animal control officials to seize or destroy a dog (in its owner's possession) without giving its owners notice and a hearing.[12] The case of Missy, a black Labrador that was reported to have bitten three children, provides a good example. The county Department of Animal Regulation ordered the dog's owner to confine Missy to an enclosed kennel. Several years later, when the owner had to go into the hospital, her son and daughter-in-law took the dog to their house. When Missy allegedly bit another child, the department ordered the dog seized and destroyed.

The county ordinance did not provide for any notice or hearing before destroying a dog, but the county conducted a "courtesy" hearing at the request of Missy's owner. The hearing officer ruled that Missy should be destroyed. A trial judge agreed.

Finally, an appellate court reversed the lower court ruling and declared that Missy "shall live and 'enjoy the noonday sun.'" The county ordinance was unconstitutional, the court said, because it didn't require a hearing before a dog was taken and destroyed. The courtesy hearing was not enough to satisfy the law.[13]

Enforcement by humane societies. Local animal regulations are usually enforced by city and county animal control, health, and police departments. Sometimes, however, a humane society or Society for the Prevention of Cruelty to Animals (SPCA) provides animal control services under a contract with the city or county. Or it may have limited powers— for example, to take charge of injured or abandoned animals, or arrest people at an organized dog fight without first getting a warrant. When it is acting in an official capacity, a quasi-public organization such as a humane society is subject to the same constitutional requirements as any other government agency. That means it must respect dog owners' due process rights, discussed above.

Overzealous Enforcement

When officers from the Pasadena, California, Humane Society, who enforce that city's leash law, spotted a familiar dog running loose on a golf course, they gave chase. But the dog, a beagle named Toby, dashed home and slipped inside the back door. When the officers caught up, they saw the door ajar; concerned that a burglar might have broken in, they called police, who searched the house. All they turned up was Toby, relaxing on his owners' bed. They shut him in the bedroom.

The humane society officers weren't ready to give up, though; they asked for police permission to go inside and nab Toby. The police agreed, but only because they thought the dog was a stray.

Toby was impounded—for the 15th time in 4½ years—and his owners socked with a $500 fine and two years' probation. The owners then sued, claiming that their constitutional right to be free of unreasonable searches and seizures had been violated. The trial court ruled for the government, but an appellate court took the side of the dog and its owners. Taking Toby from his home without a warrant was not justified by violation of the leash law, a minor offense, the court ruled. Once the dog was safely secured in the house, the officers should have gracefully withdrawn. (*Conway v. Pasadena Humane Society*, 45 Cal. App. 4th 163, 52 Cal. Rptr. 2d 777 (1996), *petition for rev. denied* (1996).)

What Happens to Impounded Dogs

So many dogs show up at animal shelters every day—strays, dogs abandoned by their owners, dogs declared vicious by courts—that many facilities are strained to the breaking point. They can't keep all those animals forever; many dispose of dogs after only three to seven days. For a dog there are only four ways out of the shelter: it may be reclaimed by its owner, adopted, sold, or destroyed.

Reclaiming a dog. If your dog is impounded, you can probably bail it out by paying a fine and a per-day charge for its keep at the shelter. If you don't have one already, you'll also have to buy a dog license and get any necessary vaccinations for the dog before it will be released to you.

Finding out that your dog has been picked up may be the tricky part. All shelters are supposed to notify owners whose dogs they impound. Of course, unless yours is an exceptionally smart and articulate dog, the only way the shelter knows you're the owner is to read the dog's identification or license tag (or unless you've outfitted the dog with a permanent ID such as a microchip; see "Lost and Found Dogs," below). Both you and the dog may be out of luck if it comes to the shelter tagless. Many shelters also have some procedure for making a public announcement about dogs they pick up. This may be posting a list online or at the shelter, city hall, and police station, publishing descriptions in the newspaper or, in small towns, making an announcement on the local radio station.

If you think your dog may have been picked up, remember that some cities have several shelters. Call all the places to which the dog might have been taken: humane societies, SPCAs, and city and county shelters. Some animal shelters don't give out information over the phone. In any case, it's much better to go in person. Leave a picture or description of the dog at each shelter. And if you don't get a satisfactory answer, keep asking. It's all too common, unfortunately, to hear stories of people who were told on the phone that their dog wasn't at the shelter and found out too late that the dog had in fact been there.

Adopting a stray. Most shelters try, of course, to find new homes for dogs they take in—private homes, rescue groups, or nonprofit agencies that will train them as assistance dogs—but they are usually defeated by the sheer numbers. There just aren't enough owners to go around.

What if someone adopts your dog? You might get it back, if you act quickly and animal control officials are sympathetic. If the shelter made a mistake—didn't notify you although it could have, or let the dog be adopted too quickly—you should have the right to your dog.

If you don't act promptly, however, the dog may be gone for good. A Georgia man, for example, couldn't get back his purebred Keeshond, which was found wandering loose without a license tag and turned over to the humane society. Nine days later, someone adopted it. The owner finally got around to inquiring at the dog shelter; when they told him a dog answering the description had been adopted, but refused to tell him the new owner's name, he sued. The court stood firm for the shelter, ruling that the city had properly used its power to dispose of dogs.[14]

Lost in the Storm

Thousands of pets were left behind during the chaos in New Orleans following Hurricane Katrina in 2005. Rescuers plucked dogs from rooftops and out of the floodwaters—and with no safe place to put them in New Orleans, took them to shelters all over the south. Many were adopted by people eager to help. Later, many determined owners tracked down their dogs, but not all the dogs' new families were willing to give them up. It wasn't always possible to prove a dog's identity (many lacked identification), and some new owners accused the former ones of neglect.

Lawsuits against new owners and rescue organizations followed. Courts generally ruled for the original owners, finding that they had not abandoned their animals and still owned them.

Following Katrina, Congress passed legislation requiring state and local emergency agencies to include pets and service animals in their evacuation plans—if they don't, they won't qualify for FEMA funds.

Selling impounded dogs. Many shelters are allowed, by law, to sell dogs that aren't adopted within a certain time. Who buys stray dogs? Research labs. Allowing public shelters to sell dogs for research is, of course, an emotional and controversial issue. (See Chapter 14, Cruelty.) Lawsuits challenging such policies on animal cruelty grounds have failed. But public pressure can be an extremely effective tool; working on legislators to change the laws, instead of fighting them in court, is probably a better strategy.

Some cities, and some states, prohibit their shelters from selling animals for research. California law requires any animal shelter, public or private, that turns dogs over to a research facility to prominently post a large sign, stating that "Animals Turned Into This Shelter May Be Used for Research Purposes."[15]

Destroying impounded dogs. Shelters across the country must destroy thousands of dogs every year; some shelters are so crowded that they can hold unlicensed dogs only for a single day. Licensed dogs, as mentioned above, usually are granted a few more days. The law often specifies only that the dogs must be destroyed in a "humane manner"; most are given a very quick and humane death by lethal injection. Some laws specifically prohibit certain methods, such as decompression (which inflicts a hideous and painful death).

What to do if your rights are violated. If the government injures or destroys your dog without giving you the notice and hearing required by law, you can sue and collect for your damages. (See Chapter 9, If a Dog Is Injured or Killed.)

Lost and Found Dogs

If a dog turns up on your doorstep, you are not free to decide that "finders are keepers" and do whatever you want with it.

If you don't want the dog, you must notify animal control authorities, who have the responsibility of trying to find the owner. You should not, unless there is an emergency, take it upon yourself to have the dog destroyed.

> **EXAMPLE:** A Louisiana man found a sick puppy, which wasn't wearing a collar, in the front yard while he was visiting his father one morning. He took the pup to a vet and, given a discouraging prognosis, two days later asked the vet to humanely destroy the dog. Only later did the dog's owners find out that the dog had been taken and destroyed. They sued and won the value of the dog.[16]

What if you do want to keep the dog? If a local or state law requires you to turn it over to the animal control authorities, ask for the first chance at adoption. But even if you're allowed to hang on to the dog, you must try to find the owner yourself. If you don't, you could be liable to the owner for the dog's value.

Here are some basic steps to take:

- If the dog has a license tag, call the animal control department and get the owner's name.

- Ask the people who live around where you found the dog.
- Put a notice in the newspaper, and notify local radio stations if they read lost dog announcements on the air.
- Post signs near where you found the dog.

Common sense should tell you what to do: if the dog is healthy and well-fed, someone is probably looking desperately for it. If it looks like it hasn't had a good meal or a bath in a while, it's unlikely that an owner is worried about it—or that it will be adopted if you leave it at a shelter.

High-Tech Dog Tags

Forget license tags—for the high-tech dog, a microchip ID is a must. A tiny microchip, injected into a dog's shoulder, provides foolproof, permanent identification. Owners can pay a veterinarian to insert a chip, which is about the size of a grain of rice, for about $25 to $50; some animal shelters also insert the chips in dogs they release for adoption.

Reading the chip requires a hand-held scanner, similar to the ones used in stores to ring up bar-coded prices. When the chip is scanned, the dog's identification number shows up on a computer screen. The person doing the scanning makes a toll-free call to the company that maintains the system, which then notifies the dog's owner.

Tens of thousands of dogs and cats have been fitted with the chips. And many veterinarians and animal shelters have scanners.

How would someone know to scan a dog? If the dog is still wearing its collar, a tag will alert finders that the dog has a microchip. But as the chips become the preferred method of identifying pets, scanning strays has become routine.

For more information, talk to your veterinarian.

Spay and Neuter Requirements

There are literally millions of unwanted pets in this country. The number is staggering, and so are the problems they create. Stray animals spread disease, bite people, attack livestock and pets, and cause traffic accidents.

Overwhelmed by the number of animals showing up in their shelters, most communities until recently had only one response: give the animals a few days of care and a humane death. National figures are impossible to come by, but no estimates are below three or four million euthanized animals each year.

That's changing now. Spurred by animal shelter workers sickened by their jobs, shelters and local governments are turning their attention to the root of the problem: the surplus of unwanted animals caused by irresponsible owners who let their animals breed.

Many animal shelters now require people who adopt dogs from the shelter to have the dogs spayed or neutered. It's the law in most states. If the animal hasn't been sterilized before it's released for adoption, the new owner may have to sign an agreement to get the animal sterilized and to put down a deposit (around $50), which can be reclaimed only with evidence that the animal has been spayed or neutered. Low-cost sterilization is available in many cities.

A much more far-reaching (and controversial) policy is mandatory spaying or neutering of all pets unless the owner acquires a special permit. So far, this approach has been tried in only a few places. Denver, Colorado, requires dogs over six months old to be sterilized unless their owners buy a permit each year. Fort Wayne, Indiana, requires a breeder's permit for anyone who intentionally or accidentally causes the breeding of a dog or cat.[17] In San Mateo County, California, the County Board of Supervisors, pressed by Humane Society staff—who put to death up to 10,000 animals every year—declared that such large-scale euthanasia was not a cost-effective, acceptable, or ethical solution to the problem of pet overpopulation.

The San Mateo law requires all dogs and cats over six months old to be spayed or neutered unless the owner buys a permit allowing an animal to be kept unaltered. Before an "unaltered animal" permit is issued, the owner must sign a statement promising that the animal will not be allowed to breed until a breeding permit is issued.[18] Violators can be fined $100 for a first offense, and up to $500 for subsequent offenses. The law, which went into effect in 1996, resulted in a significant drop in the number of incoming homeless animals.

> ## Felons and Dogs
>
> In Illinois, the law forbids certain felons from owning unaltered dogs, or any dog that has been declared vicious, for ten years after their release from prison. (729 Ill. Comp. Stat. § 5/12-36.)

Pooper-Scooper Laws

Dog droppings have become a scourge, a form of environmental pollution no less dangerous and degrading than the poisons that we exude and dump into our air and water.

—New Jersey Superior Court[19]

Anyone who has stumbled into the particular form of pollution dogs are prone to leave is likely to become, instantaneously, a committed environmentalist. While dog droppings on the bottom of a shoe aren't the most serious urban problem we face, the experience doesn't brighten anyone's day, either. Many local governments have declared that enough is enough and have passed ordinances making owners responsible for dogs that hit and run. Crowded cities such as New York led the way, but many other municipalities, small and large, have followed suit.

A typical ordinance simply requires dog owners to immediately dispose of, in a sanitary manner, droppings deposited anywhere except on their own property. If they don't, they face a fine of about $20 to $50. In New York City, the tab can go as high as $250.

Still, as anyone who's walked around the block lately knows, many dog owners neglect this law, not to mention basic good manners. People who would never dream of dropping a soft drink can in a park literally look the other way as their pets deposit unsightly and unsanitary droppings in public places. It's these owners who are giving dogs—who, after all, are only doing what comes naturally—a bad name.

Service dogs. Owners of trained service dogs are often exempt from pooper-scooper laws. (See Chapter 8, Assistance Dogs.)

Pooper-Scoopers in the Big Cities

The New York statute requiring dog owners to clean up after their pets was challenged on the ground that it interfered with the free exercise of religion—because Orthodox Jews are forbidden from picking up litter on the Sabbath. The court said the law was reasonable, anyway.[20]

There are no pooper-scooper laws at all in Paris, where dogs are welcome at most fine restaurants—including Maxim's, where many humans aren't welcome. Instead, the city regularly sweeps the sidewalk with vehicles specially designed to scoop up droppings.

Dogs in Vehicles

We've all seen dogs riding in the back of pickup trucks as the trucks fly down the highway. The dogs look to be having fun, but by living in the fast lane they risk injury from flying objects. Eye injuries are common, but there is an even greater danger: according to a California state legislator, approximately 100,000 dogs a year nationwide are killed because they jump or are thrown from a pickup. There's no reliable way of estimating how much damage and how many serious accidents such incidents cause.

Many local and state governments, and some states, now regulate how dogs can be carried in pickup beds. California, for example, requires dogs in the open back of a pickup to be either in a cage or cross-tied to the truck unless the sides of the truck are at least 46 inches high. The laws don't apply to cattle or sheep dogs being used by farmers and ranchers. Violators can be fined $50 to $100 for a first offense and up to $250 for a third offense.[21]

If you're worried about your dog bouncing around inside the car, or if you just want to keep it out of your way while you're driving, many pet supply stores and mail order companies sell seat belts and car seats designed just for dogs.

Parked cars. Dogs in parked cars are also at risk in hot weather; an enclosed car heats up in minutes, and the heat can kill a dog. Owners can be punished for leaving a dog in a car, under anticruelty statutes or laws that specifically forbid leaving a dog in a parked vehicle without adequate ventilation. (See Chapter 14, Cruelty.)

Animal Burial Restrictions

Used to be, you could lay Fido to rest in the field he had happily run through during his life. But no more—at least, not legally. Although enforcement is spotty, most towns and cities prohibit burying an animal anywhere but in an established cemetery. Outside the city limits, you may be allowed to bury an animal as long as you meet county health regulations. That means, in all likelihood, that you must bury the dog fairly deep, and away from water supplies. Contact your county health or animal control department for specifics.

Most people ask their veterinarian to take care of disposing of their dog's remains. Many cities will also, for a fee of about $25 to $50, pick up and dispose of a pet's remains. You can find out local policy by calling your city or county health department or the community animal shelter.

Pet Cemeteries

More and more people are putting their pets' remains to rest in special pet cemeteries. Having a pet buried in a cemetery can cost several hundred to several thousand dollars. Cremation is a less expensive option, just as it is for humans.

If you've got a coon dog—a dog used to hunt raccoons—it's eligible for burial in the Coon Dog Memorial Graveyard (www.coondog cemetery.com) of northwest Alabama. More than 185 coon dogs are buried in the cemetery, which was begun in 1937. The dogs don't have to be purebred, but they must be genuine coon dogs. The cemetery doesn't accept household pets—and went so far as to dig up an impostor whose owner had tried to pass it off as a coonhound.

Endnotes

1 3 Pa. Cons. Stat. Ann. § 459-201.

2 For example, see Mich. Comp. Laws § 287.286b.

3 For example, see *Ramm v. City of Seattle*, 66 Wash. App. 15, 830 P.2d 395 (1992); *Gates v. City of Sanford*, 566 So. 2d 47, rev. dis. 576 So. 2d 287 (Fla. App. 1990).

4 *Zageris v. City of Whitehall,* 72 Ohio App. 3d 178, 594 N.E.2d 129 (1991), quoting *Downing v. Cook,* 69 Ohio St. 2d 149, 431 N.E.2d (1982).

5 *Bal Harbour Village v. Welsh*, 879 So. 2d 1265 (Fla. App. 2004); *Foster v. State*, No. S00A2054 (Sup. Ct. Ga., Mar. 19, 2001).

6 *Foster v. State*, No. S00A2054 (Sup. Ct. Ga., Mar. 19, 2001).

7 *Brotemarkle v. Snyder*, 99 Cal. App. 2d 388, 221 P.2d 992 (1950).

8 For example, see 3 Pa. Cons. Stat. Ann. § 459-305.

9 Los Angeles County Superior Court, January 1987.

10 *Smith v. Costello*, 77 Idaho 205, 290 P.2d 742 (1955).

11 Op. Mich. Atty. Gen. No. 6024, p. 524 (1982).

12 For example, see *Fucelli v. American Soc. for Prevention of Cruelty to Animals,* 23 N.Y.S. 2d 983 (1940) (court ordered dog returned to owner after it had been seized by New York City Department of Health without a hearing).

13 *Phillips v. Director of the Dept. of Animal Regulation*, 183 Cal. App. 3d 372, 228 Cal. Rptr. 101 (1986).

14 *Johnston v. Atlanta Humane Soc.*, 326 S.E.2d 585 (Ga. App. 1985).

15 Cal. Civ. Code § 1834.7.

16 *Lincecum v. Smith*, 287 So. 2d 625 (La. App. 1973).

17 Fort Wayne, Ind., Ord. § 91.055.

18 San Mateo County Ord. Code § 6.12.030.

19 *Town of Nutley v. Forney*, 283 A.2d 142, 116 N.J. Super. 567 (1971).

20 *Schnapp v. Lefkowitz*, 101 Misc. 2d 1075, 422 N.Y.S. 2d 798 (1979).

21 Cal. Veh. Code §§ 23117, 42001.4; N.H. Rev. Stat. Ann. § 644:8-f.; Mass. Gen. Laws Ann., ch. 90 § 22H.

Buying and Selling Dogs

T wo kinds of laws come into play when a dog is sold: those that restrict how sellers can operate, and those that protect buyers, giving them the right to certain information before the sale and some rights after the sale. This chapter looks at what the law requires sellers to tell buyers, how to put a sales agreement in writing, and what to do if you're unhappy after you buy a pet.

Regulating Sellers

Many of the laws controlling dog sellers are aimed at pet shops, but some also affect anyone who advertises "adorable puppies for sale" after the family dog has a litter of pups. Here are the basics.

Local Bans or Restrictions

Some cities have begun to essentially outlaw pet stores that sell puppies or kittens. Albuquerque, New Mexico, for example, forbids pet stores from selling companion animals, which are defined as purebred dogs or cats.[1]

Special License Requirements

If you keep more than a certain number of dogs, or if you breed or sell even one of them, you may need a kennel or breeder's license from your city. And to get a kennel license, you may have to show that local zoning laws allow a kennel on your property.

Letting your dog have a litter of puppies just might make you a "dog breeder" under your local laws. Even if you don't make money from your kennel, you may need a "hobby kennel" license if you keep more than a certain number of dogs, although puppies less than a few months old usually aren't counted for this purpose.

The city of Los Angeles, for example, requires anyone "who sells or offers for sale any dog or cat" to buy an annual breeder's license. It also forbids advertising a dog for sale unless the ad contains the owner's license number. If you breed more than one litter a year, Los Angeles law requires you to have a kennel license, which carries its own set of restrictions and requirements. (Licenses are discussed in Chapter 2, State and Local Regulation.)

Health and Age of Dogs Sold

It is illegal to sell dogs that are diseased. Anyone who does may be penalized, and will at least have to return the buyer's money. (See "Warranties: What Did the Seller Promise?" below). Retail sellers may also be fined for selling unhealthy dogs. Many states do not allow puppies to be sold before they are a certain age, usually about six to 12 weeks.

Pet Shop Regulations

Most states impose only the most basic requirements on pet shop operators: sanitary conditions, proper heating and ventilation, enough food, and humane treatment of animals. Some also require animals to be inspected by a licensed veterinarian before they are sold. Most violations are misdemeanors and can be punished by fines or, rarely, short jail sentences. (Pet shop operators are sometimes also charged with more serious criminal offenses because of their treatment of animals; see Chapter 14, Cruelty.)

Because problems with animals from pet shops are so common, however, several states now require pet stores to make detailed disclosures to prospective buyers, and give purchasers stronger legal rights after the sale. These laws are discussed below.

What Sellers Must Tell You

Some states require sellers to disclose certain facts about the dog's health, age, and history. These disclosures are no substitute for a complete contract (discussed below), but they're a step in the right direction, because getting all the information you are legally entitled to may help you avoid problems. If your state doesn't require these disclosures by law, ask for the

The Puppy Mill–Pet Shop Connection

People who buy expensive purebred puppies in well-lit pet stores at the local shopping mall don't know that they may actually be supporting "puppy mills," where dogs spend their short lives in filthy, crowded cages. But puppy mills and pet shops couldn't survive without each other.

Most reputable dog breeders refuse to sell their dogs to pet shops. In fact, the code of ethics of some breeders' groups expressly forbids selling to pet retailers. So most pet shops across the country buy their dogs from midwestern puppy mills, where "the health of the dogs is disregarded in order to maintain a low overhead and maximize profits," as one court put it.[2] As their name implies, these places churn out puppies like factories turn out auto parts. And their purpose is the same: to make money.

Investigators from humane societies and law enforcement agencies have documented many instances of overcrowding and neglect of animals in these operations. At a typical puppy mill, you'll find:

- overbreeding
- inbreeding
- minimal veterinary care
- poor quality food and shelter
- continuous confinement in crowded cages (often made of wire, causing injuries)
- lack of socialization, and
- extreme neglect.

Many dogs suffer from malnutrition, parasites, and chronic disease. Many are destroyed or discarded once they can no longer produce puppies.

The ASPCA encourages people to pledge not to buy anything at a store that sells dogs, and warns that dogs sold online are often from puppy mills. See www.nopetstorepuppies.com. In 2011, the Humane Society of the United States sued Purebred Breeders LLC, a company that it says operates hundreds of websites and sells thousands of puppies online each year. HSUS, joined by people who bought dogs from the company, alleged that the company sold sick pets and misled buyers into believing that they were buying from local breeders.

information anyway. You should be wary of any seller who can't or won't give you answers.

New Hampshire, for example, requires retail sellers to show prospective buyers a health certificate for any dog or cat that's for sale.[3] California goes further and requires every retail seller of a dog to fill out and give the buyer a written form, which is provided by the state Department of Consumer Affairs.[4] The form documents the dog's medical history and origin, among other things.

Retailers must also post conspicuously on each cage the state in which the dog was bred.[5]

First Things to Ask the Seller

- Where the dog came from
- When it was born
- What immunizations it has had
- What medications or veterinary treatment it has had.

Dangerous dogs. A seller should always tell a prospective buyer if the dog has bitten someone or has shown very aggressive behavior. State law may require certain specific disclosures. In Ohio, for example, someone who knows a dog is vicious and sells or gives it away must give the new owner, the local board of health, and the county dog warden a form which contains the answers to several specific questions about the dog's behavior, including: "Has the dog ever chased or attempted to attack or bite a person? If yes, describe the incident(s) in which the behavior occurred."[6] (For more on the specific laws controlling dangerous dogs, see Chapter 12, Dangerous Dogs.)

Alternatives to Pet Stores

Pet shops charge high prices for purebred dogs. But keep in mind that purebred status alone tells you absolutely nothing about the health or temperament of the dog. Mixed-breed dogs make wonderful pets.

Reputable breeders. If you have your heart set on a purebred dog, go to a reputable breeder. You'll probably pay less because there's no middleman—and you'll be able to see the conditions under which your pet was raised. If you find a breeder on the Internet, be sure to check references (ask for the phone number and address of other customers) and ask the Better Business Bureau if it has gotten any complaints. Some buyers have been duped by online scam artists who never deliver.

Shelters. Shelters are full of adoptable dogs—including purebreds. Remember that there may be several shelters in your area, run by both public and private agencies.

Rescue groups. Many rescue groups specialize in finding good homes for dogs of a certain breed, while others handle mixed-breed dogs as well. A local humane society may be able to direct you to such a group. Or look on the Internet; a search for the name of the breed you're interested in will turn up information from a rescue group and photos of dogs who need homes. You can also try www.petfinder.org, which links to shelters and rescue groups—you can search by breed and location.

Putting a Sales Agreement in Writing

You can do one simple thing to avoid problems when you buy a dog: get your agreement in writing. Even if you think you and the person you're dealing with agree on everything, it is always useful to spell out the understanding on each side. You may not know until you sit down with pen and paper that the other person expects something quite different from what you do.

What belongs in a contract depends on why you're buying the dog. If you want a purebred dog that can be registered with the American Kennel

Club, that belongs in the agreement. If you just want a healthy mixed-breed dog, obviously there's no need to worry about pedigrees.

People who are in the business of buying and selling dogs may have their own contracts, covering all the subjects they've found important over the years. If you're not in the dog business, the checklist below lists areas to think about when drawing up an agreement.

Checklist for a Sales Agreement

Health. The seller should set out any health problems the dog has or may have, and should guarantee that the dog is otherwise healthy. Has the dog been examined by a veterinarian? Can you return the dog, or get reimbursed for your vet bills, if the vet finds a serious problem within a couple of weeks?

Vaccinations. List the vaccinations the dog has had and when they were given. It's also helpful to say what further vaccinations the dog will need, and when. List the veterinarian or clinic that gave the vaccination in case you need documentation—which may be the case when it's time to buy a dog license.

History. Where did the dog come from? You don't want a dog from a puppy mill, where inhumane conditions are the rule.

Training. If the dog is supposed to be trained for a particular purpose (hunting, obedience), document the extent of the training.

Pedigree. If the dog's lineage is important, spell it out and attach a copy of the parents' pedigrees.

Quality. If the dog is purebred but of only "pet quality"—that is, not up to competition in dog shows—specify that in the contract.

Price. Does it include vaccinations, or the cost of spaying or neutering?

Warranties. What kind of guarantees is the seller making? (Warranties are discussed in detail in the next section.)

Here is a sample bill of sale that may be modified for your needs. It's adapted from the bills of sale in *101 Law Forms for Personal Use,* by Robin Leonard and Ralph Warner (Nolo).

Sample Bill of Sale

1. _____ , Seller, sells to

   _____ , Buyer, the dog described in paragraph 2.

2. The dog being sold is:

   Name _____

   Breed _____

   Sex _____   Birthdate _____

3. The full purchase price is $_____ .

4. Buyer has paid Seller:

   ☐ the full purchase price.

   ☐ $_____ , balance due on _____ .

5. Seller is the legal owner of the dog described in paragraph 2.

6. Seller believes that the dog is healthy and in good condition except for the following:

   _____

   _____

   _____

   _____

   _____

7. The dog has had the following vaccinations:

Vaccination	Date	Veterinarian

The dog will need these vaccinations next:

Vaccination	Date	Veterinarian

8. Seller obtained the dog from: _____

_____ on _____ .

9. The dog has had the following special training:

_____

_____

_____

10. The dog ☐ is purebred   ☐ is not purebred.

The dog ☐ is registerable with the American Kennel Club.

☐ is registered with the American Kennel Club.

11. ☐ Buyer agrees to take possession of dog immediately.

☐ Seller will ship dog to Buyer.

Date of shipment: _____ Method : _____

To be paid for by: _____

☐ Dog will be insured for $_____

12. Other terms. _____

_____

_____

_____

_____

Seller: _____ Date: _____

Buyer: _____ Date: _____

Special State "Lemon Laws"

Laws regulating pet stores have been notably unsuccessful at stemming the tide of consumer complaints about sick animals bought at pet shops. So some states have passed laws that are aimed not at policing sellers but at protecting buyers. Following the example set by "lemon laws," which give car buyers a procedure to get a refund or a new car if theirs turns out to be a hopeless lemon, some states have adopted similar laws for pet buyers.[7]

States With "Lemon Laws" for Dogs		
Arizona	Massachusetts	Oregon
Arkansas	Minnesota	Pennsylvania
California	Nebraska	Rhode Island
Connecticut	Nevada	South Carolina
Delaware	New Hampshire	Vermont
Florida	New Jersey	Virginia
Maine	New York	

Generally, these laws allow buyers to return an unhealthy dog to the seller for a refund or another animal. In most states the owner has one to two weeks to return the animal, with a certificate from a veterinarian stating that the dog has a serious disease or congenital defect that was present when the dog was sold. If the dog suffers from a congenital disorder, the owner may have up to a year to return it to the pet store.

These statutes give owners who find themselves with sick pets one or more of these choices:

- Returning the animal for a refund, including the cost of reasonable veterinary services directly related to the examination that showed the animal was ill, and emergency treatment to relieve suffering.
- Exchanging the animal for another, and also getting reimbursement for the same veterinary expenses.
- Keeping the animal and receiving reimbursement for reasonable veterinary costs of trying to cure the animal. The amount of

reimbursement is limited, however, to the purchase price of the pet (150% of that amount in California).

To make sure consumers know their rights under these laws, several states require pet stores to give buyers a written notice explaining them. In some states, the form must contain a certificate for a veterinarian to complete if the animal turns out to have a serious illness or congenital defect.

Warranties: What Did the Seller Promise?

Even if your state doesn't have a specific law that applies to sales of dogs, if you're a dissatisfied buyer you may be entitled to a refund or replacement under general warranty (guarantee) law. Because dogs are considered property, their sale is subject to essentially the same rules as the sale of a washing machine or a lampshade. These rules, however, vary from state to state.[8] Usually, the result depends on what promises, if any, the seller made to the buyer.

Express Warranties

If the seller promises you something (say, that the dog is a rare purebred Albanian lizard hound) and you base the decision to buy on that promise ("I would *never* have bought the dog if I had known it was half Albanian lizard hound and half poodle!"), the promise is called an "express warranty." If the express warranty is violated, you can sue to get back the purchase price.

> **EXAMPLE:** A man paid $3,000 for a dog he intended to enter in bird dog field trials. He claimed the seller had expressly promised that the dog was trained and ready to compete in major field trials. Once he had the dog, however, he discovered that it was infected with heartworms and was not trained well enough for major competition. He sued, and a jury believed him and ordered the seller to give him back what he'd paid.[9]

What's the difference between an express warranty and mere sales talk? Not surprisingly, buyers and sellers sometimes disagree. The general rule is that if something the seller said really becomes part of the reason the deal is made, it's a warranty. But if the seller just natters on and on about how her dogs are the smartest or prettiest or happiest dogs in the world, most courts wouldn't hold her to that promise. But who wants to argue about such things? You'll save your breath, and lots of time, money, and aggravation, if you get all of the agreement in writing.

Implied Warranties

Even if a seller doesn't make explicit promises, implied promises often float about when a sale is being negotiated. If you're an unhappy buyer, you can rely on an implied promise just like you can rely on an express one—that is, you can sue to get your money back if the promise isn't kept. But you don't want to. Implied promises are by their nature hard to prove, and you'll spend a lot of time fighting over who said what.

You may, however, be stuck with an unsatisfactory dog and only the seller's implied promises. So, briefly, here are the two kinds of implied warranties:

Merchantability. One promise that is implied in most sales is that whatever is being sold will perform as well as items of its type should. In the context of the sale of a dog, this means that the dog should be healthy and not suffering from any kind of abnormal defect. For example, it doesn't matter that a seller doesn't promise, specifically, that a dog doesn't have mange; you have the right to expect that a dog offered for sale is healthy.

Fitness for a particular purpose. This kind of implied promise arises if the seller recommends a certain product for a certain purpose. Let's say you want a guard dog to roam around your used car parts lot at night, and a kennel owner, knowing this, recommends a Doberman named Spooky. By making the recommendation, the seller impliedly warranties Spooky as a guard dog. Spooky looks fine to you, so you buy him. It turns out later that the seller neglected to tell you that Spooky, traumatized as a pup, turns tail and hides if anyone so much as looks crossly at him. The seller breached the implied warranty of fitness, and you're entitled to your money back.

What to Do If You're Unhappy After the Sale

Consumer protection, warranty, and breach of contract laws differ from state to state. But some advice generally applies:

- If you are dissatisfied after buying a dog, promptly tell the seller so, in writing. If you have a written agreement, refer to it. Keep a copy of your letter.
- If your state has a "lemon law" for pets, check its provisions and see what you must do to exercise your rights under the law.
- If the seller doesn't make things right by giving you a new dog or your money back within about 30 days, think about bringing a lawsuit in small claims court.
- If you file in small claims court, don't worry about learning all the ins and outs of warranty or contract law. The judge will probably decide more on the basis of fairness than on legal technicalities.
- You can help the judge come to the conclusion you want by bringing to court any evidence you have of the laws or warranties you think have been breached. You may want to take an advertisement, or witnesses who heard what the seller told you. For example, if you bought your dog after answering a classified ad that offered "AKC-registered, champion-sired Brittany spaniels for sale," but the pups turn out to lack a pedigree, bring the ad with you.

RESOURCE

Everybody's Guide to Small Claims Court, by Ralph Warner (Nolo), discusses warranties and explains how to present your case to the judge.

(For more on how small claims court works, see Chapter 7, Barking Dogs.)

Class Action Lawsuits

Some angry dog owners who bought seriously ill pets from a chain pet store have banded together and sued the stores. Such a lawsuit may bring greater pressure on the stores, but is much more complicated than a small claims court suit and generally requires the assistance of a lawyer.

Endnotes

1 Albuquerque Code of Ordinances 9-2-3-12.

2 *Avenson v. Zegart*, 577 F. Supp. 958 (D. Minn. 1984).

3 N.H. Rev. Stat. Ann. § 437:10.

4 Cal. Health & Safety Code § 122140.

5 Cal. Health & Safety Code § 122215.

6 Ohio Rev. Code Ann. § 955.11.

7 Ariz. Rev. Stat. § 44-1799.05 and following; Ark. Code Ann. § 4-97-101 and following; Cal. Health & Safety Code § 122070 and following; Conn. Gen. Stat. Ann. § 22-344b; Del. Code Ann. tit. 6, § 4001 and following; Fla. Stat. § 828.31; Me. Rev. Stat. Ann., tit. 7, § 4151 and following; Mass. Dept. of Food and Agric. Regs., 330 C.M.R. 12.05; Minn. Stat. § 325F.791; Neb. Rev. Stat. Ann. § 54-644 and following; Nev. Rev. Stat. § 574.490; N.H. Rev. Stat. Ann. § 437:13; N.J. Admin. Code 13:45A-12.1; N.Y. Gen. Bus. Law § 753; 73; Or. Rev. Stat. § 646A.077; Pa. Cons. Stat. § 201-9.3; R.I. Gen Laws § 4-25-5; S.C. Code Ann. § 47-13-160; Va. Code Ann. § 3.1-796.78; Vt. Stat. Ann., tit. 20, § 4301 to 4303.

8 Both state and federal law may affect what happens when a buyer is unhappy after a sale. State laws are based on the Uniform Commercial Code (U.C.C.), a set of laws that every state has adopted, with small changes. A federal law that applies in all states, the Magnuson-Moss Consumer Warranty Act, requires warranties to be written in understandable language.

9 *Brown v. Faircloth*, 66 So. 2d 232 (Fla. 1953).

Landlords and Dogs

The conventional wisdom is that dogs and apartments don't mix. This is a particularly unhappy state of affairs as households shrink, and more and more people live in rentals. If you haven't given up and gotten a gerbil, read on. And take heart: with a little cooperation among landlord, tenant, and dog, many dog-owning tenants can live happily in rental housing.

This chapter discusses how a landlord and prospective tenant can work out a lease or rental agreement that's fair to both sides. It also looks at no-pets clauses in leases: when they apply and when they don't.

Assistance dogs. Landlords may not legally refuse to rent to tenants who need a dog because they have a disability. (See Chapter 8, Assistance Dogs.)

Negotiating a Fair Lease

Some landlords prefer to rent to pet owners, finding them a more responsible class of tenants. Some allow small dogs. A trend that seems to be growing in popularity among landlords—but not tenants—is "pet rent." In addition to any extra pet-related security deposit, and in addition to the regular rent, the landlord tacks on an extra monthly fee (pet rent) for each pet. At $10 to $40 a month for each pet, these extra payments add up quickly.

Some landlords will make an exception to their usual no-dogs rule if they become convinced that they're dealing with a responsible owner—which means that an official no-dogs policy isn't always the final word. If you want to negotiate something with a property owner or manager, be realistic. It's obvious why many landlords are reluctant to rent to dog owners: dogs can cause serious damage to apartments and yards, they can be a nuisance if they bark and a menace if they bite or frighten people. Landlords' concerns are reasonable: they risk losing time and money and, in some instances, may even face legal liability if the dog injures someone.

Before agreeing to rent to you and your dog, a landlord has a reasonable right to expect both convincing evidence that the dog won't cause problems, and provisions in the lease or rental agreement that spell out your responsibilities. The checklist below should help you work something out.

Convincing a Skeptical Landlord

- Get references from previous landlords or neighbors—brief letters saying what a nice, well-mannered pet you have.
- Show the landlord anything else that indicates the dog will be a good tenant: obedience school certificates, proof of spaying or neutering, vaccination and licensing records.
- Bring the dog along on a second visit to the new place, if the landlord agrees.
- Have the dog spayed or neutered, if you haven't already. Many problems are caused by female dogs in heat, which attract noisy and persistent suitors. And having the dog sterilized shows that you're a responsible owner.
- Offer to put down a substantial damage deposit, over and above what the landlord usually charges, to show your confidence in the dog's good behavior. (State or local law may limit the amount of the deposit; California, for example, limits security deposits to twice the amount of the monthly rent, or three times the rent for a furnished apartment.)[1]

Whatever agreement you work out, it should always be clearly set out in writing—no exceptions. If you have a dog, never sign a lease that contains a standard "no-pets" clause, even if the owner or manager has offered oral assurances that it's all right to have the dog. If the landlord later reconsiders, or sells the property to a new owner, you could land in the middle of a legal battle. (This is discussed more fully in "Enforcing a No-Pets Clause After Allowing a Dog," below).

You can modify a rental agreement or add a separate addendum to cover pets. Here are some clauses you can modify to fit your situation and add to a standard rental agreement or lease.

- "Tenant may have one dog, his Miniature Schnauzer named Pepper, on the premises."
- "Tenant may have one dog, which weighs less than 50 pounds, on the premises."
- "Tenant will remove dog droppings from the yard daily [or, if the yard is private, weekly]."
- "Tenant will repair, or pay for repair of, any damage done to yard or house by dog."

- "Tenant will keep the dog inside between the hours of 10 p.m. and 7 a.m."
- "Tenant will pay a $300 refundable security deposit, in addition to the standard security deposit of $500, to cover any damage that may be caused by the dog."
- "In lieu of paying an increased security deposit, tenant will pay for steam cleaning of the carpets when she moves out."
- "Tenant will keep $100,000 of liability insurance to cover injuries or damage caused by the dog." This clause is necessary only if there's some reason to fear the dog might injure someone. (See "Landlord Liability for Tenants' Dogs," below.)

Opening Landlords' Doors to Pets

Several organizations concerned about animals and people have programs to help landlords and pet-owning tenants get along.

Project Open Door, an ambitious program of the San Francisco Society for the Prevention of Cruelty to Animals (SPCA), seeks to show landlords how to make renting to pet-owning tenants a satisfying and profitable experience. The SPCA offers:

- checklists to help landlords screen pet-owning tenants
- model policies for tenants with dogs or cats
- model agreements to add to standard leases and rental agreements, and
- free mediation if landlords and tenants have problems.

Tenants can get good materials, too, on how to negotiate with a landlord.

Other animal welfare organizations, including the Humane Society of the United States and the Massachusetts SPCA, also publish guidelines for tenants and property managers.

For more information, contact the San Francisco SPCA at 2500 16th St., San Francisco, CA 94103, 415-554-3000. Or check out its website at www.sfspca.org. You can reach the Humane Society of the United States at 2100 L Street, NW, Washington, DC 20037, www.humanesociety.org. The Massachusetts SPCA is at 350 South Huntington Ave., Boston, MA 02130, 617-522-7400, www.mspca.org.

Mobile Home Parks
Special laws may apply to tenants in mobile home parks. For example, in California a mobile home park cannot prohibit pets, and cannot charge a fee for keeping pets unless it actually provides special facilities or services for pets.[2] In Oregon, a tenant may keep a pet that's legally living there, if the landlord adds a no-pets clause to the rules.[3]

Elderly Tenants or Tenants With Disabilities

The special place pets occupy in the lives of older people or people living with disabilities is well recognized. Finally, at least in some places, the law is taking that special bond into account.

Subsidized Housing

Older or disabled people, living in government-subsidized housing, being forced to give up pets that are their cherished companions—it doesn't make for good press for the bureaucrats responsible. Pressure on those government officials has yielded results.

Tenants in "federally assisted" housing for the elderly or handicapped are allowed by law to own pets.[4] This rule applies even if the federal government does not own the rental housing—it's enough that a federal agency (the U.S. Department of Housing and Urban Development, for example) subsidizes it. Owners and managers may place reasonable regulations on pets, after consulting with tenants.[5] Contact a local HUD office or your county Housing Authority to find out if a particular rental is covered.

Several states have also taken action. In California, residents of public housing developments (those owned and operated by a state, county, city, or district agency) who are over the age of 60 or have a disability may keep up to two small pets per apartment.[6] Arizona, Connecticut, the District of Columbia, Massachusetts, Minnesota, and New Hampshire have similar rules, allowing tenants in state-owned housing developments for the elderly or disabled to have pets.[7] (In Connecticut, a tenant may have a pet if the housing project allowed pets when the person applied for admission.)

The laws allow the public agencies to make reasonable regulations about pets. In Massachusetts, for example, policy guidelines issued by the state limit tenants to one pet; a dog must not weigh more than 40 pounds, and it must be spayed or neutered. The Arizona statute forbids requiring a tenant to pay a deposit of more than one month's rent.

But regardless of standard lease terms, landlords must make "reasonable accommodations" for tenants with disabilities, as long as the accommodations don't impose undue hardship on the operation of the property.[8] For example, a New Jersey court ruled that a man with paraplegia might be allowed to have a dog that was bigger than the 20-pound limit imposed by the standard lease. The man had trained the dog to retrieve objects for him, and two doctors stated that keeping the dog was important to his emotional well-being. The landlord could not automatically exclude the dog, the court said, without an inquiry into whether allowing the dog to stay was a reasonable accommodation for the tenant.[9]

Similarly, a Massachusetts woman with a psychiatric disability was allowed to keep her cat, despite a no-pets rule in her subsidized apartment complex. At her eviction trial, experts testified that she was emotionally attached to her pet and had "perhaps even psychological dependence" on it. A state appeals court ruled that accommodating the tenant was required under the law; the animal had caused no problems or complaints, and allowing her to keep it would not pose a hardship for the management of the apartments.[10]

However, a man failed in his efforts to keep a dog despite a no-pets clause in his lease. He claimed that the dog helped his health because it prompted him to walk and because he had formed an emotional attachment to it, but did not present evidence of any psychiatric disability or psychological dependence on his dog, He also did not show any connection between his physical ailments and his attachment to the dog.[11]

If the management makes reasonable accommodations and the pet still creates problems, the tenant may be evicted. For example, a Connecticut housing complex for the elderly and disabled had trouble with a tenant whose dog frightened and bothered other residents. The dog's owner, a chronic schizophrenic, did not walk his dog in the designated areas or clean up after it, and left it in his apartment for long periods of time. Despite the efforts of a social worker and the dog trainer whom she enlisted to help, problems persisted. A court reluctantly concluded that the management had made the reasonable accommodations required by law, and could proceed with an eviction.[12]

Private Housing

Landlords must make "reasonable accommodations" for tenants who have a disability, and that includes modifying a no-pets policy if necessary. This is a requirement of federal law, the Fair Housing Act. For more on tenants' rights and landlords' responsibilities, see "Rental Housing" in Chapter 8, Assistance Dogs.

States may also offer their own protections. In Arizona, the District of Columbia, Minnesota, and New Jersey, elderly tenants have rights to keep pets in either public or private housing. In Montgomery County, Maryland, a tenant 60 years old or older may keep a pet unless pets are specifically prohibited, in writing, when the tenant takes occupancy.[13]

New Jersey, for example, guarantees the right of senior citizens in any "senior citizen housing project" to have pets. Any building with three or more units, intended for and solely occupied by persons 62 or older, is covered by the law. (Owner-occupied buildings with less than three units are exempted.) Residents can have a dog, cat, or any other animal that doesn't constitute a health or safety hazard. A landlord who unreasonably refuses to renew a tenant's lease because of a pet that is properly cared for and not a nuisance can be fined up to $500.[14]

Why It Matters

Many elderly people wouldn't move to better housing if it meant giving up their pets, according to a new study. Researchers talked to 2,300 older people in Evanston, Illinois, nearly one-third of whom owned pets. Of the pet owners, 86% said pet ownership dictated where they lived.[15]

Public Housing

Federal law allows tenants in public housing to keep companion animals, subject to reasonable regulations established by the public housing agency.[16] The agency can charge pet deposits or fees, and can, for example, restrict the size, weight, or number of pets. It can make other restrictions based on the particular property—for example, a high-rise building could reasonably have rules quite different from a smaller building with backyards.

Enforcing No-Pets Clauses

> *In today's troubled world and times, the need to communicate and reach out and care for other human beings and other forms of comforting animal life ... should not be inhibited .... Instead, the court should attempt to preserve decent and reasonable rules by which mankind and animals may live together in harmony.*
>
> —New York City Civil Court, Queens County[17]

As all pet-owning tenants know, most standard leases and rental agreements contain no-pets clauses. Such provisions are legal everywhere, and courts generally allow a landlord to evict a tenant who acquires a pet in violation of a lease clause and refuses to give it up.

In certain situations, however, a landlord may not be able to enforce a no-pets clause if a tenant and dog are already living in a rental unit and:

- The landlord tries to add a no-pets clause to a rental agreement; or
- The landlords tries to enforce an existing no-pets clause, after knowing about but not objecting to a tenant's dog for a significant period; or
- The landlord agreed, no matter what the lease says, that the tenant could have a dog; or
- The tenant has a disability and allowing a dog is a reasonable accommodation; or
- The tenant can prove that keeping a dog is necessary for security reasons.

You don't want to go to court to argue about any of these theories if you can possibly avoid it. So if a landlord tries to get rid of you or your pet, sit down together and try to work things out. You may end up paying a little more rent or putting down a bigger security deposit, but it will be cheaper than court.

Landlord-Tenant Mediation

Before you run to court to hash out a disagreement with your landlord, remember that, usually, everyone loses when fights go to court. You lose money and time, and legal procedures have a way of escalating tensions, so that even petty differences start looking like life-and-death matters of principle.

One good alternative to court is mediation—getting together with a neutral third person who helps you and the other person work out the problem. The mediator doesn't have power to impose a settlement, but is trained to help people come up with their own solutions. Mediation is quick and usually cheap or free.

Many cities have free programs specifically designed to mediate landlord-tenant disputes. The mediators are familiar with the common problems that crop up between landlords and tenants—and dogs are certainly one of them. To find out if such a program is available in your area, call your local small claims court, Rent Control Board (if your city has rent control), or a Tenants' Union, Landlords' Association, bar association, or community mediation organization.

A local humane society may even provide mediators specifically for landlord-tenant disputes about pets. The San Francisco SPCA, for example, provides this service as part of its "Open Door" program.

(For more on how mediation works, see Chapter 7, Barking Dogs.)

Adding a No-Pets Clause to a Lease

Even though landlords may refuse to rent to someone with a pet, it's harder for a landlord to change the rules if a tenant already has a pet. The landlord's legal right to change the terms of the tenancy usually depends on whether the landlord and tenant signed a rental agreement or a lease.

- A **lease** is an agreement that lasts for a specified time. Neither the landlord nor tenant can unilaterally change the terms of the lease while it is in effect. When the lease comes up for renewal, generally a landlord is free to change its terms. But, as discussed just below, a landlord who hasn't objected to a dog for a long time may have lost the chance.
- A **rental agreement** is open-ended. Commonly, it runs from month to month, and allows the landlord to change the terms of the rental agreement with 30 days' notice to the tenant. Local rent control ordinances, or the rental agreement itself, may limit the landlord's right to make such changes. (If the landlord and tenant didn't sign anything, but simply agreed that the tenant would pay a certain amount of rent every month, the law says that they have a month-to-month rental agreement.)

Some special local rules may apply, however. Some cities, recognizing that adding a no-pets provision is often just a way to get rid of a tenant for another reason, have restricted the practice. Check your local ordinances or call the city to find out.

Enforcing a No-Pets Clause After Allowing a Dog

A landlord who doesn't object to a tenant's pet for several months or years may lose the right to enforce a written no-pets clause. By not acting promptly, the landlord waives the right to object. (Some landlords get around this rule by including a clause in the lease saying that a landlord who fails to enforce a lease clause when it's first violated can still enforce it later.)

How long a landlord can wait to enforce depends on the circumstances. A few days, obviously, isn't too long, as an Indiana tenant found out when his landlord told him to get rid of a cat three days after he moved in.[18] But a tenant who has had a pet for several months or a year may have a strong legal argument for getting to keep it.[19] For example, tenants who kept a dog for six years could not be evicted under their lease's no-pets clause, a New York court ruled.[20] It may be enough, by the way, that the landlord's agent—the apartment manager, if there is one—knows of the pet.

In New York City, a landlord has three months, after finding out about a tenant's pet, to start enforcing a no-pets clause in a lease. If the clause isn't enforced during that period, the landlord loses the right to enforce it (again, of course, unless the pet is a nuisance).[21] The ordinance mentions only leases; it doesn't say whether or not a landlord who has allowed a pet can add a no-pets clause to a month-to-month rental agreement.

Separate Agreement With the Landlord

What if a landlord or manager tells you it's all right to move in with a pet, even though the standard printed lease they signed says no-pets are allowed? If you relied on the landlord's promise that it was all right to have a dog (bought a dog, or moved into the apartment just because dogs were allowed there), a court might rule that the landlord could not later try to get out of the agreement. In the end, it comes down to basic fairness.

For example, a New Jersey court ruled that tenants who had kept a dog for more than ten years could not be kicked out of their apartment because they refused to accept a no-pets clause when they renewed their lease. The apartment manager had told the tenants that they could have a dog because they were such good tenants. The court found that because the tenants had relied on that promise, buying and becoming attached to a purebred dog, they should not have to get rid of their pet "on the basis of a landlord's whim or caprice."[22]

What If You Need a Dog for Protection?

Security is a big factor in many people's decisions to get dogs, and it can be a big factor in a judge's decision as well. A tenant who can prove that a dog is necessary for personal safety and peace of mind because of well-grounded fears of crime may be able to override a no-pets restriction. Evidence of a well-founded fear is a history of crime in the neighborhood, drug deals in the building, or break-ins at the apartment.

If the dog is not a nuisance, the tenant will probably at least get a chance to argue that the no-pets clause is unreasonable and shouldn't be enforced. Some courts, however, have flatly rejected this argument.[23]

Condominiums and Planned Developments

People looking to buy a condominium or planned subdivision unit (frequently called planned unit development or P.U.D.) should be prepared for rules. Lots of rules, covering everything from the kind of shutters you can have on the windows to how many pets you can have and what color you can paint the doghouse.

These rules can be found in the development's "Covenants, Conditions, and Restrictions" (CC&Rs), the bylaws or declarations of a condominium owners' association or other document. They often forbid or strictly limit the number of animals that residents can have, and residents can do little to get around them. If a resident violates a no-pets rule, the condominium governing body can get a court order (injunction) that prohibits the resident from keeping the pet.[24]

A resident who wants to challenge a no-pets rule successfully must prove one of three things:

* the rule is being enforced arbitrarily or unfairly
* it is unreasonable, or
* it was not adopted by the proper procedure.

Unfair enforcement. If a no-pets rule isn't enforced evenly—if, for example, some owners are singled out for enforcement and others are left alone—the targeted owners may be able to challenge the enforcers. In most cases, this is the strongest tack to take. For example, a Florida man won the right to keep his dog after a condominium association tried to enforce a pet restriction retroactively. The association passed a rule that residents could not keep dogs unless the pets were replacements for dogs that had been registered with the association a year earlier. A court struck down the rule.[25]

Reasonableness. This avenue of attack is not promising when it comes to a condominium rule that forbids pets or allows only one small pet. Courts always say no-pets restrictions in condominiums are reasonable, given residents' concerns about "potentially offensive odors, noise, possible health hazards, clean-up and maintenance problems, and the fact that pets can and do defile hallways, elevators, and other common areas."[26] Rules that allow residents to keep the dogs they have, but not to replace them if they die, have also been upheld in some states.[27] Subdivisions, where residents are more widely spaced, rarely ban dogs, and such a prohibition might be more vulnerable to a reasonableness challenge.

Improperly adopted rules. Every condominium has a decision-making group made up of some or all the unit owners. Whatever its form, it must follow its own rules when it adopts regulations that affect all the unit owners. That means following the requirements for voting, giving notice to owners, and holding meetings. As a practical matter, it may not matter that a rule was improperly adopted; after all, the rule-makers can probably just go do it again, this time getting the procedure right. But if the improper procedure really did make a difference—so that a new owner didn't know about the rule, for example—it's possible that a resident might get to hang on to a pet as a result.

For example, the board of directors of a Massachusetts condominium complex adopted a rule that prohibited animals outside of the units, and sued a couple for walking their golden retriever in the common areas. An appeals court ruled that the inside-only rule was invalid and unenforceable because it had never been put to a vote of the unit owners and wasn't, as required by state law, in the bylaws or master deed of the condo organization.[28]

The Aloha State Welcomes Pets

In Hawaii, if bylaws don't forbid pets, any condominium owner who has a pet may replace that pet if it dies.

People who rent from condominium owners are subject to the same restrictions the owners are. Bylaws may not forbid tenants from keeping pets if owners are allowed to keep them, and the owner of the unit agrees.[29]

Landlord Liability for Illegal Evictions

A tenant who is evicted illegally, in violation of a state statute or local rent control ordinance, may be able to sue the landlord for the damages suffered as a result. And a tenant who is forced to give up a dog because of an illegal eviction may be able to recover money specifically for that loss. A landlord in Hayward, California, agreed to pay a ten-year-old boy $5,000 for the emotional distress the boy suffered when he had to give up his dog. The landlord had evicted the boy's family from their apartment in violation of the city's rent control ordinance, and the dog was not allowed in their new apartment.[30] (How to put a dollar figure on the emotional distress you suffer when you lose a dog is discussed in Chapter 9, If a Dog Is Injured or Killed.)

Landlord Liability for Tenants' Dogs

One of the reasons landlords are reluctant to rent to tenants with pets is that in some circumstances, a landlord may be financially responsible for damage or injury caused by a tenant's dog. In other words, if the injured person sues the landlord, the landlord, as well as the dog's owner, may end up paying. Tenants must be prepared to deal with the landlord's fear of liability.

It's very rare, however, for a landlord to be found liable for injuries inflicted by a tenant's dog. Just leasing premises to a tenant with a dog usually isn't enough, by itself, to make a landlord legally responsible for a tenant's dog. For example, if a tenant's apparently friendly dog bites someone, the landlord isn't liable for the injury.[31]

In general, when a tenant's dog injures someone, courts hold the landlord liable only if the landlord:

- knew the dog was dangerous and could have had the dog removed; *or*
- "harbored" or "kept" the tenant's dog—that is, cared for or had some control over the dog.

These factors are discussed just below. They apply to homeowners' associations, which control common areas in their developments, as well as traditional landlords.[32]

If a landlord is found financially liable, the liability coverage of the building owner's insurance may cover the loss. (Liability insurance is discussed in Chapter 11, Dog Bites.)

Knowing About and Having Power to Remove the Dog

In many states, someone trying to hold a landlord liable for injuries caused by a tenant's dog must prove both that the landlord knew that the dog was dangerous and that the landlord had the power, legally, to make the tenant get rid of the dog or move out.[33] Sometimes, courts put this requirement in terms of the landlord's general duty to keep the property in a safe condition.[34] As one court put it, a property owner cannot "sit idly by in the face of the known danger to others."[35]

But not all states use this rule. Under some laws, landlords are not liable even when they know a tenant's dog is likely to hurt someone. A Montana rancher, for example, knew that a dog belonging to his foreman (who lived on the rancher's property) had bitten someone. But when the dog later bit a utility company meter-reader, the rancher wasn't held liable. If, however, the rancher had exercised some control over the animal—was a "keeper" under the law—he would have been liable.[36]

A court may also refuse to find a landlord liable if the landlord does not control the area on which the dog bite occurred. For example, an Iowa court found that a landlord was not liable when a tenant's dog bit a visitor because the rental was a single-family house, and the landlord "did not retain control of the area in which the injury occurred." As a result, the landlord did not have a duty to keep that area safe; the responsibility was the tenant's.[37]

Actual knowledge. To be held liable, a landlord must actually know that a tenant's dog is a danger to others. Dogs aren't presumed to be dangerous. So only a landlord who has specific knowledge of the dog's dangerous disposition is legally responsible if it injures someone. A Pennsylvania landlord, for example, was not liable for injuries suffered by a boy bitten by a tenant's dog, because there was no evidence that the landlord had actual knowledge that the dog was dangerous.[38] In practice, that means the landlord must know that the dog has already threatened or injured someone.

For example, a landlord who knows only that a tenant's dog is kept chained and barks at people who approach probably will not be held liable if the dog bites someone. A New York court, given those circumstances, did not hold a landlord liable for the injury her tenant's dog had inflicted.

Especially in light of the town's leash law, the court ruled, the landlord shouldn't be expected to infer that a dog is dangerous just because it is kept enclosed in a yard.[39]

Generally, knowing or believing that a tenant's dog is a pit bull terrier isn't the same as knowing the dog is dangerous—though there's a possible exception in cities and states that have declared all "pit bull type" dogs dangerous or banned them outright. (See Chapter 12, Dangerous Dogs.) For example, a Massachusetts landlord was sued after his tenant's dog, identified as a pit bull terrier, bit a child. The court ruled that the landlord could not be held liable just on the basis of the dog's breed, but that breed propensities could be taken into account in determining whether the landlord had been negligent.[40] And a New Jersey court ruled that without expert evidence of the propensity of a particular breed to aggressiveness, a jury's decision would be "rooted solely on passion, prejudice, or partiality, which is an impermissible result."[41]

If the dog is particularly threatening, however, that may be enough evidence of a dangerous tendency, as a Colorado landlord found out. Before signing a lease, the landlord took care of two dogs that belonged to a prospective tenant. During the two weeks he had the dogs, they threatened his grandchild. Nevertheless, he rented to the tenants. When the dogs later severely injured a child, a court found the landlord liable for the injuries. The court ruled that by leasing the premises to the tenants, the landlord knowingly created a "clear potential for injury."[42]

Courts generally say that a landlord who rents to a tenant with a dog doesn't have to observe the dog's behavior or check public records for complaints about the dog. For example, a California company rented a house to a family and specified in the rental agreement that they could keep a German shepherd named Thunder. The 100-pound dog chased a cable television installer out of the yard, making him injure his shoulder as he dove headlong over a fence to get away. The landlord was not held liable for the injury. There was no evidence that the landlord knew the dog was dangerous, and the court ruled that the landlord didn't need to assume that a German shepherd called Thunder would be vicious. After all, the court said, "it is not uncommon for an owner of a St. Bernard or a Great Dane to name the dog Tiny."[43]

(For a more detailed discussion of what kinds of facts put someone on notice that a dog is dangerous, see "The Common Law 'One-Bite' Rule" in Chapter 11, Dog Bites.)

A landlord who ignores overwhelming evidence of the danger posed by a tenant's dog does so at his peril. Such an irresponsible landlord may be punished by being made to pay extra damages (called punitive damages) over the amount needed to compensate the victim. That's what happened in an Alaska case, after a six-year-old girl was mauled by two dogs that belonged to her next-door neighbor in an Anchorage mobile home park. When she sued the mobile home park, a jury awarded her $235,000 in compensatory damages and $550,000 in punitive damages. On appeal, the court ruled that the mobile home park's inaction, after it knew of incidents involving the tenant's dogs, had been such "blatant disregard of its tenants' safety" that it justified the extra damages.[44]

On the other hand, some Ohio landlords were not liable for injuries caused when a tenant's dog bit a child, even though they knew the dog had bitten another child nine days earlier. The landlords said, in sworn statements, that they thought the dog had been destroyed after the first incident. The court ruled that this reasonable belief meant that they had no duty to take further action.[45] Whether other courts would let a landlord off the hook in similar circumstances is questionable; most courts hold landlords liable for knowing about conditions (including the presence of a dangerous dog) on their property.

Power to remove the dog. Obviously, it wouldn't be fair to hold a landlord responsible for a dog he is powerless to control or have removed. For example, say a landlord buys a building that is already occupied by a tenant who has both a one-year lease and a dangerous dog. The landlord probably won't be liable for any injuries the dog causes, because the landlord may not be able to order the dog removed. But if the tenant has a month-to-month rental agreement, which can be terminated on 30 days' notice, the landlord who does nothing after finding out the tenant has a dangerous dog may be liable if the dog later hurts someone. (Remember, however, that local laws may restrict a landlord's ability to terminate a rental agreement.)

In a North Carolina case, a tenant's two rottweilers attacked a visitor. The lease gave the landlord the right to demand that the tenant remove his dogs within 48 hours if the landlord decided that they were a nuisance or simply "undesirable." The court concluded that this provision gave the landlord control over the tenant's dogs, and he could have eliminated the danger they posed.[46]

A landlord who acquires a potentially dangerous or troublesome dog along with the property can still take measures to avoid liability and be fair to the tenants. Eviction may be possible if the dog is a nuisance, or if the tenants are violating a law that prohibits keeping a dog. A landlord who doesn't think getting rid of the dog is necessary may still want to take precautions, such as fencing in a yard or asking the tenant to keep the dog inside or post warning signs.

Injuries Off the Landlord's Property

A landlord may be liable for injuries caused by a tenant's dog even if the injuries don't occur on the rented property. The Supreme Court of Oregon ruled that a landlord can be liable if the landlord knew that the dog posed an unreasonable risk of harm to persons off the rental property. In that case, the landlord knew that the dog had been declared "potentially dangerous" by the county after it bit a child, and that the dog was sometimes allowed to roam.[47]

A California Court of Appeal ruled similarly, stating that liability for a dog bite off the premises depends on the same factors as liability for an injury on the premises. If, for example, a dog escapes because of defects in the landlord's property, the landlord would be liable for off-site injuries caused by the dog.[48] A Florida court ruled that a landlord might be liable for a dog bite that occurred in a park adjacent to the property, because the landlord had advertised the park as an amenity and the tenants understood that there was a close relationship between the apartment complex and the park.[49] Some courts, however, have ruled that a landlord has no duty to prevent injuries to third parties caused by a tenant's dog off the premises.[50]

Harboring a Tenant's Dog

Someone who "keeps" or "harbors" a dog—that is, cares for or exercises some control over it—is usually treated just like the dog's legal owner when it comes to liability for injury the dog causes. A landlord who does more than merely rent to a tenant who has a dog may be considered a "keeper" for purposes of liability. Here are some examples that show how courts evaluate such situations:

- An Illinois landlord rented half of his building to a tenant and occupied the other half himself. The tenant's dog, which was kept to guard the building, roamed all of it. When the dog bit someone, the landlord and the tenant were both held liable.[51]
- A landlord who lived off the premises hired a manager to take care of his Illinois apartment building. The manager allowed one tenant to fence in the building's backyard, which all the tenants used, and keep his dog there. One day the 65-pound dog leaped over the fence and bit a boy's nose, requiring plastic surgery to repair the damage. The Illinois Supreme Court ruled that the landlord had not harbored the dog within the meaning of the law. "Harboring," the court said, means more than simply allowing the tenants to keep a dog on the premises. Without "some degree of care, custody or control," the landlord was not liable.[52]
- Connecticut landlords rented an apartment to dog owners, but didn't ever feed or take care of the dog. The dog was not allowed to roam in or use the yard abutting the building. A court ruled that the landlords were not "keepers" of the dog, and so were not liable to a guest of the tenants who was bitten by the dog.[53]
- The landlord of a mobile home park was not a keeper of a tenant's dog, under the Minnesota dog-bite statute, because the landlord never tried to control or manage the dog. When the dog attacked a two-year-old on the landlord's property, the landlord could not be found liable, a court ruled.[54]
- A Wisconsin landlord was held not to be a keeper or harborer of her tenant's dogs and wolf-dog hybrids, which were kept in a wooded area near where the tenant and landlord lived. The court also ruled that landlords "who do not have control over or custody of" dogs

could not be liable, on general principles of negligence, for injuries caused by those dogs.[55]

(The liability of owners and those who "keep" or "harbor" dogs is discussed more fully in Chapter 11, Dog Bites.)

Endnotes

[1] Cal. Civ. Code § 1950.5.

[2] Cal. Civ. Code § 798.33.

[3] Or. Rev. Stat. § 90.530.

[4] Housing and Urban-Rural Recovery Act of 1983, 12 U.S.C. § 1701r-1.

[5] 24 C.F.R. § 5.300 and following.

[6] Cal. Health & Safety Code § 19901.

[7] Ariz. Rev. Stat. Ann. § 36-1409.01; Conn. Gen. Stat. § 8-116b; D.C. Code Ann. § 8-2032; Mass. Gen. Laws Ann., ch. 23B, § 3(u); Minn. Stat. § 504B.261; N.H. Rev. Stat. Ann. § 161-F: 31.

[8] Section 504 of the Rehabilitation Act of 1973, 29 U.S.C. § 794; 45 C.F.R. § 85.53.

[9] *Oras v. Housing Authority of City of Bayonne*, 373 N.J. Super. 302, 861 A.2d 194 (N.J. Super. A.D. 2004).

[10] *Whittier Terrace Associates v. Hampshire,* 26 Mass. App. Ct. 1020, 532 N.E.2d 712 (1989); see also *Majors v. Housing Authority of DeKalb*, 652 F.2d 454 (5th Cir. 1981).

[11] *Everett Housing Authority v. Auger*, 1998 WL 1181682 (Mass. Super. 1998).

[12] *Woodside Village v. Hertzmark*, 1993 Conn. Super. LEXIS 1726, app. dismissed, 647 A.2d 759 (1994).

[13] Md. Code Ann. [Real Property] § 8-214.

[14] N.J. Stat. Ann.§ 2A: 42-103 and following.

[15] "Pets Determine Where Elderly Choose to Live," *San Francisco Chronicle*, April 10, 1992.

[16] Pet Ownership in Public Housing Act, 42 U.S.C. § 1437z-3.

[17] *New York Life Ins. Co. v. Dick*, 71 Misc. 2d 52 (N.Y.C. Civ. Ct. 1972) (landlord could not enforce no-pets clause against tenants who had had dog for nine years).

[18] *Chuchwell v. Coller Stoner Building Co.*, 385 N.E.2d 492 (Ind. App. 1979).

[19] For example, see *Mutual Redevelopment Houses, Inc. v. Hanft*, 42 Misc. 2d 1044, 249 N.Y.S.2d 988 (1964) (landlord was aware of tenants' dog for many months); *Capital View Realty Co. v. Meigs*, 92 A.2d 765 (D.C. Mun. Ct. 1952) (tenants kept dog for almost two years with knowledge of resident manager).

[20] *Landmark Properties v. Olina*, Index No. SP1148/02 (N.Y. Dist. Ct. 2002).

[21] New York City Admin. Code § 27-2009.1; *Toledo Mut. Housing Corp. v. Schwartz,* 934 N.Y.S.2d 283 (2011); *Seward Park Housing Corp. v. Cohen,* 287 A.D.2d 157, 734 N.Y.S.2d 42 (2001).

[22] *Royal Associates v. Concannon,* 490 A.2d 357 (N.J. Super. 1985). See also *Kerrigan Avenue Realty, Inc. v. Lecaro,* 2006 WL 3228772 (N.J. Super. App. Div. 2006).

[23] *East River Housing Corp. v. Matonis,* 34 A.D.2d 937, 312 N.Y.S.2d 461 (1970).

[24] See, for example, *Board of Directors of 175 East Delaware Place Homeowners Ass'n. v. Hinojosa,* 287 Ill. App. 3d 886 (1997); *Gesemyer v. State,* 429 So. 2d 438 (Fla. App. 1983).

[25] *Winston Towers 200 Assoc., Inc. v. Saverio,* 360 So. 2d 470 (Fla. App. 1978).

[26] *Dulaney Towers Maintenance Corp. v. O'Brey,* 418 A.2d 1233 (Md. App. 1980). See also *Nahrstedt v. Lakeside Village Condominium Assoc., Inc.,* 8 Cal. 4th 361, 878 P.2d 1275, 33 Cal. Rptr. 2d 63 (1994); *Noble v. Murphy,* 34 Mass. App. Ct. 452, 612 N.E.2d 266 (1993).

[27] See, for example, *Wilshire Condominium Assoc., Inc. v. Kohlbrand,* 368 So. 2d 629 (Fla. App. 1979).

[28] *Granby Heights Assoc., Inc. v. Dean,* 38 Mass. App. Ct. 266; 647 N.E.2d 75 (1995).

[29] Haw. Rev. Stat. §§ 514A-82.5, 82.6.

[30] *San Francisco Daily Journal,* Nov. 17, 1987.

[31] See, for example, *Georgianna v. Gizzy,* 483 N.Y.S.2d 892, 126 Misc. 2d 766 (1984); and *Gilbert v. Christiansen,* 259 N.W.2d 896 (Minn. 1977).

[32] See *Barrwood Homeowners Assoc., Inc. v. Maser,* 675 So. 2d 983 (Fla. App. 1996), *reh'g denied* (1996).

[33] See, for example, *Park v. Hoffard,* 111 Or. App. 340, 826 P.2d 79 (1992), aff'd as modified, 847 P.2d 852 (Or. 1993).

[34] See, for example, *Gentle v. Pine Valley Apts.,* 631 So. 2d 928 (Ala. 1994) (dangerous dog in common areas of apartment building is a "dangerous condition," and landlord has duty to prevent injuries); *Nelson v. United States,* 838 F.2d 1280 (D.C. Cir. 1988) (U.S. government liable to girl injured by serviceman's dog on Air Force base; base security knew the dog had attacked children before and should have gotten rid of it to keep the base safe).

[35] *Linebaugh v. Hyndman,* 213 N.J. Super. 117, 516 A.2d 638 (1986), aff'd, 106 N.J. 556, 524 A.2d 1255 (1987) (landlord liable for injury caused by tenant's dog because landlord knew dog had bitten someone before).

[36] *Criswell v. Brewer,* 44 Mont. 1408, 741 P.2d 418 (1987).

[37] *Patterson v. Rank,* 797 N.W.2d 131 (Iowa App. 2010).

[38] *Rosenberry v. Evans,* 2012 WL 1383051 (Pa. Super. 2012).

[39] *Gill v. Welch*, 524 N.Y.S.2d 692 (1988).

[40] *Nutt v. Florio,* 75 Mass. App. Ct. 448.

[41] *Casatelli v. Dressler*, 2011 WL 2518857 (N.J. Super., App. Div. 2011).

[42] *Vigil ex rel. Vigil v. Payne*, 725 P.2d 1155 (Colo. App. 1986). A similar result was reached in a New York case, *Strunk v. Zoltanski*, 62 N.Y.2d 572, 479 N.Y.S.2d 175, 468 N.E.2d 13 (1984).

[43] *Lundy v. California Realty*, 170 Cal. App. 3d 813, 216 Cal. Rptr. 575 (1985).

[44] *Alaskan Village v. Smalley ex rel. Smalley*, 720 P.2d 945 (Alaska 1986).

[45] *Parker v. Sutton*, 72 Ohio App. 3d 296, 594 N.E.2d 659 (1991).

[46] *Holcomb v. Colonial Associates*, LLC, 58 N.C. 501, 597 S.E.2d 710 (N.C. 2004).

[47] *Park v. Hoffard*, 315 Or. 624, 847 P.2d 853 (1993).

[48] *Donchin v. Guerrero*, 34 Cal. App. 4th 1832, 41 Cal. Rptr. 2d 192 (1995).

[49] *Ramirez v. M.L. Management Co., Inc.*, 920 So.2d 36 (Fla. App. 2005).

[50] *Tran v. Bancroft*, 648 So. 2d 314 (Fla. App. 1995).

[51] *Edelstein v. Costelli*, 85 Ill. App. 2d 81, 229 N.E.2d 557 (1967).

[52] *Steinberg v. Petta*, 114 Ill. 2d 496, 103 Ill. Dec. 725, 501 N.E.2d 1263 (1986).

[53] *Buturla v. St. Onge,* 9 Conn. App. 495, 519 A.2d 1235 (1987).

[54] *Wojciechowski v. Harer*, 496 N.W.2d 844 (Minn. App. 1993). The court based its decision on the dog-bite statute only; it did not discuss whether or not the landlords knew the dog was dangerous.

[55] *Smaxwell v. Bayard*, 274 Wis. 2d 278, 682 N.W.2d 923 (2004); see also *Ladewig ex rel. Grischke v. Tremmel*, 802 N.W.2d 511 (Wis. App. 2011).

Veterinarians

For many people, finding a veterinarian they trust to take care of their animals ranks close behind finding a good family doctor.

This chapter discusses the legal relationship between pet owner and vet, gives some tips on how they can maintain a good relationship, and suggests what to do if something goes wrong.

The Owner-Veterinarian Relationship

The most important thing pet owners can do to ensure a smooth relationship with a veterinarian is to find a vet they trust and establish a personal relationship. As one veterinarian put it, some people expect to use veterinary services like they use a dry cleaner or fast food outlet—and then get upset when their animal is treated like a piece of laundry or a hamburger.

Disputes between pet owners and veterinarians are likely to arise for the same reason most other disputes arise: a failure of communication. Owners misunderstand diagnoses, instructions, and fees, and busy vets are often guilty of not explaining things as well as they should.

Pet owners should ask questions. Make sure you understand just what the vet thinks is wrong with your pet, what the dog needs, how serious the problem is, and how much time, effort, and money you will have to spend correcting it. If you're embarking on a long-term or expensive course of treatment, such as surgery and follow-up therapy, get an agreement about fees in writing. You may not be able to set exact amounts, but it will help to put down estimates. If you're unhappy with your vet, because of inadequate or excessive treatment, high bills, or any other reason, get a second opinion.

New Specialties for Veterinarians

As a broader range of treatments become available to pets, veterinarians are specializing; the American Veterinary Medical Association recognizes more than a dozen specialty boards. There are veterinarians who have special training in treatments ranging from acupuncture to dentistry.

Veterinarians should take the time to explain what they're doing, and make sure the owner understands completely. It will avoid a lot of misunderstandings and unpleasantness. And remember that satisfied pet owners recommend a competent and accessible vet to their pet-owning friends.

A sample agreement between a client and veterinarian concerning extensive fees and treatment for a sick dog is shown below. The agreement could be modified to suit most circumstances. It addresses not only the issue of fees, but also builds in full disclosure from the vet about the likelihood of the dog's complete recovery.

Sample Agreement

Geoffrey Livingstone and Alice Schweitzer, D.V.M., agree that:

1. Dr. Schweitzer is treating Mr. Livingstone's dog, Stanley, for a serious hip condition. Treatment will probably require surgery, followed by several months of examinations and medication.

2. Dr. Schweitzer estimates the cost of this treatment will be between approximately $700 and $1,200. Her office will bill Mr. Livingstone monthly.

3. Mr. Livingstone will pay up to $1,200 for Stanley's treatment. If Dr. Schweitzer discovers that the cost will exceed $1,200, she will notify Mr. Livingstone as soon as is reasonably possible. When $1,200 in fees has been billed to Mr. Livingstone, Dr. Schweitzer will not proceed with treatment without authorization from Mr. Livingstone.

4. Because of the dog's injury, the proposed course of treatment may not completely restore Stanley's leg to normal condition. The dog may always have a slight limp. The dog will suffer some pain from the surgery and recovery, but this will be kept to the minimum level reasonably possible.

Geoffrey Livingstone   Date

Alice Schweitzer, D.V.M.   Date

If you do get into a dispute, try to work something out, with or without the help of a third person, before turning the problem into a legal battle. Filing a lawsuit should always be a last resort.

Disputes over fees. If your problem is with a veterinarian's bill for services—if, for example, you think it's excessive, or you didn't authorize the treatment—talk to the vet. If you haven't paid the bill, pay what you think is fair and include a written explanation with your check. If you have paid, you should send the vet a letter explaining exactly why you think the bill was excessive and how much money you think should be returned to you. If you and the vet don't come to an agreement, you can always sue in small claims court.

Disputes over treatment. If you lose a pet through what may have been the vet's carelessness or incompetence, it's difficult to discuss the matter dispassionately. The same goes for a veterinarian who is wrongly accused of incompetence or worse. That's why a mediator, who can help people work something out themselves, may be a great help. At this stage, a lawyer probably won't be helpful. Although a good lawyer should try to settle a dispute before it gets to court, involving a lawyer often instantly raises tension and acrimony. (Chapter 7, Barking Dogs, discusses the mediation and small claims court process in detail.)

A Reminder From Uncle Sam

You may think of your dog as a dependent member of the family, but the IRS doesn't. That means you can't deduct your dog's medical expenses from your federal income tax.[1]

Health Insurance for Dogs

Health insurance for dogs and cats is looking better and better to pet owners who have paid big veterinary bills. The average dog owner spends about $250 a year on routine veterinary care, according to the American Pet Products Association (AAPA). Surgery or other procedures can cost thousands. More than two million dogs are now insured, according to a pet owners' survey conducted by the APPA.

One reason for getting insurance is that it reduces the chances that you'll have to put a dollar value on the life of your pet. That unhappy task can arise if you are forced to choose between paying for the sophisticated and extremely expensive procedures now available (laser treatment, CAT scans, chemotherapy) or destroying a dog that might be saved.

The amount of the premium depends on the coverage you choose, where you live, and the dog's age. You'll spend from $2,000 to $6,000 on insurance over a dog's lifetime, on average. Certain costs are generally not covered: congenital or hereditary defects, elective procedures, vaccination, food, grooming, behavioral problems, parasites, orthodontics, routine teeth cleaning, and conditions present before the policy effective date. Before you sign up, read the actual policy carefully and be sure you understand all the fine print.

You may also want to check out the veterinary equivalent of a health maintenance organization. For a monthly fee, your pet's veterinary needs will be taken care of.

If a Dog Injures a Veterinarian

Whether or not you want to believe it, there are circumstances in which your dog would bite someone. Even if your dog patiently suffers all sorts of indignities without protest (children pulling its tail, having its toenails clipped), if a dog is frightened, threatened, or hurt enough, it will bite.

The law presumes that veterinarians know this, even if not all owners do. Courts have ruled that because veterinarians knowingly take the risk of injury as part of the job, and should know from experience how to guard against it, they can't sue an owner if they are injured while handling a dog. As one court put it, "a veterinarian cannot assume a normally gentle dog will act gently while receiving treatment."[2]

The same rule generally applies to veterinary assistants and others who knowingly take the risk of handling animals in the course of their jobs. A veterinarian's employee might, however, be able to sue a vet who exposes the employee to an unnecessary risk.

Of course, there may be exceptions to this rule. If, for example, a dog was known to be dangerous, but its owner concealed that from the vet, the law might hold the owner responsible if the dog injures the vet.[3]

Even dog-bite statutes, which make owners liable for any injury their dog causes, don't usually apply when veterinarians are injured. Courts follow different logical paths to arrive at this conclusion. Some say that because veterinarians take dogs under their control, they themselves are "owners" under the statutes that make owners liable.[4] The Florida Supreme Court, however, in the case of a kennel employee bitten by a dog being boarded there, ruled that under the state's dog-bite statute, a kennel owner or veterinarian who is caring for a dog is not the dog's owner. The Court also ruled that dog owners are liable unless one of the specific exceptions in the statute applies—and noted that the Florida statute does not contain an exception for kennel or veterinary employees.[5]

Other courts say that a veterinarian, by treating a dog, provokes it to bite; provocation is a defense under most dog-bite statutes.[6] Provocation doesn't have to be deliberate or cruel; it can be completely innocent, as when you accidentally step on a dog's tail. (These statutes are discussed in Chapter 11, Dog Bites.)

The Collar Purple

"Where retailers used to carry a basic leather leash, today customers want fine nylon leashes, and in a spectrum of colors so they can color-coordinate. If your dog has a red sweater, you wouldn't want to take him out in public with a green leash."[7] Except at Christmas, of course.

Veterinarians' Duty to Treat Animals

In most cases, a veterinarian is under no legal duty to treat an injured animal. But once a vet agrees to treat a pet, stopping while the animal still needs attention may lead to malpractice liability.

Stray Dogs

Many vets treat injured or sick strays that wander in, just because they love animals. Some states—Massachusetts, for example—reimburse a vet a nominal amount for taking in a stray dog that is sick or injured.[8]

A vet may humanely destroy (euthanize) a dog without the owner's consent in an emergency. If, for example, a critically injured dog is taken to a veterinarian, and the owner is unknown or unreachable, the veterinarian will not be held liable for damages for euthanizing the dog if the owner is later found and objects.[9]

Abandoned Dogs

Some owners bring pets to a veterinarian, leave them, and never return. When this happens, the vet is not responsible for feeding and caring for an animal indefinitely. To be fair to both vet and owner, many states now have laws that set out a procedure for veterinarians to follow.

California law, for example, deems an animal abandoned if its owner doesn't pick it up within 14 days of the time agreed on by the vet and owner. The law requires a veterinarian to try, for at least ten days, to find a home for the animal. A vet who can't place an animal with a new owner may humanely destroy it. The vet may not turn the dog over to a pound or let it be used for scientific experimentation.[10] Dog owners are to be notified of these rules by a prominent sign in the vet's office or a conspicuous notice on a receipt.

I'm a Basset Hound, My Cheeks Are *Supposed* to Sag

It had to happen: cosmetic surgery for pets. Some veterinarians are now offering tummy tucks, wrinkle removal, even hair transplants.[11] Just the thing if you want your shar-pei to look as sleek as a greyhound.

Euthanasia

Euthanasia—"putting a dog to sleep"—is something that almost every pet owner must eventually consider. Many veterinary clinics have rules that govern the circumstances under which they will euthanize a dog. For example, many veterinarians will not euthanize healthy animals on demand. They ask the owners why they want the dog destroyed and try to suggest alternatives. Sometimes behavioral problems can be corrected, or the dog can be found a new home.

Complaining About a Vet

Veterinarians, like doctors, contractors, architects, and other professionals, are licensed by the state. Without a license, it's illegal for them to refer to themselves as veterinarians or to perform certain acts, such as operating on animals or prescribing medication.

A pet owner who is unhappy with a veterinarian's services may complain to a local veterinary association or the state licensing agency, which will investigate the vet and may bring disciplinary proceedings. To find the name and number of your state's licensing agency, look in a directory of state agencies on your state's official website, or call your public library and ask. You can also contact the American Veterinary Medical Association at 800-248-2862, www.avma.org. Many state laws provide that "gross malpractice," as well as many other forms of misconduct, may justify suspending or revoking a vet's license. But again, trying to resolve problems without resorting to formal complaints or legal action is likely to bring a much more satisfying result.

Veterinary Malpractice

The law of veterinary malpractice is pretty much like that of its theoretical ancestor, medical malpractice. And although the numbers are tiny compared to medical malpractice, more veterinary malpractice suits are filed every year.

The fact is that for a dog owner, pursuing a malpractice lawsuit is rarely practical. By the time you factor in attorney fees, fees for an expert witness, and all the other miscellaneous costs of a lawsuit, the cost of going to court will probably exceed the amount eventually recovered. Obviously, it's best to settle the matter outside the courtroom. Many veterinarians carry malpractice insurance, and a dog owner may well be able to reach a settlement with the insurance company without going to court.

RESOURCE

How to Win Your Personal Injury Claim, by Joseph Matthews (Nolo), discusses how to deal with an insurance company when you're injured, but many of its tips can be helpful when you're negotiating with a veterinarian's insurer.

What's Malpractice?

Malpractice is an error that a professional, who is expected to have a certain level of competence because of special training and experience, shouldn't make. For example, if a veterinarian looks at a dog with mange and treats it for heartworm, that's probably malpractice, because the vet should know better.

Only issues of a veterinarian's professional competence and judgment are malpractice issues. Acts of simple negligence (carelessness that is unreasonable under the circumstances) for which anyone, not just a vet, would be liable do not constitute malpractice.

Some examples may help illustrate the point. Here are some actions that may constitute malpractice:

- misdiagnosing a dog's illness
- prescribing the wrong course of treatment, or
- stopping treatment while a dog still needs veterinary attention.

Here are some that may be simple negligence:

- leaving a dog on a heating pad too long[12]
- letting a dog escape through a door carelessly left open, or
- failing to turn over a dog's body to a funeral organization.

The distinction between negligence and malpractice is important for two reasons:

- **It may be easier for a pet owner to win a malpractice lawsuit.** Someone suing a vet for negligence must show that the vet acted unreasonably—that is, not as an average, reasonable person would have acted. In a lawsuit for malpractice, the vet is held to a higher standard of conduct: to escape liability, the vet's behavior must measure up to that of the average veterinarian (taking into account education and experience) under the circumstances.

  > **EXAMPLE:** Robin takes her dog, Sherlock, to the vet, afraid that the dog sprained a hind leg jumping for a Frisbee. That's the vet's diagnosis, too, but he's wrong; the dog actually has a fracture. Is Robin's vet liable for malpractice? Yes, if the average vet would have correctly diagnosed the problem.

  > Now let's say that after this bumbling vet keeps Sherlock for observation, he goes off for the weekend and forgets to leave the dog any food. Is that more malpractice? No. It is, however, simple negligence, if the average reasonable person wouldn't have done it under the circumstances.

- **There may be different deadlines for filing different kinds of lawsuits.** State law may set different time limits for bringing a lawsuit for malpractice and bringing one for negligence. (This issue is discussed below.)

Injuries to People

Veterinarians may be liable not only for injuries to animals they treat, but to people as well.

For example, if a veterinarian allows a dog's owner to restrain the dog during treatment, when it is foreseeable that the dog might bite, the veterinarian could be liable for the injury. Or a veterinarian could prescribe a drug that harmed a pet owner in some way. A veterinarian might also be held responsible for failing to warn a pet owner about a disease—for example, roundworms in puppies—that can be transmitted from animals to humans.[13]

Who Is Liable

Obviously, a veterinarian can be sued for veterinary malpractice. But the veterinarian may also be legally liable for the actions of employees—the technicians and assistants who may be responsible for much of the hands-on treatment of a dog. And it may be a kind of malpractice if a veterinarian lets untrained or unsupervised employees take care of animals.

When Lawsuits Can Be Brought

In most states, both malpractice and simple negligence cases must be filed within one to three years of the injury. If you don't discover the injury until later, you may be able to start counting the one- or three-year period from the time you discover the injury.

As a rule, lawsuits do not improve with age; if attempts at settlement don't work, file promptly. If you are in doubt about when you must file, see a lawyer or look up your state's law (usually called the "statute of limitations").

Suits against a government agency (for example, if the vet at a city-run clinic neutered a dog but bungled the surgery) must usually be preceded by a claim against the government made within about 100 days. If the claim is denied, a lawsuit may be filed.

What Courts Can Be Used

What court a lawsuit belongs in depends on how much money is being sued for. Small claims court is available, and advisable, for smaller disputes. Few states allow claims larger than $10,000 to be filed in small claims court.

(Small claims court procedures, and the claim limits for each state, are discussed in more detail in Chapter 7, Barking Dogs.)

Compensating an Owner

Putting a dollar value on the death or injury of a pet is difficult, to say the least, and the rules are different in different states. Here is a summary of what a pet owner may be able to sue for and collect:

- cost of treatment necessary to fix damage caused by the malpractice
- market or replacement value of the pet
- special or sentimental value (in some states only)
- emotional distress (under certain circumstances), and
- punitive damages (if the veterinarian's conduct was outrageous or intentional).

(Chapter 9, If a Dog Is Injured or Killed, discusses the law in detail and gives examples of cases, including cases against veterinarians, in which dog owners recovered damages for each of these items.)

What an Owner Must Prove

To win a malpractice lawsuit, a pet owner must prove two things in court:

- the veterinarian acted incompetently or carelessly, and
- the incompetence caused an injury.

Proving Incompetence

A veterinarian is responsible for conforming to professional standards of conduct. One who doesn't is liable for any injury that results.

The standard of conduct for veterinarians. A dog owner must prove that the vet acted incompetently—that is, not as competently as other veterinarians. Then the question is: what other veterinarians? The ones in the town, state, or the whole country? Specialists or general practitioners? The most highly skilled vets or the hypothetical "average" one?

In general, a veterinarian's skill and diligence are judged against those of an average practitioner, not a specialist or unusually skilled one. A vet who is certified as a specialist by a veterinary specialty board, as more and more are these days, is held to a higher standard.

> **EXAMPLE:** Robin's Frisbee-chasing dog, Sherlock, has a hairline fracture of his leg, which a veterinarian of ordinary competence could miss. Robin takes Sherlock to Bones-R-Us, a clinic staffed by vets who specialize in orthopedics and charge extra for their expertise. A specialist there who missed the fracture, when a competent orthopedic vet would have caught it, would be guilty of malpractice.

Some states say that a veterinarian's competence is to be judged against that of other veterinarians "in the community." A local standard may not promote competence; instead, it may protect vets who don't live up to statewide or national standards.

Other states hold vets to the standard of care that would be provided by vets who are "similarly situated" or in a similar locality.[14] This reduces the standard of care in the community to just one factor for a jury to consider.[15] Other factors include available facilities and size and location of the town.

Evidence of incompetence. In some cases, it is obvious that a veterinarian made a serious mistake. If a dog has fleas which the vet treats for ringworm, that obviously falls short of professional competence. Very often, however, it's necessary to get an expert witness—that is, another veterinarian—to testify about the appropriateness of the first veterinarian's actions. Courts in several states have ruled that expert testimony is necessary to prove veterinary malpractice, because without it, jurors can't be expected to know what kind of care should have been given.[16] You may need an expert even in small claims court. In one New York case, a pet owner had won $250 in small claims court, based on her claim that a veterinary clinic had released her dog too soon after surgery and without enough sedation. When the clinic appealed, the court ruled that the dog owner shouldn't have won, because she had not presented any expert testimony to prove that the clinic's treatment deviated from accepted veterinary standards.[17]

The expert will testify about what care a veterinarian should have given under the circumstances.

For example, a negligent misdiagnosis can be malpractice.[18] But the fact that a veterinarian doesn't correctly diagnose an animal's illness doesn't mean that the vet fell below the required standard of "care and diligence." Perhaps it was a difficult case, with contradictory symptoms, and would have confused any veterinarian of normal competency.[19] If that's true, the veterinarian was as competent as the law requires.

Small claims court evidence rules. In small claims court, letters and similar kinds of evidence are admissible. If you can take the dog to an out-of-town vet and get a written second opinion, the vet won't have to show up at your court hearing in person to testify. In some states, including California, testimony can even be taken over the phone.

In small claims court, where evidence rules are much less strict than in regular court, it may be enough simply to report that another veterinarian quickly diagnosed or fixed a condition that baffled the veterinarian who's being sued. For example, an Ohio couple took their dog to a vet for an ear problem. The veterinarian prescribed (three times) antibiotic eardrops, but the condition kept worsening. A second veterinarian immediately spotted a tumor in the dog's ear; the dog required extensive surgery. An appeals court ruled that the dogs' owners had met their burden of proof.[20]

Proving the Malpractice Caused the Injury

It's not enough to show that a vet did something and your pet was injured; the connection between the act and the injury must be proven. Again, expert medical testimony is often necessary.

> **EXAMPLE 1:** A woman sued a veterinarian, claiming that her horse turned into a "killer" after the vet negligently operated on its leg. She offered no proof of a connection between the surgery and the change in disposition except that the horse's behavior deteriorated after the operation. She lost her case.[21]

> **EXAMPLE 2:** An owner brought a German shepherd, who was having trouble giving birth, to a veterinary hospital. The veterinarian on duty called in a surgeon. The surgeon arrived later that evening and performed a cesarean section, but only two pups lived. The owner sued for malpractice, but no expert testimony was presented at trial. The court ruled that the owner had not proven that the veterinarians' actions caused the injury.[22]

 RESOURCE

Everybody's Guide to Small Claims Court, by Ralph Warner (Nolo), shows how to prepare and present a winning small claims court suit. *Represent Yourself in Court*, by Paul Bergman and Sara Berman (Nolo), explains how to conduct a trial without an attorney.

Other Lawsuits Against Veterinarians

Not every complaint against a veterinarian is necessarily a malpractice case. If you think you might have a malpractice claim, check to see if your situation falls into one of the categories discussed here. But be warned that this short list doesn't come close to covering all the possible kinds of lawsuits veterinarians might come in for. If you have a situation that doesn't fit in any of these pigeonholes, you may want to find out your options from a lawyer.

If a Dog Dies at the Vet's

If your dog dies at the vet's, and you don't know why or how—or what happened at all—the law in most states helps you by making the vet responsible for proving that the death wasn't caused by malpractice or negligence.

The way you take advantage of this rule is by suing for negligent bailment. "Bailment" is the legal term for the relationship that results when some item of property—in this case, a dog—is left in someone else's care. Under the law of bailment (which may vary from state to state), if a dog is left with a vet and the dog dies, the vet is presumed, legally, to be negligent. The vet must then prove otherwise or be liable to the dog's owner for the value of the dog.

> **EXAMPLE:** A woman boarded her healthy, eight-year-old dog with a New York veterinarian. When she returned two weeks later, she was told the dog had died a few days before. The vet gave no satisfactory explanation of the dog's death, so the owner was entitled to recover for the value of the dog.[23]

When Vets Are Liable for Taking a Dog

A veterinarian who takes your dog without permission is liable to you for the value of the dog. The vet may also be guilty of theft, but that's a criminal matter to be handled by the police and district attorney. You can bring a civil lawsuit for "conversion." (No, this doesn't mean you can sue your vet for kidnapping your Protestant poodle and converting her to canine Catholicism.)

> **EXAMPLE:** An Oregon woman asked a vet to humanely destroy her dog, which had been shot and was in extreme pain. Instead, the vet gave the dog to two assistants who had grown attached to it. The original owner sued when she found out, and was awarded $500 for the vet's conversion of the dog. She was also awarded $4,000 for her mental anguish and $700 in punitive damages.[24]

Endnotes

[1] *Schoen v. Commissioner*, T.C.M. (P-H) 1975-167.

[2] *Nelson v. Hall*, 165 Cal. App. 3d 709, 211 Cal. Rptr. 668 (1985); see also *Cohen v. McIntyre*, 16 Cal. App. 4th 650, 20 Cal. Rptr. 2d 143 (Cal. App. 1993) (owner not liable to veterinarian bitten by dog).

[3] See *Willenberg v. Superior Court*, 185 Cal. App. 3d 185, 229 Cal. Rptr. 625 (1986).

[4] See, for example, *Armstrong v. Milwaukee Mut. Ins. Co.*, 549 N.W.2d 723 (Wis. 1996); *Tschida v. Berdusco*, 462 N.W.2d 410 (Minn. App. 1990); *Wilcoxen v. Paige*, 174 Ill. App. 3d 541, 124 Ill. Dec. 213, 528 N.E.2d 1104 (1988).

[5] *Wipperfurth v. Huie*, 654 So.2d 116 (Fla. 1995).

[6] For example, *Mulcahy v. Damron*, 168 Ariz. 11, 816 P.2d 270 (Ariz. App. 1991).

[7] Terry Boyd, president of the Pet Industry Distributors Ass'n.

[8] Mass. Gen. Laws Ann. ch. 140, § 151B.

[9] For example, see R.I. Gen. Laws § 4-15-15.

[10] Cal. Civ. Code §§ 1834.5, 1834.6.

[11] "What to Do When a Dog Is a Dog," *San Francisco Chronicle*, Mar. 30, 1989.

[12] *Knowles Animal Hospital, Inc. v. Wills*, 360 So. 2d 37 (Fla. App. 1978).

[13] "Medical-Legal Aspects of Veterinary Public Health in Private Practice," by Jerrold Tannenbaum, *Seminars in Veterinary Medicine and Surgery (Small Animal)*, Vol. 6, No. 3, p. 175 (August 1991).

[14] For example, see *Swan v. Lamb*, 584 P.2d 814 (Utah 1978).

[15] *Ruden v. Hansen*, 206 N.W.2d 713 (Iowa 1973).

[16] *Williamson v. Prida*, 89 Cal. Rptr. 2d 868 (Cal. App. 1999); *Baechler v. Beaunaux*, 167 Wash. App. 128 (2012).

[17] *Juliano v. S.I. Vet Care*, 34 Misc. 3d 147(A) (N.Y. App. Term 2012).

[18] *Boom v. Reed*, 23 N.Y.S. 421 (1923).

[19] *Brockett v. Abbe*, 3 Conn. Cir. 12, 206 A.2d 447 (1964) (suit for misdiagnosis dismissed because no evidence that misdiagnosis was negligent).

[20] *Lewis v. Hendrickson*, 2003 WL 21652177 (Ohio App. 2003).

[21] *Southall v. Gabel*, 293 N.E.2d 891 (Ohio 1972).

[22] *Denaro v. New Haven Central Hospital*, 2004 WL 203943 (Conn. Super. 2004).

[23] *Brousseau v. Rosenthal*, 110 Misc. 2d 1054, 443 N.Y.S.2d 285 (1980).

[24] *Fredeen v. Stride*, 525 P.2d 166 (Or. 1974).

Traveling With Your Dog

When novelist John Steinbeck set off to drive through America in 1960, his only companion was a big poodle named Charley. "He is a good friend and traveling companion, and would rather travel about than anything he can imagine," Steinbeck wrote in *Travels With Charley*. "A dog, particularly an exotic like Charley, is a bond between strangers. Many conversations en route began with 'What degree of a dog is that?'"

Today's travelers, if they want to take their dogs with them, are probably still best off to imitate Steinbeck and take to the highways. More modern modes of transportation, such as commercial jets, are best avoided.

The Not-So-Friendly Skies

Commercial airlines are not deliberately cruel or even particularly careless when it comes to shipping dogs; they just aren't set up to deal with pets efficiently. Unless a dog is small enough to carry on board the plane, air travel is a risky way for it to go. The U.S. Department of Transportation, which tracks animal injuries and deaths during air transport, reports that 122 dogs died while being transported during the five-year period ending in May 2010. Another 88 were reported lost or injured. (You can see the breakdown by breed at http://airconsumer.dot.gov/publications/Deceased%20Canines%20in%20Transit.pdf.)

The basic problem is that to an airline, your pet is just an especially bothersome piece of baggage. And as everyone knows, baggage slip-ups are inevitable, given connecting flights scheduled too close together, long delays, and human error in a stress-filled, overloaded system. When a mistake means your luggage goes to Minneapolis while you go to Atlanta, you'll survive the inconvenience. But if your dog goes to the wrong city or is forgotten on a luggage carousel, it may not survive.

Special rules for service dogs. Service dogs travel with their owners, in the airliner's cabin. (See Chapter 8, Assistance Dogs.)

Airline Rules

For information on a specific airline's rules regarding animals, contact the carrier. Also check out the American Kennel Club's summary of airline animal shipping policies, available at www.akc.org.

The Problems With Flying

Put simply, a lot of things can go wrong when a dog goes on a commercial flight. Most problems occur on the ground, not during a flight. (Conditions on the plane are described in "How Dogs Travel on Airlines," below.) Here are some of the more common problems you should be aware of before you ship a dog.

- **The dog escapes from a cage.** This can lead to tragic results, as it did in 1988 for a small dog named Loekie. Loekie, on a TWA flight from Dallas to Los Angeles, got out of his cage during a stopover in St. Louis. The dog was killed by a car on an airport road.

- **The cage gets tipped or crushed during transport.** Sturdy travel kennels alleviate this problem to some degree, but mishandling—for example, putting a pet carrier on a regular baggage carousel—can toss an animal around.

- **The plane is delayed on the ground, with the dog in it.** During flight, the cargo area in which pets travel is pressurized, and the temperature is controlled. But on the ground, no fresh air gets in, and the temperature can fluctuate dramatically in a short time. If you've ever sat in a hot, stuffy plane during the summer, waiting to take off or pull up to a gate, you can imagine how an animal feels in the even hotter baggage compartment.

- **Baggage handlers remove the dog from the plane during a stopover and then forget to load it on again.** Animals are shipped in a compartment near the door of the plane where baggage is loaded. Unknown to the owner sitting on the plane, they may be removed during a stopover (so that other baggage can be unloaded more easily) and inadvertently not reloaded.

- **The dog is shipped to the wrong place.** Just like a suitcase, a dog can end up in the wrong place. Because few airports are equipped to handle animals well, a dog flown to the wrong destination can have a bad or even life-threatening experience waiting for another flight or for you to show up and claim it.
- **The dog is left in the heat, cold, or rain.** An animal left outside at an airport may be subject to extreme heat or cold. Many airlines do not accept pets during the summer, and federal regulations prohibit shipping animals if they will be exposed to temperatures below 45 degrees or above 85 degrees for more than four hours.
- **The dog is left unattended, without food or water, in a "lost luggage" storage area.** Because most airlines don't have special places for live animals, animals can sometimes end up abandoned with misplaced baggage. Usually, employees care for the dog as best they can. But if a dog is scared and snappish, as it may well be, it may get little care. Employees may not even know a pet is there.

Even if you plan carefully and everything goes as planned, air travel is frightening and stressful for a dog. And you often can't cope with problems as they come up, because you and your dog are separated during the critical times.

Reported Problems

Airlines are required to report any incident involving an animal who is injured, lost, or killed to the Secretary of Transportation. Complaint figures are published in the Department of Transportation's monthly publication, *Air Travel Consumer Reports*, available at www.dot.gov/airconsumer. Very few problems are reported.

Animal-Only Air Carriers

PetAirways (www.petairways.com) is devoted entirely to transporting pets—or "pawsengers," as the airline calls them. The airline uses small turboprop planes, which the big commercial carriers use on short flights. Pets get regular potty breaks and fly in their crates, regularly monitored by pet attendants along the way. PetAirways serves nine cities, including New York, Los Angeles, Washington DC, Chicago, Atlanta, Denver, and more.

How Dogs Travel on Airlines

Some airlines don't accept pets at all, or allow them only in the passenger cabin. Others offer three options. From most to least desirable, they are:

- in the passenger cabin
- as excess baggage, or
- as cargo.

With You in the Cabin

If your dog is a trained service dog or is tiny enough—generally under 20 pounds—to be comfortable in a pet carrier that fits under an airline seat, you can take it on the plane with you. You can find out the exact measurements of the under-seat space from the airline. Most airlines allow only a few animals in the cabin per flight, so don't just show up with your dog; make arrangements when you purchase your own ticket.

Most airlines charge about $125 for the animal's one-way fare, regardless of destination. Service dogs accompanying their owners fly for free (See Chapter 8.) Many will also rent or sell you a kennel that will fit under the seat.

This is by far the best way to fly with your dog. Aside from being stuck in a carrier for a while (and not being able to stick its head out the window), it's not much different for the dog than a car ride.

Even Zsa-Zsa Must Follow the Rules

Police escorted Zsa-Zsa Gabor off a Delta Airlines flight several years ago after she refused, according to airline officials, to keep her two dogs in cages. A Delta agent told the press that Zsa-Zsa's language was "less than ladylike."

On Your Flight as Checked Baggage

If you're traveling with your dog, some airlines will allow the dog to travel as checked baggage. The fee will probably be about $250 for a domestic flight, no matter what the destination. Some airlines base their charge on the dog's size or weight.

The dog travels on the same plane you do, in a cargo compartment that's pressurized, lighted, and heated. It's where fragile items (flowers and musical instruments, for example) travel, according to airline officials. Notify the airline in advance that you want to ship a dog as baggage. A plane will only carry a few animals, and certain items—things being kept cold with dry ice, for example—can't be put into the compartment with live animals.

You must provide a travel kennel for each animal, big enough for the dog to sit, stand, turn around and lie down in.

Common restrictions include:

- **Summer travel.** Most major carriers won't take dogs as baggage during the summer months.
- **Ban on short-nosed breeds.** Some airlines refuse to transport short-nosed breeds such as bulldogs, pugs, and Lhasa Apsos, either all year or during the summer.
- **Ban on "dangerous" breeds.** Until 2012, United Airlines refused to accept pit bull terriers, American Staffordshire terriers, and several other less common breeds. An online petition drive, started by a woman who owned a pit bull mix, persuaded United to change its policy.[1]
- **Health.** Many airlines require a recent veterinarian's certificate, saying that the dog is healthy and has had a rabies vaccination, before they will accept it as checked baggage. You must present the certificate when you check in with the dog before your flight. Many airlines require that the certificate have been signed no more than 30 days before the flight.
- **Size and weight.** Generally, a dog and carrier that together weigh over 100 pounds (a large carrier weighs about 25 to 30 pounds) must travel as air freight instead of baggage. That means if you have an extra-large dog, you may have to pay an extra-large price to ship it.

> ### Short Nose? Stay on the Ground
>
> When you fly, leave your Pekingese, bulldog, or pug at home. For these pug-nosed breeds, breathing—never easy—is just too difficult at high altitude. From 2005 to 2010, about half of the dogs that died while being shipped as cargo were "short-faced" breeds, according to the U.S. Department of Transportation. They had a significantly higher mortality rate than did other breeds; English bulldogs accounted for almost a quarter of total deaths. You can see the breakdown by breed at http://airconsumer.dot.gov/publications/Deceased%20Canines%20in%20Transit.pdf.

Cargo

If you're not traveling with your dog, or if your dog is too big to meet excess baggage size limitations, or the airline doesn't accept pets as baggage, the only alternative may be air freight. It's a poor option, for lots of reasons.

First of all, it is tremendously expensive. If you think of it as sending an overnight mail letter that weighs 100 pounds or so, you'll get the idea.

Additional regulations may apply to dogs shipped as cargo. For example, you may need a health certificate signed by a veterinarian and rabies vaccination certificate.

Airline Liability Limits

Whenever you ship a dog, you run the risk that the dog will be injured. What you may not realize is that unless you buy extra liability coverage for a dog you ship by air, and something does happen to the dog, you may get stuck with the airline's decision about how much it will pay for your loss—no matter how much you lose.

International flights. Claims for damage that occurs during international flights are covered by special rules. (See "International Travel," below.)

How Liability Limits Work

Airlines limit their liability for loss, delay, or damage to baggage to the minimum required by the federal government, which is currently $3,300.

The only way around this limit is to declare (before the flight) a higher value for your baggage and pay an additional fee. Remember, your dog is classified as baggage (carry-on or excess) unless you ship it air cargo. Similar liability limits also apply to air cargo.

If you suffer a loss of more than $3,300, and the airline refuses to make it good, you can challenge the liability limit in court (including small claims court, if the amount you're asking for is within your state's small claims court limit). In general, for a liability limit written in fine print to hold up in court, the passenger must have had:

• notice of the limit, and
• an opportunity to declare a higher value for the baggage.

Notice of the limit. If, as a passenger, you honestly have no reason to know about a liability limit, it isn't reasonable to bind you to its terms. If the liability provision is buried in the fine print on the back of a ticket or available only in an obscure place on the airline's website, a court might rule that you weren't given adequate notice.

But if you're familiar with flying and with baggage liability limits, and you had your ticket days or weeks in advance, you will probably be held responsible for knowing what's written on it. The same is true if you were notified in some other way—by a conspicuous sign on the ticket counter, for example, or by an airline employee.

A chance to declare a higher value for the baggage. The airline must also give you a fair opportunity to declare a higher value for your dog, and pay a correspondingly higher shipping fee. If it didn't, you won't be held to the liability limit.

Most airlines do allow passengers to declare a higher value for baggage. The ticket will probably only inform you that you have this option; to find out how much the added liability coverage will cost you, you'll have to ask the airline. (See "Getting Extra Coverage," below.)

> **EXAMPLE:** In 1983, Thomas Deiro shipped nine racing greyhounds by air from Portland to Boston. The airline left the dogs in their cages on a baggage cart in the sun, in 97° heat, during a stopover in Dallas. Seven of them died, and the others were injured. Deiro sued American Airlines for $900,000.

The court awarded him $750, the liability limit at the time.[2]

The court analyzed the factors discussed above and upheld the airline's baggage liability limit. It reasoned that Deiro, who was an experienced traveler and regularly shipped dogs by air, should have declared a higher value for his greyhounds. "We find it difficult," the court stated, "to imagine how any passenger with Deiro's experience, planning to check a quarter of a million dollars worth of baggage, could have had more opportunity or incentive to familiarize himself with the baggage liability provisions."

Deiro had received his ticket nine days before his flight, but hadn't bothered to read all the print on the back. He paid dearly for his casual attitude.

Getting Extra Coverage

If you don't want to abide by an airline's liability limit, you can either get extra liability coverage from the airline or buy insurance from a private insurer. Obviously, if you're shipping economically valuable dogs, it will be worth your while to investigate. You can find out how much the airline charges for extra coverage by getting a copy of the airline's "contract of carriage," which is available at the ticket counter.

To get the airline to agree to a higher liability limit, you must declare that the dog's value is over the liability limit. The airline will charge you a higher fee, and if anything happens to the dog, you will be covered for the value you declared. For example, say you are shipping a show dog worth $10,000 as excess baggage, and the airline limits its liability to $3,300. Before the trip, tell the airline that you want to declare a higher value on the dog. The airline will charge you an extra fee based on the $6,700 of excess declared value.

The airline may limit the amount you can declare to a few thousand dollars. Above that amount, you will have to talk to private insurance companies to get coverage. Obviously, this all takes lots of time—another reason you should make your arrangements well ahead of time. Don't expect to take care of everything when you show up to get your boarding pass.

The same goes for air freight. Airlines limit their liability to about $9.07 per pound. Say you're shipping a 100-pound dog as air freight. The dog and carrier together weigh 125 pounds. So unless you declare a higher value, the airline's liability is limited to $1,133.75 (that is, $9.07 x 125 pounds).

How to Figure Your Losses

If the dog is injured or killed during air travel, you must put a dollar amount on your loss in order to make a claim to the airline. If your dog performs in races or shows, it may be relatively easy to put a dollar value on your claim. But if you got your dog free from a shelter, and its value is emotional rather than economic, what must the airline pay you in damages? It's a difficult question, and the answer seems to be changing as more and more courts become willing to take into account noneconomic factors. (How to put a value on your economic loss and emotional distress is discussed in Chapter 9, If a Dog Is Injured or Killed.)

Settling With the Airline

Even though airlines may not be legally bound to compensate pet owners for their emotional distress at losing a pet, lawsuits over such incidents are bad publicity, and an airline may be willing to settle a suit rather than go to trial.

American Airlines agreed to pay $15,000 to the owner of a dog that died in transit. The dog had been left in the cargo hold of an airplane—in 115-degree heat—when the plane was delayed on the runway for more than an hour.[3] When the owner, Andrew Gluckman, sued the airline, it first offered just $1,250, the standard amount for lost baggage at that time.[4]

Advice for Air Travelers

If you must ship a dog, it's up to you to make sure the dog is on the plane every time you take off. Ask a flight attendant for confirmation from the baggage handlers that the dog is on board—or talk to the baggage people yourself. And if there's an extended delay, ask that the dog be taken off the plane. Be polite, but be persistent.

If you can, book a nonstop flight, even if it means choosing a less convenient schedule or airport. Most problems occur in airports, not during flights. Missed connections are a prime source of complications when you're shipping a dog; if you can't get a nonstop, make sure there is enough time between flights to get all the baggage loaded on the connecting flight. You can also do valuable research on how often a certain flight is delayed; statistics are now available from the airlines. When you tentatively schedule a flight, ask the airline representative what the on-time percentage is for that flight. Avoiding peak times (holiday weekends, for example) may also get you more cooperation from airline personnel. During hot weather, avoid flights in the hottest part of the day. During cold weather, try to schedule a stopover in a southern city instead of a cold northern one.

Be sure to get a well-made kennel for your dog. Watch out for ones that use wing nuts to attach the top and bottom. The wing nuts have been known to come off because of the vibration of the plane. You may also want to put a note on the outside of your dog's cage. The note should include the dog's name, your name, destination, flight numbers, and any special instructions or cautions.

If You're Moving

If you want help arranging transport of your dog, you may find it from the Independent Pet and Animal Transportation Association International (IPATA), a trade association of animal handlers, pet moving providers, kennel operators, veterinarians, and others. Its member organizations use regularly scheduled flights on commercial airlines to ship pets, primarily for people who are moving, not traveling. They can help with pick-up and delivery, find flights with airlines and schedules that are best for your pet, provide flight kennels that meet legal and airline requirements, and help with health certificates and with documents that may be required for international travel.

The IPATA website is at www.ipata.com; you can call them at 903-769-2267. Another company that offers similar services is AirAnimal, at www.airanimal.com or 800-635-3448.

Checklist for Air Travel

- Did you book the most direct and reliable flight?
- Does the airline know you're bringing an animal? Do you know all the airline's rules? Most airlines put their rules and regulations on their websites. For example, the "JetPaws" section of the JetBlue website sets out everything you need to know to fly with a pet on that airline and offers pet carriers and other products for sale. Read the rules—don't rely on what an airline employee tells you on the phone.
- Have you obtained health or vaccination certificates, if necessary?
- Is the kennel big enough for the dog to stand up, lie down, and turn around in comfortably?
- Is the kennel sturdy and well ventilated? Have you lined the bottom with shredded paper or other absorbent material?
- Have you securely attached your name, contact information, and any special instructions to the outside and inside of the kennel?
- Have you labeled the kennel "Live Animal" and "This End Up" in letters at least an inch high?
- Is the dog wearing an identification tag and a snug but comfortable collar or harness (not a chain collar, which could get caught on something and choke the dog)?
- Have you obtained adequate liability coverage for your dog from the airline or an outside insurer?

Don't feed your animal for six hours before the flight, but attach containers of food and water to the outside of the carrier, if possible. This will allow someone to feed and water the dog without opening the cage. Opening the cage is to be avoided as much as is possible: it not only makes the handler risk getting bitten, but also might let the dog escape.

Your dog, of course, should be wearing an identification tag—but not just one that gives the address you've just left, where there may be nobody home. Attach a tag with your destination, including a phone number where you can be reached. Even better, get your dog microchipped, so that it can be identified even if it slips out of a collar or harness.

What about mildly tranquilizing your dog? The answer depends on the dog's temperament, health, and metabolism. Tranquilized dogs may be more susceptible to breathing problems, especially if they get overheated. And tranquilizers slow down an animal's metabolism, which is also affected by the change in pressure during flight. A less drastic alternative is motion sickness medication, which a veterinarian can prescribe. Talk to a vet who's familiar with your animal before you decide on a strategy.

Special Hawaii Rules

Unless you're crossing national borders, you don't usually need to worry about special restrictions on taking your dog with you. But if you want to take your pet for a tropical vacation, you need to know that Hawaii has very strict entry regulations, designed to keep the islands rabies-free.

In recent years, the rules have been relaxed, so that your dog may be inspected upon arrival and then released directly to you from the airport. But if you haven't gotten the right vaccinations, done all the tests, and submitted the right paperwork ahead of time, your dog could be quarantined for up to four months.

Direct Release or Five-Day Quarantine

You can qualify for the five-days-or-less program if you've taken all these required steps before the dog arrives in Hawaii:

- the dog must have received at least two rabies vaccinations, not less than three months apart, the most recent one not less than 90 days before arriving in Hawaii
- the dog must have had a microchip identification implanted by a veterinarian, and
- a blood sample, identified by the microchip ID number, must have been tested for rabies antibodies 120 days to 36 months before the dog arrives in the state.

There are many detailed rules about what paperwork is required and when fees must be paid. (And how they must be paid—you need a cashier's check, because personal checks aren't accepted.) All documents must be received by the Hawaii Rabies Quarantine Branch more than ten days before the dog arrives. Make sure you get all the information you need well in advance—keep in mind that there's a 120-day waiting period after the blood test, and if you arrive sooner, the dog will have to stay quarantined until the 120-day period elapses.

If your dog arrives at the quarantine facility during normal inspection hours (8 a.m. to 5 p.m., seven days a week), it may be released to you the same day. Because transport from the airport to the quarantine facility can take up to an hour, be sure to book a flight that arrives at the airport by 3:30 in the afternoon.

The fee for direct release is $165; it costs up to $224 for up to five days of quarantine.

If the airline you're using participates in the Hawaii program, your dog can be released to you from the airports at Kona (Big Island), Lihue (Kauai), or Kahului (Maui). The requirements for the shorter quarantine are the same as for Honolulu, except that all required documents must be submitted earlier—at least 30 days before you arrive. You must make a reservation with a local veterinary hospital or humane society for a pre-release inspection of the dog.

For a checklist of how to request direct release of your dog, see the Hawaii Department of Agriculture website at http://hawaii.gov/hdoa/ai/ aqs/Checklist%20for%20NII%2001%202012.pdf.

120-Day Quarantine

If you don't qualify for the five-days-or-less program, your pet will be quarantined for up to 120 days. Not only do you have to give up your pet, you have to pay for it: the current cost is $1,080 for 120 days. Airlines deliver pets directly to a state holding facility, and the state takes them to the quarantine station on the island of Oahu. Dogs are kept in individual outdoor runs. Owners can visit their dogs during afternoon visiting hours but cannot take the animals out of the kennel.

State officials stress that it's important for owners to arrange, in advance, for a private animal hospital to provide emergency veterinary care. The quarantine center handles minor ailments, but it does not have facilities for major medical problems. Unless a veterinary hospital has agreed in advance to accept an ill pet, the state will not take the animal to a private hospital.

Special Rules for Service Dogs

Different rules apply to service dogs, as a result of a lawsuit by guide dog users.[5] If you meet certain requirements, you can keep your dog with you after only a brief examination in the Honolulu airport. Before you go, you must:

- Get a letter from a physician setting out your disability, unless your dog is a guide dog.
- Get an ID card or certificate that shows that the dog was trained at a specialized school.
- Have an identifying microchip implanted in the dog.
- Make sure your dog's rabies vaccination is current, and have documentation.
- Have the dog undergo a blood test for rabies.
- Get a health certificate issued within two weeks before arrival.
- Notify the animal quarantine station at least 24 hours before you arrive, so they'll be ready to take an immediate blood sample from the dog when you get there.

When the dog arrives in Honolulu, airline personnel will take it to the Airport Animal Quarantine Holding Facility. There, the quarantine officials will examine the paperwork and the dog. If everything is in order, you should be able to leave, with your dog, in about 15 to 20 minutes.

As you can see, these rules are complicated; they also change from time to time. Make sure you have up-to-date information by checking the state's website, and get your specific questions answered by contacting the quarantine station directly.

Hawaii Quarantine Information

Animal Quarantine Station
99-951 Halawa Valley Street
Aiea, Hawaii 96701
808-483-7151
www.hawaii.gov/hdoa/ai/aqs/info
email: rabiesfree@hawaii.gov

International Travel

International travel involves a whole new set of considerations and regulations. If you're taking a dog abroad, be sure to investigate restrictions well in advance of your trip.

Entrance Restrictions

Some countries require health certificates and proof of rabies vaccination before they will admit a dog; others have mandatory quarantine periods for all animals entering the country. To find out what rules apply to you, contact the nearest consulate of the country to which you want to take your dog.

Injuries During International Flights

A person whose animal is injured during an international flight must notify the airline in writing within seven days of receiving the injured animal. If, however, the animal has been lost or killed—not just injured—such notice isn't required, according to at least one United States court.[6]

As always when flying, it's a good idea to check the airline's liability limitations before you fly. You may want to declare a higher value for your dog. (See "Airline Liability Limits," above.)

On the Road

Transporting your dog in a car instead of a plane obviously gives you more flexibility and control. It has its own problems, of course: heat, space, food and water and, especially, accommodations along the way.

Federal law requires motels and hotels to allow service dogs, even if they don't accept pets.[7] But the number of hotels and motels willing to accept—and welcome—dogs has been increasing, according to surveys conducted by the American Automobile Association. These businesses are realizing that they can profit from attracting loyal customers who will appreciate, and pay more for, amenities that cater to dogs—everything from exercise areas to dog beds to gourmet doggy room service.

Some counties and states impose restrictions on how dogs can be transported in vehicles. Several states, for example, require dogs in open pickup truck beds to be in cages or cross-tied, so that they don't get thrown from the truck. (See Chapter 2, State and Local Regulation.)

 RESOURCE
Barkbuckleup.com offers safety tips, pet travel products, and a list of the top ten cars for pet safety.

Dogfriendly.com has links to several big hotel chains that welcome pets as well as information about pet-friendly car rental companies, restaurants, and more.

Buses, Trains, and Ships

If you want to transport a dog by bus, train, or ship, your options are limited. Amtrak does not accept animals, except assistance dogs. Many bus lines also don't accept pets.

But if your pet wants a luxury cruise, you can book a spot on the Queen Mary 2, which has a kennel for passengers' dogs and cats. Animals can also be walked in a special area on one deck, but are not allowed anywhere else on the ship. For more information, contact the Cunard Line, 555 Fifth Ave., New York, NY 10017, 800-221-4770, www.cunardline.com.

Endnotes

1 "Pit Bulls, Other Breeds No Longer Banned on United," ABC News, May 9, 2012.

2 *Deiro v. American Airlines, Inc.*, 816 F.2d 1360 (9th Cir. 1987).

3 *HSUS News*, Vol. 40, No. 3, p. 33 (Summer 1995).

4 "Dog Who Died in Airplane's Hold Is Defined as Luggage by a Judge," *New York Times*, Feb. 16, 1994.

5 *Crowder v. Kitagawa*, 81 F.3d 1480 (9th Cir. 1996).

6 *Dalton v. Delta Airlines*, 570 F.2d 1244 (5th Cir. 1978).

7 28 C.F.R. § 36.502(c).

Barking Dogs

[T]he very best of [dogs] can, with less effort and in a shorter space of time, make themselves more of a nuisance to the square inch than any other domestic quadruped of which we have any knowledge.

—California Court of Appeal[1]

Probably the most common complaint about dogs is the noise they make. Barking dogs may "murder sleep," said one judge who presumably had some first-hand experience. The good news for neighbors is that usually problems can be resolved without resorting to legal means, through informal negotiation or mediation. And if that fails, there is almost always a law against dogs that make a nuisance of themselves by barking, howling, or whining.

If you can't get these laws enforced to your satisfaction, you can sue the dog owner to get the nuisance stopped and to recover money damages. But substituting a major hassle with expensive lawyers for a small one with a bad-mannered spaniel isn't much progress. (Keep in mind Ambrose Bierce's definition of a lawsuit: "A machine which you go into as a pig and come out of as a sausage.") Lawsuits are especially undesirable when the other party is a neighbor—after all, you'll still be next door to each other no matter who wins.

This chapter discusses the most promising ways to resolve neighborhood dog disputes out of court and stay on relatively good terms with the neighbors.

Talking to Your Neighbor

There is no such thing as a difficult dog, only an inexperienced owner.

—Barbara Woodhouse, *No Bad Dogs*

The obvious first step—asking the dog's owner to stop the noise—is either ignored or botched by a surprising number of people. Perhaps it's not all that surprising; approaching someone with a complaint can be unpleasant and in some cases intimidating. And if you're afraid of your neighbor's burly watchdog, which snarls at you whenever you come near its owner's house, you're probably not eager to drop by to discuss things.

How to Solve a Barking Dog Problem

Here is a checklist of actions to take when you're losing patience (or sleep) over a neighbor's noisy dog. Each step is discussed in detail in the chapter.

- Ask your neighbor to keep the dog quiet.
- Try mediation, especially if you and the neighbor have other issues.
- Contact animal control authorities and request that they enforce local laws restricting noise.
- Call the police.
- Bring a nuisance lawsuit in small claims court.

Talking to your neighbor calmly and reasonably is an essential first step. Even if you do eventually end up in court, a judge isn't likely to be too sympathetic if you didn't make at least some effort to work things out first. So it's a no-lose situation, and if you approach it with a modicum of tact, you may be pleasantly surprised by the neighbor's willingness to work toward a solution.

Sometimes owners are blissfully unaware that there's a problem. If a dog barks for hours every day—but only when it's left alone—the owner may not know that a neighbor is being driven crazy by a dog the owner thinks is quiet and well-mannered. Even if you're sure the neighbor does know about the dog's antisocial behavior, it may be better to proceed as though she doesn't: "I knew you'd want to know that Rusty was digging up my zucchini, so that you could prevent it from happening again."

What, *My* Dog a Problem?

If you're the target of a complaint about your dog's behavior, you should at least be willing to talk about the problem, even if you think your neighbor is being completely unreasonable. It's in your interest to solve the problem quickly, before it escalates and your neighbor calls the police or retaliates for your dog's offenses by parking in front of your driveway.

Try to find out the exact problem. It may be easily solved—or the real problem may not be the dog at all.

Some common problems, such as barking or digging under fences, may be relatively easy to correct with proper training of both the dog and the owner. Often, local humane societies offer free advice and referrals to trainers or obedience schools. The San Francisco SPCA, for example, has a "hotline" owners can call. A staff member answers questions and suggests solutions for hundreds of frustrated pet owners every year. Before you talk to your neighbor, make a few phone calls and see if there are some resources you can suggest during your talk.

Here are some suggestions on how to get the most from your negotiations:

- Write a friendly note or call to arrange a convenient time to talk. Don't blunder up some rainy evening when the neighbor is trying to drag groceries and kids in the house after work.

- If you think it's appropriate, take a little something to the meeting to break the ice: some vegetables from your garden, perhaps.

- Don't threaten legal action (or worse, illegal action). There will be plenty of time to discuss legal remedies if relations deteriorate.

- Offer positive suggestions. Once you have established some rapport, you may want to suggest, tactfully, that the owner get help with the dog. Try saying something like: "You know, my friend Tom had the same problem with his dog, and since he's been taking the dog to ABC Obedience School classes, he and his neighbors are much happier." Of course, if you make suggestions too early in the process, the neighbor may resent your "interference."

- Try to agree on specific actions to alleviate the problem: for example, that the dog will be kept inside between 10 p.m. and 8 a.m.

- After you agree on a plan, set a date to talk again in a couple of weeks. If your next meeting is already arranged, it will be easier for you to talk again. It won't look like you're badgering your neighbor, but will show that you're serious about getting the problem solved.

Mediation: Getting Another Person to Help

If talking to your neighbor directly doesn't work, or you're convinced it's hopeless, consider getting some help from a mediator. A mediator won't make a decision for you, but will help you and your neighbor agree on a resolution of the problem.

Mediators, both professional and volunteers, are trained to listen to both sides, identify problems, keep everyone focused on the real problems, and suggest compromises. Going through the process helps both people feel they've been heard (a more constructive version of the satisfaction of "having your day in court") and often puts people on better terms.

Mediation provides a safe, structured way for neighbors to talk. They meet informally with one or more mediators, and first agree on ground rules—basic guidelines, such as no name-calling or interrupting. Then, each person briefly states a view of the problem. The mediator may summarize the problem and its history before moving on to discuss possible solutions.

The key to mediation is that unlike a lawsuit, it is not an adversarial process. You do *not* go to mediation to argue your side. No judge-like person makes a decision for you. So there is nothing to gain from the lying and manipulation common to the courtroom; the outcome is in the hands of the people who have the dispute. Until both agree, there is no resolution. People can become amazingly cooperative when they realize it's in their power—and no one else's—to resolve their problem.

A frequent consequence of mediation is that those involved in the dispute discover that the problem they think they have—a nuisance dog, for example—isn't the main problem at all. It may turn out that the reason one neighbor hasn't controlled her dog better is that she's upset about the other's plum tree, which drops messy fruit on her side of the fence. Mediation often brings out these hidden agendas. A neighbor who solves the tree problem by pruning a few overhanging branches may find that his neighbor suddenly finds a way to make her dog behave.

When two people do agree on how to alleviate the problem, it's best to put the agreement in writing. The goal is not to make it legally binding—the whole point of mediation is not to rely on some outside authority, like the courts, to make or enforce decisions. But writing down the agreement helps clarify everyone's expectations. And it's invaluable if later memories grow fuzzy, as they almost always do, about who agreed to do what. A sample agreement is shown later in this chapter.

Where to Find a Mediator

The best place to look for a free or low-cost mediator for this kind of dispute is a community mediation group. Many cities—unfortunately, by no means all—have government or nonprofit organizations that provide trained mediators for neighborhood disagreements. To find a program near you, check the website of the National Association for Community Mediation at www.nafcm.org.

These mediators are likely to be familiar with dog disputes; Community Boards, a pioneering San Francisco program, estimates that about one in ten of its complaints involve pets. (A typical Community Boards mediation session is outlined below.)

Someone who doesn't have any formal training may make a fine mediator. For example, someone active in a neighborhood association, if neutral about the dispute and willing to stay neutral during mediation, might make a good amateur mediator. For that matter, anyone who's respected by the people involved in the dispute might be able to help. Someone who's lived in the area a long time may have some good ideas for solutions, but you'll never know unless you ask.

Here are some other places that may be able to refer you to a mediation service:

- the small claims court clerk's office
- the local district attorney's office—try the consumer complaint division, if there is one
- radio or television stations that offer help with consumer problems
- state or local bar associations. Many state bar associations publish directories of all local dispute resolution programs in the state.

Some people make a living as professional mediators. Many of them, however, are lawyers and specialize in an area such as divorces or child custody matters. Their fees may not be worth it to you unless your only alternative is the costly one of hiring a lawyer and going to court.

Mediating Dogfights

Here's an example, based on an actual dispute, of a typical mediation from Community Boards, a San Francisco organization of volunteer mediators.

EXAMPLE: Maxine called the SPCA and police because her neighbor's dog frightened her and woke her with its barking. The police suggested Community Boards. Don, the dog's owner, was anxious to stop what he considered Maxine's harassment and readily agreed to mediation. A Community Boards volunteer talked to Maxine and Don separately, wrote a short summary ("case report") outlining the problem, and scheduled a hearing.

At the hearing, after the introductions and preliminaries, one of the volunteer mediators read the case report. The problem was that Don's dog growled and barked at Maxine when she came home from work late each night, and woke her in the morning when it barked at anyone who rang the doorbell of Don's house. She called the SPCA because she thought the dog barked because it was being mistreated. She hadn't approached Don directly because she was afraid of the dog.

Don was upset and embarrassed by visits from police and letters from the SPCA. He'd had his dog, Aspen, for five years without any problems. He considered himself a responsible pet owner, and Aspen a good dog and a positive addition to the community.

Maxine was the first to give her opinion of the problem.

Maxine: "I'm so tired of all that barking and snarling! That dog is vicious, and he ought to be put away!"

Don: "Aspen serves as a watchdog, and in our neighborhood that's really needed. He only barks at strangers and unfriendly people like Maxine. He wouldn't need to bark if you didn't make those threatening gestures."

The mediators, Kate and Joe, step in to keep Maxine and Don, who are obviously angry and uncomfortable, talking civilly about the issues.

Joe: "We would like you to talk to each other about your conflict directly. Please turn your chairs to face each other."

Maxine: "I don't want to talk to him. Why can't you just tell him to get rid of the dog?"

Joe: "Our job is to help both of you reach your own solution. Please talk to Don directly."

Maxine: "Well, I don't think this will do any good. I can't talk to anyone who says I am harassing him. All I want is peace in my own home without being awakened or jumped on by a dangerous dog."

Don: "I really resent that! Aspen's not dangerous. He's just protecting his home. If you'd stop yelling at him, he wouldn't bark or jump at you."

Kate: "Maxine, you mentioned two noise problems, during the day while you're trying to sleep, and when you are home at night, right?"

Maxine: "The dog wakes me up around 9 or 10 in the morning. It seems like every morning … then I can't get back to sleep."

Don: "If those salesmen and religious fanatics and political freaks would stop ringing the doorbell and leaving their literature—that's why he barks. He's just protecting his home."

Maxine: "From what? Someone collecting signatures on a petition? Why does he throw himself against the fence and growl and show his teeth when I come from work? It scares me so much that some nights I don't even want to come home!"

Kate: "So Don's yard is right next to your front door?"

Maxine: "Yes. I let myself in along the side of the building, and that dog is always there in the yard. He growls while I'm trying to get my door unlocked. It's scary. I'm afraid he'll break the fence down and attack me."

Kate: "Don, can you repeat what Maxine just said?"

Don: "Yes, she said she was scared. But if she would take the time to meet Aspen, he wouldn't growl because he would know her."

Kate: "Would you tell Maxine that, please?"

Don: "You're afraid that Aspen will attack you."

Maxine: "Yes, I got bitten badly when I was growing up, and I'm afraid of dogs."

Don: "Aspen's very gentle. He doesn't ever bark at people he knows. Maybe if he got to know you, you would see that you don't need to be afraid of him."

Joe: "Don, please tell Maxine about having the police come to your home."

Don: "It's so embarrassing! I'm afraid that the landlady will find out and get mad, and make me move or get rid of Aspen. Also, I don't want my neighbors thinking I'm a drug dealer or something."

After some more discussion, the mediators began to help Maxine and Don clarify their progress.

Joe: "Maxine, do you understand Don's position now?"

Maxine: "I realize that Don's dog wasn't barking or threatening me on purpose. Also I know that he wants to be a good neighbor."

Don: "I realize now that Maxine was frightened of dogs because of her childhood experience and that she was really afraid Aspen would hurt her. Also, she called the police because she didn't think I would listen to her."

Kate: "Maxine, if the dog's noise bothers you again, what might you do differently?

Maxine: "I wouldn't call the police, at least not if I could talk to Don first."

Kate: "What about you, Don?"

Don: "I would try to take care of the noise problem, and try to make Maxine feel welcome in the neighborhood."

Next, the mediators helped Maxine and Don work together on a written resolution. One mediator read from the notes taken during the hearing, and suggested areas of agreement. Their agreement is shown below.

Sample Agreement

Maxine Green and Don Kaufman wish to settle a dispute over Don's dog, Aspen. Don recognizes that Aspen frightens Maxine and bothers her with his barking. Maxine recognizes that by her behavior she has sometimes inadvertently provoked the dog's barking, and that she has exacerbated the problem between Don and herself by calling the police when the dog barks.

Maxine and Don agree that:

- Maxine will call Don instead of the police or humane society when Aspen barks.
- Don will disconnect his doorbell during the day to prevent Aspen from barking.
- Maxine will come over and meet Aspen this week, so he will become familiar with her.
- Don will stay up a few nights next week and meet Maxine, with Aspen, when she comes home from work, so that Aspen knows Maxine is friendly.
- If they have future disputes, Maxine and Don will again try to talk, with or without a mediator, to work things out amicably.

_____   _____
Maxine Green   Date

_____   _____
Don Kaufman   Date

State and Local Laws

If the situation doesn't improve after your efforts to work something out, it's time to check your local laws and see what your legal options are. Armed with this knowledge, you'll be better prepared to approach your neighbor again or go to animal control authorities, the police, or a small claims court judge.

In some places, barking dogs are covered by a specific state or local ordinance. For example, Massachusetts law allows neighbors to make a formal complaint to the town's board of selectmen (city council) about a dog that is a nuisance because of "excessive barking."[2] The board holds a hearing and makes whatever order is necessary to stop the nuisance—including, in some cases, ordering the owner to get rid of the dog.[3]

Similarly, state law in Oregon declares any dog that disturbs someone with "frequent or prolonged noises" is a public nuisance.[4] The county investigates complaints. The terms may sound a little vague, but courts have ruled that they are clear enough to let dog owners know what isn't allowed. For example, the Supreme Court of North Dakota concluded that a local ordinance prohibiting "excessive, continuous, or untimely barking" was not unconstitutionally vague.[5]

Keeping a dog whose barking is a nuisance may even be a minor criminal offense. In 2006, a Pennsylvania judge sentenced a woman to ten days in jail because the noise from her five dogs was "torturing the neighbors." He offered, however, to cancel the $300 fine and the jail sentence if she could find new homes for three of the dogs.[6]

If there's no law aimed specifically at dogs, a general nuisance or noise ordinance will make the owner responsible. Local law may forbid loud noise after 10 p.m., for example, or prohibit any "unreasonable" noise. And someone who allows a dog to bark, after numerous warnings from police, may be arrested for disturbing the peace. (Dealing with the police is discussed below.)

A Tennessee judge imposed a fine of $6,200 on a man whose dogs—up to 19 of them, at times—disturbed his neighbors. The steep fine came after the dog owner said, in court, that he didn't care what the neighbors said.[7]

To find out what the law is where you live, go online or to a law library and check the state statutes and city or county ordinances yourself. Look up "noise," "dogs," "animals," or "nuisance." You can probably also find out about local laws by calling the local animal control agency or city attorney.

Other Common Complaints

The laws of many towns and counties cover, in addition to barking dogs:
- dogs that run at large
- dogs that damage property or threaten people, and
- the number of dogs allowed per household.

(See Chapter 2, State and Local Regulation.)

Animal Control Authorities

If your efforts at working something out with your neighbor haven't succeeded, talk to the animal control department in your city or county. The people there are likely to be more receptive than the police or other municipal officials.

When you call, don't just make your complaint and hang up. If it's really a persistent problem, you need to be persistent, too. Find out how to follow up and get results. Ask the person you talk to—and write down his name, so you won't have to explain your problem every time you call—about the department's procedures. Find out what the department will do, and when. For example, if the problem is a barking dog, the department may need to receive a certain number of complaints within a certain time before it will act. If that's the case, you may want to discuss the problem with neighbors; if they feel as you do, enlist their help.

Some cities have set up special programs to handle dog complaints. The animal control department establishes a simple procedure for making a complaint, and follows up promptly—and repeatedly, if necessary. This is a great idea, for two main reasons. First, it gives a specific city official or department—usually the health, police, or public safety department—responsibility for the problem. Otherwise, if it's not clear who's primarily responsible, someone with a complaint is likely to get shuffled from department to department, explaining the problem to six different people during each call.

A dog complaint program also lets everyone—dog owners and their neighbors—know what they can expect. A predictable system of warnings and sanctions tells dog owners what's expected of them and lets neighbors know what it will take to solve a problem before it drives everyone in the neighborhood batty. Of course, it doesn't do much good unless these rules are published and readily available—which, unfortunately, is rare.

If the Collar Works, Wear It

Dog owners in Berkeley, California, who can't quiet their dogs can rent an antibarking collar from the Berkeley Dispute Resolution Center. There are three kinds of collars: one squirts citronella (a smell most dogs detest) when the dog barks, another emits a high-frequency sound, and the third gives the dog an electric shock. That most severe kind of collar—banned as too cruel in some other countries—is appropriate only when the only other option is destroying the dog.

Police

The police may not be very interested in barking dog problems, and you can't much blame them. Unless you live in an exceptionally quiet and peaceful place, police have lots more serious problems on their hands. But a note or oral warning from the police can be very effective; people don't want visits from police. You may be able to make your complaint anonymously, to avoid worsening what may already be strained relations with your neighbor.

The police have the power to enforce local noise laws and laws that prohibit disturbing the peace. As when you're dealing with animal control people, don't be afraid to ask the police exactly what you and other neighbors must do to get them to take action. You may well have to make more than one call or written complaint.

The Los Angeles Solution

A program that should serve as a model is the Los Angeles system, which is administered by the city's Department of Animal Regulation.[8] This program, aimed at solving the problems of noisy dogs and dogs that run at large, is quick and easy to use, and makes good use of mediation techniques.

All it takes to get the department into action is one written complaint describing the noise and giving the name, address, and phone number of the person making the complaint. The department then sends the dog's owner a letter, saying it has received a complaint and requesting that steps be taken immediately to abate the noise.

The department also notifies the person who complained that a letter has been sent to the dog owner. It asks the person to wait 15 days and then, if the situation hasn't improved, to call the department. About 75% of barking dog problems are solved by the first letter.

If the dog doesn't stop being a nuisance and the neighbor complains again, the department sends an officer to the problem dog's house. The officer listens to the dog and looks at where the dog is kept in relation to the neighbor's windows. Next the department schedules a mandatory meeting of an animal control officer, the dog owner, and the neighbor. The animal control officer makes more suggestions about stopping the noise. The department estimates that another 15% of problems are solved by this stage.

The most stubborn cases—the remaining 10%— are resolved at a hearing. The officer who conducts the hearing has the power to fine the dog owner, but that's rarely done. Most often, the officer has the dog license reissued with conditions attached. For example, the owner may be required to keep the dog inside at night, get training for the dog, or have it neutered. If the conditions aren't met, the license is revoked, and the owner must get rid of the dog. The owner isn't allowed another license for a year.

Small Claims Court

If nothing you've tried helps, you can sue the owner of a barking dog, on the ground that the dog is a nuisance that interferes with your use and enjoyment of your home. The least painful route is through small claims court. Small claims court procedures are simple and designed to be used without a lawyer. In some states, including California, lawyers are barred from small claims court. Even if they aren't banned, you will rarely see one there because most people find it too expensive to hire them. Fees in small claims court are also low, and the process is relatively fast—which means you'll get to court in a few weeks or months, not years.

Winning a lawsuit in small claims court can get you money (and satisfaction), but probably nothing else. In most states, small claims court judges only have the power to order someone to pay money. They can't give you what you really want: a court order telling your neighbor to make the problematic pooch be quiet.

Still, making your neighbor fork over some money may be even more effective than a simple court order in convincing your neighbor to clean up his (or his dog's) act. And you can keep going back to court and asking for more as long as the nuisance continues.

If you absolutely must have a court order telling the neighbor to stop (the technical term for this kind of order is an injunction), you may have to go to "regular" court (often called circuit, superior, or district court) instead of small claims court. For that, you'll probably need a lawyer, though you can bring a straightforward nuisance suit yourself, if you're willing to spend some time and effort finding out how to draw up the papers and submit them to the court.

RESOURCE

Represent Yourself in Court, by Paul Bergman and Sara Berman (Nolo), explains how to represent yourself in a lawsuit without a lawyer.

> ## Before You Sue
>
> - **Try to negotiate with the dog's owner.** Many states require proof that you have tried to reach some settlement of the dispute, or at least that you have demanded payment, in writing, before you sue.
> - **Check the deadline for bringing suit.** There is always a limit on how long you have to file a lawsuit after an incident occurs. Usually, it's a year or two. If the problem is ongoing, you have the right to sue as many times as you want (or are willing to) until it stops.
> - **Decide how much to sue for.** You'll have to put a dollar amount on the harm you've suffered because of the neighbor's dog. (See below.) If you want to ask for more than your state's small claims court limits (listed below), you'll have to sue in regular court.
> - **Gather proof that the dog is, legally, a nuisance.** You'll need witnesses, photos, or other evidence that the dog is a nuisance. (See below.)

How Much to Sue For

How much money should you ask for? There is, obviously, no formula to translate your annoyance into dollars. Start with your actual out-of-pocket losses—costs to replace a dead rose bush or damaged fence, for example. Don't spend much time computing your less tangible losses like lost sleep, pain and suffering, or time spent cleaning up dog droppings. Small claims courts put a pretty low ceiling on what you can request, anyway, and the judge will make the final decision on what you get. If you've been suffering every day for months, even a small amount, multiplied by all those days, can add up.

Proving the Dog Is a Nuisance

If you're ready to sue your neighbor in small claims court, you're already convinced that the dog you're complaining about is a nuisance. "Nuisance," however, has a special legal meaning, which has been developing since the Normans conquered England in the 11th century.

Small Claims Court Limits

Alabama	$3,000	Montana	$7,000
Alaska	$10,000	Nebraska	$3,500
Arizona	$2,500	Nevada	$7,500
Arkansas	$5,000	New Hampshire	$7,500
California	$10,000	New Jersey	$3,000[1]
Colorado	$7,500	New Mexico	$10,000
Connecticut	$5,000	New York	$5,000
Delaware	$15,000	North Carolina	$5,000
District of Columbia	$5,000	North Dakota	$10,000
Florida	$5,000	Ohio	$3,000
Georgia	$15,000	Oklahoma	$6,000
Hawaii	$5,000	Oregon	$7,500
Idaho	$5,000	Pennsylvania	$12,000
Illinois	$10,000	Rhode Island	$2,500
Indiana	$6,000	South Carolina	$7,500
Iowa	$5,000	South Dakota	$12,000
Kansas	$4,000	Tennessee	$25,000
Kentucky	$2,500	Texas	$10,000
Louisiana	$3,000	Utah	$10,000
Maine	$6,000	Vermont	$5,000
Maryland	$5,000	Virginia	$5,000
Massachusetts	$7,000	Washington	$5,000
Michigan	$3,000	West Virginia	$5,000
Minnesota	$7,500	Wisconsin	$10,000
Mississippi	$3,500	Wyoming	$6,000
Missouri	$5,000	[1] $15,000 Special Civil Part, Superior Court.	

And you know that anything lawyers have had their hands on that long is bound to be complicated.

Nuisance is defined broadly: it generally includes any unreasonable or unlawful condition that interferes with the use of someone's property. Noisy parties in the middle of the night, smelly garbage, and dogs that won't stop barking are all nuisances to the person whose enjoyment of property is affected.

Rules vary from state to state, but you will probably have to prove that the noise (or other problem) is excessive and unreasonable. You may also have to prove that the nuisance causes you actual physical discomfort and annoyance. The key question to ask yourself is this: Is the activity you're complaining about unreasonable under the circumstances?

> **EXAMPLE 1:** Aaron lives next door to Flo, who has two beagles, Flash and Flood. The dogs are well behaved and quiet, and Flo is considerate of her neighbors, never letting the dogs run loose. But beagles are hounds, and hounds howl. Whenever Flash and Flood hear a fire truck's siren, they turn their muzzles skyward and let out mournful howls until the siren has faded from hearing. Sirens are a pretty rare occurrence in this quiet neighborhood. Just the same, Aaron hates the howling.

Is the beagles' baying a legal nuisance to Aaron? Probably not. It's infrequent and doesn't last long. And while it's mildly annoying, it doesn't substantially interfere with his enjoyment of his property; after all, the siren is probably already making more noise than the dogs. Unless a court were prepared to say that it's never reasonable to have dogs in a city, it couldn't really conclude that it's unreasonable for hounds to howl occasionally.

> **EXAMPLE 2:** Mattie lives next door to Fred, who keeps two German shepherds and one unclassifiable little yapper in his relatively small back yard. The dogs are always outside, and almost always, it seems to Mattie, barking. Their favorite time to chime in together is 6 a.m., when Fred goes out to feed them. Their barking goes on a good five minutes until Fred shuts them up, by yelling at least as loudly as the dogs bark. The commotion often wakes up Mattie, who lies in bed

fuming and having revenge fantasies until she can go back to sleep. Mattie is also often bothered by an unpleasant smell from Fred's yard; it's gotten so that she doesn't even open her windows on the side of the house bordering Fred's. And as if that weren't enough, the dogs sometimes leave droppings in Mattie's front yard.

Is Fred's menagerie a nuisance? You bet. The noise is persistent, at its worst at a time when many people are sleeping, and isn't reasonable by any normal community standards. The smell and the droppings are also interfering with Mattie's use of her property.

How to Sue

Small claims court procedures are supposed to be simple for nonlawyers to use, and they usually are—but you've got to know where to start. Many courts have booklets (sometimes downloadable from the court website) that explain how to proceed with a suit. Usually, all you need do is complete a fill-in-the-boxes form and file it with a small filing fee. Be sure to get whatever materials your local court has, so you understand its special rules and way of doing things.

Courts in some parts of New York, California, and several other states offer free professional help to people who are going to appear in small claims court. In these courts, advisers (lawyers or trained paralegals) answer questions and help people prepare for their court appearances. It's a valuable service which, unfortunately, hasn't caught on everywhere.

RESOURCE
Everybody's Guide to Small Claims Court, by Ralph Warner (Nolo), shows how to prepare and present a winning small claims court suit.

Preparing for Court

The most important part of your small claims case comes before you ever set foot in the courtroom. In other words, good preparation is essential.

You need to organize your case logically to present it to the judge. First, make a list of the points you want to get across. Let's take the example of Mattie and Fred, outlined above. Mattie decides she's had enough of the noise and smell of Fred's dogs. She's already tried, unsuccessfully, to get Fred to agree to mediation. The city health department hasn't taken action, either, so she decides to go to small claims court.

Her first stop is her city's website, for a look at the city ordinances. It turns out the city allows three dogs per household, so that won't be any help. But the city also has an ordinance saying dogs that bark loudly and disturb neighbors are a nuisance.

Before Mattie files her claim, she writes Fred a demand letter, shown below. A demand letter is required in some states, but it's always an excellent idea. Even if it doesn't bring results, it's a good way to get your thoughts organized and make sure the person you're complaining about understands your point of view. And once you're in court, it can help you convince a harried small claims court judge that you have exhausted all your other means of solving the problem.

After waiting for a reply from Fred, which never comes, Mattie files her complaint, and the court clerk sets a date for the hearing. Next, she sits down to prepare. To win her case, she needs to convince the judge of four things:

1. Fred's dogs produce noise and odors that are offensive.
2. The noise, droppings, and odor unreasonably interfere with her use of her property.
3. She should be compensated by Fred for the inconvenience, annoyance, and physical discomfort she has suffered as a result.
4. A reasonable amount of damages, figured by calculating $20 a day for the six months she's lived next door to Fred, is $3,600. The small claims court limit in Missouri is $5,000, so she can ask for the full amount. She can sue again if Fred doesn't stop the nuisance.

Now that she has an outline of what she wants to prove, Mattie must see where her evidence fits. The first item on her agenda is simply to show that the dogs are offensive, loud, and smelly. There are two main ways she can do this: with physical evidence (photographs, documents, tape recordings) or with witnesses who will testify to the conditions.

Demand Letter

September 12, 20xx

Fred Little
445 Euclid St.
Augusta, Missouri

Dear Mr. Little:

I have spoken to you several times about the problems your three dogs create for the neighborhood: the droppings left on my lawn are a nuisance, the noise and smell emanating from your yard make it difficult for me to use my yard, and I am frequently awakened at night by the dogs' prolonged barking. This is even more bothersome in the early morning; the dogs' barking when you feed them at about 6 a.m. every day wakes me and keeps me awake.

I have also spoken to the city health and animal control departments, who have in turn contacted you. You have not responded to their requests to keep the dogs quiet and to clean your yard to eliminate the offensive smell. My attempts to work something out with you have been unsuccessful, and you have refused to try to resolve these problems with the help of a neutral mediator provided by our neighborhood association.

I am making one last formal demand that you stop the nuisance created by your dogs. If you do not correct the problem by next week, I feel I have no alternative but to take the problem to small claims court.

Sincerely,

Mattie Hinman

Mattie Hinman
443 Euclid St.
Augusta, Missouri

Mattie decides to do both. First, she will take pictures that show how close Fred's yard is to her house, how many dogs he has in his yard, and how messy the yard is. Second, she will bring another neighbor, Sarah, as a witness. Sarah lives across the street from Fred, and the dogs' barking has bothered her, too. She can testify both to the loudness of the dogs and the timing of their early morning feeding frenzies. Mattie also asks her friend Jack to testify. He has been to her house and seen the conditions next door.

Then, testimony from Mattie will be the best way to convince the court that the odors and noise from Fred's yard interfere with her use of her property—that is, they constitute a legal nuisance. She should testify to specific instances, complete with dates and times, that illustrate the problem. For example, she can recount the story of a barbecue she tried to have in her back yard, but had to move inside because the dogs' barking next door made talking impossible, and the filthy conditions made breathing unpleasant. The testimony of a guest who was there would help convince the judge, too.

Live testimony is usually preferable: it has a greater impact, and is especially good if the other side has live witnesses, but written statements can also usually be admitted into the court's record of your case. A written statement, which should be brief and to the point, can be in the form of a letter to the court.

Below is a letter that Mattie gets from Jack, who can't testify in person on the day of Mattie's hearing.

Some courts also allow testimony by telephone if a witness is unable to make it to court. You can check with the court clerk to see if the court will let a witness who is ill or out of town testify by phone. It's a good idea to have a letter from the witness, explaining why he can't be there in person.

The third item on the agenda is convincing the judge that Fred should pay for the nuisance. That should follow directly from proving that there is a real nuisance, but Mattie should bolster her efforts by showing that she's tried unsuccessfully to work things out with Fred and to get the city animal control department to do something. That way the judge knows that small claims court is her last resort, and she really needs a judgment against Fred to get him to do something. Here, copies of police or animal control department reports will document her earlier efforts to solve the problem.

Letter in Support of Small Claims Case

Oct. 26, 20xx

Presiding Judge
Small Claims Court
Augusta, Missouri

Re: Mattie Hinman vs. Fred Little, Case #45-77889

Dear Judge:

I have visited Mattie Hinman at her home at 443 Euclid Street several times in the six months she has lived there. Twice we tried to sit on her back patio, but both times we were driven inside by the noise and smell from Mr. Little's back yard next door. The dogs (I could see two large German shepherds, and I could hear another dog) barked whenever we came out on the patio.

I'm a dog owner myself, and I know that all dogs bark sometimes. These dogs, however, went on for probably half an hour. The noise was really nerve-wracking, and the smell was sickening.

Sincerely,

Jack Oster

Jack Oster
849 Oakmont Ave.
Augusta, Missouri

When it comes to the amount Mattie is asking for, there's not too much she can do to influence the judge in addition to presenting convincing evidence about how obnoxious the dogs are. The amount that will be awarded is "within the discretion of the court"—that is, the judge will decide based on the evidence and personal judgment. There are no formal guidelines to follow. (Remember, though, that the judge is bound by the state's law limiting money awards in small claims courts.)

The Small Claims Court Hearing

If you've never been to small claims court, try to go and watch some cases a few days before your hearing is scheduled. You'll be more at ease with court procedures, and you may learn what not to do when you're in front of the judge. A few pointers:

- State your problem in an organized way. (The person bringing the lawsuit begins by summarizing the situation.) Begin with the heart of the problem—in this case, that Fred's dogs are noisy and smelly—not the background. You should be able to state the problem in less than five minutes.
- Don't read your statement. A few notes on a 3" x 5" card should be enough to help you remember key points. You're much more likely to keep the judge's attention if you talk naturally.
- Don't overload the judge with a jumble of documents. Present relevant documents in an orderly, organized way.
- Don't forget to tell the judge how much money you're asking for.

Courtroom Etiquette

- Address the judge as "Your Honor."
- Don't speak directly to your opponent; direct all your comments to the judge.
- Don't argue with or interrupt the judge or your opponent. You'll get a chance to respond.

Here's how Mattie's case against Fred went once they got into court.

Court Clerk: The next case is Mattie Hinman vs. Fred Little. Will everyone please come forward?

Judge: Good morning. Ms. Hinman, will you begin?

Mattie: Thank you, Your Honor. I brought this case because my next-door neighbor, Mr. Little, has three dogs that are a nuisance. Their barking is a terrible annoyance because often they bark for a half hour or an hour without stopping. It's especially bad very early in the morning, about 6 o'clock, when Mr. Little feeds them. The noise wakes me up, and then I have to wait until they stop and try to go back to sleep. It also makes it nearly impossible to use my back yard, because whenever I go outside the dogs start barking.

There is also a bad smell coming from Mr. Little's back yard, because he doesn't keep the yard clean of the dogs' droppings. It gets so bad sometimes that I have to keep the windows on that side of the house closed. That's another reason I can't use the back yard. And sometimes the dogs leave droppings in my front yard.

I have here a letter from a friend of mine, who has been to my house and seen the conditions I'm talking about *[Mattie hands letter to judge]*.

I've lived next door to Mr. Little for six months. I've tried to talk to him about the problem, and I wanted to get help from a community mediation panel, but Mr. Little refused. Then I called the city animal control and health departments. The health department said it would send someone out to give Mr. Little a warning, but that was two months ago and the situation is unchanged.

I have copies of my letters to the health department, Your Honor, and a copy of the letter I wrote Mr. Little demanding that he do something about the dogs. *[Mattie hands copies to court clerk or judge.]* I also brought my neighbor, Sarah Stewart, who can testify to the noise and smell.

I'm asking for $3,600 in damages to compensate me for the discomfort and loss of sleep I've suffered for six months. And as I said, I've also all but lost the use of my back yard. All I really want is some peace and quiet, but if I'm forced to live with this nuisance, I think I should be compensated. Thank you.

Judge: Ms. Stewart, do you have something to add?

Sarah: Yes. I just want to say that Mattie is completely right about the barking and the smell. I'm not as close to it as she is, so it doesn't bother me as much, but I can still hear the barking, and sometimes it does go on for a long time. I don't know how she puts up with it. And when the wind is right, I can smell Mr. Little's house even across the street. It's not sanitary, and people shouldn't have to live next to that.

Judge: All right, Mr. Little, it's your turn to explain why you haven't responded to Ms. Hinman's and the health department's requests to keep your dogs from being a nuisance.

Fred: My dogs aren't a nuisance, Your Honor! Sure, they bark now and then, but there have been burglaries in the neighborhood, and they bark when they hear something suspicious. I'd think Mattie would feel safer having my dogs next door. I've got a right to keep pets, don't I?

Judge: What about the barking early in the morning when you feed them?

Fred: Well, yeah, they do that sometimes, but I've been trying to keep them quiet ever since Mattie complained. I didn't know it bothered her until she told me, you know.

Judge: Ms. Hinman, when did you first complain to Mr. Little?

Mattie: About a month after I moved in, I think.

Fred: Anyway, I'm doing the best I can. I can't stop them from barking when I'm gone, but when I'm home I shut them up right away. I think she just doesn't like dogs, and if she were friendly to them they wouldn't bark at her when she goes in her yard.

As far as the smell, well, I live there and it doesn't bother me. I clean up the yard when I have time, but I've been real busy lately so maybe I haven't kept it quite as good as I should have.

Judge: Thank you. If no one has anything else to add, I will take the case under advisement. I'll tell you right now, however, that I intend to award Ms. Hinman some, if not all, of the damages she has requested.

The reason I'm ruling this way is that it's obvious, from the testimony presented here, that your dogs, Mr. Little, are a legal nuisance. They interfere with Ms. Hinman's use of her property and have caused her significant discomfort. You have had several opportunities to take care of the nuisance but have not done so. You'll get my final decision on the amount of damages in the mail in a few days.

Endnotes

1 *In re Ackerman*, 6 Cal. App. 5, 91 P. 429 (1907).

2 Mass. Gen. Laws Ann., ch. 140, § 157.

3 *Commonwealth v. Ferreri*, 30 Mass. App. Ct. 966, 572 N.E.2d 585 (1991).

4 Or. Rev. Stat. § 609.095(i)(f).

5 *City of Belfield v. Kilkenny*, 729 N.W.2d 120 (N.D. 2007).

6 "As barking angers neighbor, law puts bite on dogs' owner," *Harrisburg, Penn. Patriot-News*, Oct. 13, 2006.

7 "Court cites barking, bites man with fine," *Memphis Commercial Appeal*, April 13, 1996.

8 Los Angeles, Cal., Public Safety and Protection Code §§ 53.63, 53.18.5.

Assistance Dogs

One of the happiest partnerships between humans and canines is the use of dogs to help owners who have a disability—that is, any physical or mental condition that substantially limits a major life activity. A well-trained dog can vastly improve the life of its owner, who may for the first time taste some of the independence others take for granted. The law recognizes the special status of these dogs and allows them places other dogs, no matter how devoted, clever, or winsome, never see.

Old laws gave privileges only to guide dogs (also called "Seeing Eye" dogs). But nowadays all kinds of individually trained assistance or service dogs have special legal status.

Types of Assistance Dogs

Dogs have been trained to perform a truly astounding range of tasks for owners with disabilities.

The most familiar and easily identified are guide dogs trained to help the blind or sight-impaired get about. Guide dogs steer their owners around cars, other people, and all other obstacles, steadfastly ignoring all outside distractions.

Hearing or signal dogs help hearing-impaired people by alerting them with a nudge to important sounds: intruders, phones, crying babies, doorbells, and smoke alarms. Many hearing dogs also ride along in cars to alert their owners to the warnings of ambulance sirens and honking drivers.

Service or support dogs are the arms and legs of many people with a physical disability. They pull wheelchairs, carry baskets and briefcases, open doors, and turn on lights for their owners. Those who suffer from balance problems are often paired with service dogs that help steady them as they negotiate steps or terrain that was formerly off-limits.

Seizure-alert dogs warn owners of impending seizures. This uncanny ability has proven especially important in recent years, as service dogs have been matched with veterans returning from war in Iraq and Afghanistan with serious injuries, including amputations and posttraumatic stress disorder (PTSD). Many dogs that were originally trained to help veterans with mobility and balance turned out to have a gift for helping calm anxious vets and warning them in advance of stress-related seizures.[1]

Some dogs guide autistic or developmentally disabled people through everyday tasks, and may be trained to give calming, reassuring snuggles to owners who become agitated or withdrawn.

Although the lengthy and intensive training these dogs receive is expensive (most, but not all, dogs are trained in special schools), once the dogs are paired with an owner, they work cheap. One study found that people who had a service dog for a year spent 68% less on hired assistants than they had before.[2] That study found significant psychological benefits as well: All the participants (48 people with severe ambulatory disabilities) showed substantial improvements in self-esteem and psychological well-being within six months of getting a service dog.

Dogs also play an important role in the day-to-day social interactions of their owners. People with impaired hearing, for example, suffer the additional stress of having a hidden disability—one they must explain to new acquaintances. A hearing dog is a social ice-breaker, making the process easier for everyone.[3] And there is considerable evidence that people without physical disabilities are more likely to interact with people with disabilities who are accompanied by assistance dogs.[4]

Because of their general temperament and size, German shepherds, Labrador retrievers, and golden retrievers are the breeds most often trained as guide or service dogs. More excitable breeds like terriers and poodles (and all kinds of small mixed-breed dogs) often make good hearing dogs; they respond to sounds without waiting for a command from an owner. While some programs differ, most dogs are bred at the training site, then spend their first months with skilled volunteers or families who teach them simple obedience and social skills. The dogs are then returned to the training facility, where they are spayed or neutered and put through intensive schooling. Only about half graduate. Some don't have the calm demeanor required; some just can't be trained to ignore the temptations of squirrels or cats.

Potential owners must pass tests, too. They are screened and interviewed to ensure that they are in fairly good health, that they want the dog for mobility and independent living, and that the dog would have a good home and adequate exercise. Owners are then teamed with dogs that have the skills and temperament they require. In most programs, the owners stay on-site for several weeks under the supervision of trainers, who teach them handling and grooming. The owner and dog then go home to live and work together.

Therapy Dogs

Therapy dogs are not trained to help a particular owner with a disability, but provide joy to many. These dogs were first used in institutions such as nursing homes and schools for emotionally disturbed children. Volunteers now take them to hospitals, hospices, and nursing homes, where they cheer patients. Unlike individually trained assistance dogs, they do not accompany owners to public places.

Access to Public Places

A federal law, the Americans with Disabilities Act (ADA), guarantees disabled people with service animals access to public places—and requires those places to modify their practices to accommodate the dogs, if necessary.

As the U.S. Department of Justice interprets the ADA, a "service animal" is a dog that has been individually trained to do work or perform tasks for a person with a disability. The disability can be physical or mental, including sensory, psychiatric, intellectual, and other mental disabilities.[5] Under this definition, the dog is a working animal, not a pet.

Although a dog trained to calm an owner with PTSD would qualify as a service animal under the ADA, dogs whose sole function is to provide comfort or emotional support aren't considered service animals. Other federal laws (the Fair Housing Act or the Air Carrier Access Act, discussed below), define "assistance animal" more broadly. (For more information, see the U.S. Department of Justice resources at www.ada.gov/service_animals_2010.htm.)

A person with a disability can generally take a service animal anywhere that members of the public are allowed—restaurants, stores, and theaters, for example. Some other places of public accommodation are:

- hotels and motels
- schools
- parks, golf courses, and bowling alleys
- museums and libraries
- shopping centers and grocery stores
- convention centers and concert halls
- doctors' offices and hospitals.[6]

Surprisingly, people in charge of public accommodations still don't always know or respect the law. In 2004, for example, a California woman successfully sued a performing arts center after it turned away her and her service dog, a little poodle mix named Jazz. The dog had "yipped" twice before at previous performances—but only at intermission, and only when strangers had approached his owner's wheelchair. Once the dog's owner had assured Jazz everything was okay, the dog was quiet. No patrons had complained. But when the woman tried to attend a later performance, the manager not only refused to let her in with her dog, but called the police and threatened to have her arrested.[7]

In Florida, a man who stopped into a convenience store with his guide dog was ordered out by the clerk. The patron—who happened to be the president of the local chapter of the National Federation for the Blind—tried to explain the law that allowed his dog inside, but to no avail. A county judge later sentenced the clerk, who pleaded guilty to violating the rights of a person with a disability, to six months of probation and 25 hours of community service at Lighthouse for the Visually Impaired and Blind.[8]

The ADA requires places of public accommodation to modify their "policies, practices, or procedures" to permit the use of a service animal by a person with a disability.[9] For example, a restaurant must allow a service dog in its public area, despite the fact that state or local health laws prohibit animals on the premises where food is served. A business cannot isolate someone with a service dog from other customers, or charge an extra fee.

Unfortunately, people with service dogs sometimes still encounter businesses that try to exclude their animals. This seems especially common in restaurants, perhaps because employees are used to obeying health regulations forbidding animals but haven't been similarly trained on the federal law allowing service dogs.[10]

The only restrictions allowed are those that are absolutely necessary. For example, in California, zoos are allowed to keep assistance dogs out of areas where zoo animals aren't separated from the public by a physical barrier, but the zoo must maintain free kennel facilities for the dogs.[11]

Teaching Schools a Lesson

Even in the face of California's explicit law allowing service dogs in public places, a 16-year-old high school student had to sue her school district before it would allow her service dog to accompany her to school. The school had claimed that it was too inconvenient, and that the girl should ask other people, not her dog, to retrieve dropped objects for her and help her with other tasks.

The court immediately ordered the school to let her bring the dog, and chastised the school for undermining the student's legal rights as well as her dignity and self-respect.[12]

Bringing a service dog to school may not, however, always be a reasonable accommodation for a student who has a disability. In the case of a high school boy with impaired hearing, a court ruled that the school did not have to allow him to bring his newly acquired hearing dog to school with him. The court based its decision on the facts that the boy was already doing well at school with other accommodations (including an interpreter, note-taker, extra time for exams, and seating in the front row of his classes) and that the dog would pose potentially very serious health problems for allergic students and teachers. The court found that the parents had not pursued the proper administrative remedies before suing.[13]

Congress directed public accommodations to take these steps to ensure that individuals with disabilities are not separated from their service animals. Congress "intended that the broadest feasible access be provided to service animals in all places of public accommodation." In rare circumstances, places may not have to accommodate service dogs, if doing so would cause a fundamental change in the "nature of the goods, services, facilities, privileges, or accommodations offered or provided, or the safe operation of the public accommodation would be jeopardized."[14] If you must be separated from your service dog for such a reason, you will be responsible for providing for the dog's supervision and care.[15]

What Must You Prove?

It's easy to see the necessity of assistance dogs that are pulling wheelchairs or guiding owners with visual impairments. But what if the dog's function isn't obvious? For example, you can't tell just by looking that an ordinary-looking dog is actually a seizure-alert animal that could save his owner's life.

Generally, all an owner needs to do to get a service dog admitted to public places, rental housing, or a workplace is explain what the dog has been trained to do. Service dogs do not have to wear special equipment or tags, and the law does not require you to carry any special ID. If it's not obvious what work the dog will be doing for the owner, staff members at a place of public accommodation can ask only two questions:

- Is the dog a service animal required because of a disability?
- What work has the dog been trained to do?

Questions about the owner's disability are off-limits. The owner cannot be required to produce proof of a medical condition or of the dog's training, or any special identification.

If an establishment does ask these legitimate questions, it won't be found liable for violating the ADA. For example, a patron showed up at a Delaware casino with a four-month-old puppy, unleashed but outfitted in a "support dog" vest tied at the neck with clothesline. The man stated that he had a disability and wished to bring his dog in. When security personnel asked what tasks the animal had been trained to perform, the dog's owner refused to answer and was denied entry. When he complained to the state Human Relations Commission, he was awarded compensation (under a state law that's essentially the same as the federal ADA) for being denied access. The Delaware Supreme Court, however, reversed that decision, ruling that the casino security guards had asked only what they were allowed to ask by law.[16]

If you are denied access to a public place, you are perfectly within your rights to call the police. Still, many people are simply ignorant of the law, and if you want to educate them, you can show both identification for your dog and a copy of the federal regulations that allow you and your dog access to public places. Seeing the law in black and white almost always opens doors.

RESOURCE

The New York City Bar Association's material on *Access Rights of People With Disabilities and Their Service Animals*, available at www.nycbar.org, has great nuts-and-bolts information about access to public places. Although it contains some material specific to New York laws, it also covers the federal laws that apply everywhere.

RESOURCE

For more information, you can contact one of the many nonprofit organizations dedicated to fostering the connection between people and their assistance dogs. Here are just a few:

Pet Partners (formerly the Delta Society)
875 124th Ave. NE, Suite 101, Bellevue, WA 98005
425-679-5500
www.petpartners.org

Canine Companions for Independence
National office: P.O. Box 446, Santa Rosa, CA 95402-0446
For nearest regional center, call 800-572-BARK (800-572-2275)
866-CCI-DOGS (866-224-3647)
www.cci.org

Guide Dog Foundation for the Blind, Inc.
371 East Jericho Turnpike, Smithtown, NY 11787-2976
631-265-2121 or 800-548-4337
www.guidedog.org

Rental Housing

The federal Fair Housing Act requires that landlords make "reasonable accommodations" for tenants with disabilities. Allowing an animal can be such an accommodation.[17] State laws may offer additional protections.

A landlord must modify its rules, policies, or practices to allow a tenant with a disability to use an assistance animal when it's necessary to give that person an equal opportunity to use a dwelling or common area. So if a tenant with a disability needs an animal, the landlord must make an exception to its general no-pets policy. (Tenants must still follow rules regarding animals that damage the premises, or that annoy or threaten residents or guests, as discussed below.)

It's the tenant's responsibility to provide evidence of the disability and request a dog as an accommodation for that disability. Usually, all a tenant needs is a letter from a physician or therapist, stating that the person has a disability and needs an assistance animal. A landlord that refuses to make a reasonable accommodation is in violation of the Fair Housing Act.[18]

Most courts have ruled that tenants do not have to prove that their dogs meet the strict definition of a "service animal" as defined by the Americans with Disabilities Act (discussed above); the FHA uses a broader standard. As one court put it, "There is a difference between not requiring the owner of a movie theater to allow a customer to bring her emotional support dog, which is not a service animal, into the theater to watch a two-hour movie, an ADA-type issue, on one hand, and permitting the provider of housing to refuse to allow a renter to keep such an animal in her apartment in order to provide emotional support to her and to assist her to cope with her depression, an FHA-type issue, on the other."[19]

Landlords that refuse requests for reasonable accommodations can be sued. A California landlord ended up paying a tenant almost $300,000 after forcing her to get rid of her dog because it exceeded the apartment complex's new 35-pound weight limit for pets. The tenant had painful spine, muscle, and nerve problems; the dog helped her with the anxiety and depression her illness caused. Despite a doctor's note recommending a dog for therapy and classifying her dog Nellie as more than a pet, the owners wouldn't renew the tenant's lease. Eventually, she had to have the dog put down. The tenant sued, alleging discrimination because of her disability; California's Department of Fair Employment and Housing announced that the landlord had settled the lawsuit.[20]

Another company, which owned an apartment complex in Washington, DC, told prospective renters—who were actually testers from the Department of Justice—that no dogs, including guide dogs, were allowed. The company ended up paying $25,000 to compensate would-be tenants who had been discriminated against and another $20,000 penalty to the government.[21]

The law allows landlords to include reasonable regulations concerning animals in the lease or rental agreement. The owners, like all dog owners, are liable for any damage the dogs cause. In some states, however, landlords are prohibited from charging a security deposit for a service or companion animal that is needed by a tenant with a disability.[22]

Subsidized housing. In some circumstances, people with disabilities who live in government-subsidized housing are allowed by law to have dogs, whether or not the dogs have any special training. (See Chapter 4, Landlords and Dogs.)

> **RESOURCE**
>
> *Best Friends for Life* is a short book that does an excellent job of explaining the rights of people with disabilities (and others) to have animals in rental housing. It's available from the two organizations that published it:
>
> The Doris Day Animal League, 227 Massachusetts Ave. NE, Washington, DC 20002, 202-546-1761, www.ddal.org
>
> The Massachusetts Society for the Prevention of Cruelty to Animals, 350 S. Huntington Ave., Boston, MA 02130, 617-522-7400, www.mspca.org.

Assistance Dogs in the Workplace

The federal Americans with Disabilities Act forbids any kind of employment discrimination against persons with disabilities. Employers with 15 or more employees must make "reasonable accommodations" for workers with disabilities.[23] The Act doesn't say whether or not this includes allowing an employee to bring an assistance dog to work; the answer will depend on what is "reasonable" under the circumstances. The regulations interpreting the law say, however, that letting a blind employee use a guide dog at work is an example of a reasonable accommodation.[24]

An Illinois physician, who was permanently injured in an accident but returned to work using a wheelchair, asked permission to bring a service dog to work with her at a federal Veterans Administration facility. Her doctors had recommended a service dog, because years of operating her wheelchair had placed extraordinary stress on her body. The VA refused; but a federal court ruled that the facility must allow the doctor to bring the trained service dog to work because it was a reasonable accommodation to her disability.[25]

There can be other, less obvious violations of the law as well. Any kind of workplace discrimination against an employee with a disability is illegal—for example, it is illegal to deny a qualified person a job or promotion simply because the person is accompanied by a service dog.

Traveling With Assistance Dogs

Assistance dogs are allowed by law on all kinds of public transportation, including buses, planes, and trains. Companies that don't accept service animals may be found in violation of the ADA or comparable state laws. For example, after a bus company refused to transport two blind people and their guide dog, the Massachusetts Commission Against Discrimination found the company liable for discriminating against people with disabilities. The bus company was ordered to compensate the couple a total of $60,000 and pay an additional $10,000 fine.[26]

The federal Air Carrier Access Act (ACAA) guarantees that service dogs and emotional support dogs may travel with passengers who have a disability. The dogs fly free, with their owners, in the airliner's cabin. Passengers with dogs are usually placed in the front row of a section of seats, which gives the dog room to lie down in front of the owner. But federal regulations require airlines to accommodate these dogs at any seat where the passenger sits unless the dog blocks an aisle, in which case the airline needs to find another seat.[27]

Let the airline know, when you book your ticket, that you will be accompanied by the dog. If your impairment is not obvious and the dog's presence might be questioned, it's a good idea to have with you proof of your dog's special status, such as a special license tag or a certificate that documents its training.

As evidence that the dog is a service dog, the airline can accept an ID card or other document, or rely on the fact that the dog is wearing a special harness or tag. If the dog isn't a service dog (as defined by the ADA) but is an emotional support or psychiatric service animal, the passenger can be required to provide documentation. The document must be no older than a year from the date of the flight and on the letterhead of a licensed mental health professional such as a psychiatrist, psychologist, licensed clinical social worker, or medical doctor who's specifically treating the passenger's mental or emotional disability. The letter must give date the and type of the professional's license, and the state that issued it. It must state that:

- The passenger has a mental or emotional disability recognized in the fourth edition of the *Diagnostic and Statistical Manual of Mental Disorders.*
- The passenger needs the dog as an accommodation for travel or at the destination.
- The person providing the assessment is a licensed mental health professional who is caring for the passenger.

If an airline refuses to accept a dog, it must explain why, and then put the explanation in writing and deliver it to the passenger within ten days.

Don't Even Bother Telling It to the Judge

A San Francisco man was convicted of driving alone in a carpool lane, after a judge failed to be swayed by his argument that his dog should be counted as a second person in the car.

But what really got the judge upset was the man's claim that he was legally blind—and that when he drove, his dog sat in his lap and barked when she saw a car in front of his.[28]

Exemptions From Local Regulations

Specially trained service dogs are often granted exemptions from local requirements that are imposed on other dogs. As mentioned, some laws exempt only guide dogs, or only guide and hearing dogs.

Licenses

Virtually all cities give free licenses to trained service dogs. In some states (Connecticut and Michigan, for example), state law guarantees free licenses.[29] If you qualify for a free license, remember that you still must go through the motions of getting the license. Only the fee is waived; you must still show that the dog has had required vaccinations. You must also renew the license when it expires.

Some states (Ohio and North Carolina, for example) make this easier by issuing free, permanent licenses for service dogs. Owners don't have to worry about renewing the license every year.

Pooper-Scooper Laws

Many pooper-scooper laws (New York's and San Francisco's, for example) don't apply to service dogs.[30] Unfortunately, zealous police officers trying to enforce these laws may not always know, or be willing to be told, that service dogs are exempt. In San Francisco, for example, a policeman ignored a blind woman's protests that the law exempted her. As a large lunch-time crowd gathered, the officer forced the woman to clean up her guide dog's droppings and take them across the street to a garbage can. She sued and received a $17,000 settlement from the city for emotional trauma.[31]

Bans on Specific Breeds

What happens when a small town's ban on pit bulls runs into federal law allowing people with disabilities to have service dogs? In the words of one court faced with that conflict, "The national public interest in enforcement of the ADA 'trumps' the more local public interest in public health and safety" reflected in the local ordinance prohibiting pit bulls.

The case came about when James Sak, a retired police officer, moved from Chicago with his wife to a small Iowa town so they could take care of her elderly mother. They brought with them Snickers, a five-year-old dog they had acquired as a puppy. Snickers had been trained to help Sak, who had been seriously and permanently injured by a stroke, with walking, balance, and retrieving items for Sak around the house. According to Sak and his wife, Snickers had never shown any aggression; in any case, they didn't intend to use Snickers to assist Sak on trips away from their home. Snickers caused no problems in his new town.

So what was the problem? Snickers appeared to be, at least in part, a pit-bull type of dog. (There's no one breed of dog called a pit bull, but several are considered the pit bull type.) And the little town of Aurelia, Iowa, (population approximately 1,100) had passed an ordinance banning all pit bulls from the town. They asked the town to grant an exception for service dogs. Instead, they were told that they had 24 hours to get Snickers out of town. Sak and his wife obeyed the law and found a kennel for Snickers outside the town limits. While Snickers was gone, Sak fell and, without Snickers to hang onto, couldn't get back into his wheelchair; he had to call 911. Finally, Saks and his wife sued, alleging that the ordinance violated the ADA.

The U.S. District court weighed the town's argument—pit bulls can be dangerous—against the right of Mr. Sak to have his service dog, and concluded that the ordinance had to give when it came to Snickers. It also looked at guidance from the U.S. Department of Justice on interpreting the ADA. The DOJ "does not believe that it is either appropriate or consistent with the ADA to defer to local laws that prohibit certain breeds of dogs based on local concerns that these breeds may have a history of unprovoked aggression or attacks. ... State and local government entities have the ability to determine, on a case-by-case basis, whether a particular service animal can be excluded based on that particular animal's actual behavior or history—not based on fears or generalizations about how an animal or breed might behave." The court issued a preliminary injunction, prohibiting the town from banning pit bulls.[32]

Income Tax Deductions for Guide Dogs

Even the Internal Revenue Service has something for guide dogs: it recognizes them as a legitimate medical expense, which can be deducted for federal income tax purposes.[33]

Public Assistance

Some states assist low-income people with the expenses of keeping a guide, hearing, or other service dog. New York and California, for example, give a monthly payment for dog food to owners who qualify.[34]

The federal government also may pay for a service dog, including a dog trained to help someone with posttraumatic stress disorder or mental illness, for a veteran who is entitled to federal disability compensation.[35] The costs paid for may include travel expenses incurred when the veteran goes to pick up the dog from a training center.

Assistance Dogs and Creditors

Generally, a creditor who has won a lawsuit against a person with a disability and is trying to collect the amount of the judgment cannot seize the person's guide, service, or hearing dog to satisfy the judgment. In New York, the dog's food is also exempt.[36] More states prohibit creditors from taking a debtor's "health aids," which should include assistance dogs.

Penalties for Injuring Guide Dogs

Unfortunately, many guide dogs suffer attacks from other dogs—incidents that can be traumatic for both dog and owner. Although exact numbers aren't available, several surveys of guide dogs users have reported that a significant percentage of the teams—more than 40%—have experienced some form of attack on the dog.[37]

Many states apply special laws when a guide dog, or a blind person using a guide dog, is injured. For example, if another dog injures a guide dog, Rhode Island law makes the owner of the guilty dog liable for twice the amount of damages the blind person incurs. If the dog hurts a guide dog or owner again, the tab goes up to three times the amount of damages.[38] And in Nevada, anyone who beats or interferes with a service animal may be sentenced to up to a year in jail, fined up to $5,000, or both.[39] Pennsylvania and some other states also apply such laws to all service dogs.[40] You can find links to all states' laws on the website of Guide Dogs for the Blind, www.guidedogs.com.

Endnotes

[1] "Veterans Helped By Healing Paws," *New York Times*, Nov. 11, 2008.

[2] "The Value of Service Dogs for People With Severe Ambulatory Disabilities," by Karen Allen and Jim Blascovich, Journal of the American Medical Association, April 3, 1996.

[3] "The Socializing Role of Hearing Dogs," by Lynette Hart, R. Lee Zasloff, and Anne Marie Benfatto, presented at the national conference of the Animal Behavior Society (July 1996).

[4] See, for example, "Social acknowledgements for children with disabilities: effects of service dogs," by B. Mader and L.A. Hart, Child Development, 60: 1529-1534 (1989).

[5] 28 C.F.R. § 36.104, 28 C.F.R. § 35.104.

[6] 28 C.F.R. § 36.104

[7] *Lentini v. California Center for the Arts*, 370 F.3d 837 (9th Cir. 2004).

[8] *LRP Disability Compliance Bulletin*, Mar. 16, 2006.

[9] 42 U.S.C. § 12181; 28 C.F.R. § 36.302.

[10] For example, see "Macomb County restaurant refuses to serve disabled man with service dog," *Downriver News-Herald*, Jan. 8, 2012; "Popeyes apologizes to man with service dog," *Atlanta Journal-Constitution*, May 22, 2012.

[11] Cal. Civ. Code § 54.7.

[12] *Sullivan, ex rel. Sullivan v. Vallejo City Unified School District*, 731 F. Supp. 947 (E.D. Cal. 1990).

[13] *Cave v. East Meadow Union Free School Dist.*, 480 F. Supp. 2d 610 (2007).

[14] 28 C.F.R. § 36.301.

[15] 28 C.F.R. § 36.302(c).

[16] *Thompson v. Dover Downs, Inc.*, 887 A.2d 458 (Del. 2005).

[17] The Fair Housing Amendments Act, 42 U.S.C. §§ 3601–3619.

[18] For example, see *Sun Harbor Homeowners' Ass'n. Inc. v. Bonura*, No. 4D10-3038, Fla. Dist. Ct. of Appeal, June 13, 2012.

[19] *Fair Housing of the Dakotas, Inc. v. Goldmark Property Management, Inc.*, 778 F. Supp. 2d 1028 (D. N.D. 2011).

[20] "Landlords to pay $300,000 for evicting woman's helper dog," *San Francisco Chronicle*, Nov. 21, 2009.

[21] *United States v. Douglass Management, Inc.*, consent order, 2006.

[22] For example, see Del. Code Ann. Tit. 25, § 5514; Or. Rev. Stat. § 90.300.

[23] 42 U.S.C. § 12111.

[24] 29 C.F.R. Part 1630, Appendix.

[25] *Branson v. West*, 1999 WL 311717 (N.D. Ill. 1999).

[26] *LRP Disability Compliance Bulletin*, Aug. 2, 2007

[27] 14 C.F.R. Part 382, Subpart H, § 382.117.

[28] *San Francisco Examiner*, Dec. 1990.

[29] Mich. Comp. Laws Ann. § 287.291; Conn. Gen. Stat. Ann. § 22-345.

[30] N.Y. Pub. Health Law § 1310; S.F. Health Code, art. 1, § 40.

[31] *San Francisco Chronicle*, Aug. 16, 1988.

[32] *Sak v. City of Aurelia, Iowa,* No. C 11–4111–MWB. 2011 WL 6826146 ____ F. Supp. ____ (N.D. Iowa 2011).

[33] Treas. Reg. § 1.213-1(e)(1)(iii).

[34] N.Y. Soc. Serv. Law § 303-a; Cal. Welf. & Inst. Code § 12553.

[35] 38 U.S.C. § 1714(b).

[36] N.Y. Civ. Prac. Law § 5205(h)(2).

[37] Godley and Gillard, "Assisting Handlers Following Attacks on Dog Guides: Implications for Dog Guide Teams," Journal of Visual Impairment & Blindness, October-November 2011.

[38] R.I. Gen. Laws § 4-13-16.1.

[39] Nev. Rev. Stat. § 426.790.

[40] 18 Pa. Cons. Stat. Ann. § 5511.

If a Dog Is Injured or Killed

We acknowledge that the dog is man's best friend ...
—California Court of Appeal[1]

What can a dog owner do if a dog dies because of someone's deliberate or careless act? It can happen: a dog is hit by a car, shot while chasing a farmer's chickens, euthanized after being picked up by animal control officers, or carelessly treated by a veterinarian, to name just a few scenarios.

The lawyer's standard answer—"sue the bastard!"—will not comfort anyone familiar with how the legal system works. If possible, working out a settlement is less painful, less expensive, and quicker than battling in court. And when the dispute centers on how much money a dog is worth—which is often relatively little—going to court is unlikely to be worth your while, and negotiation and mediation are preferable. (Chapter 7, Barking Dogs, contains a detailed discussion of mediation, which is not repeated here.) In general, only if those methods don't work should you consider whether or not a lawsuit makes sense. If you do have to go to court, small claims court is usually the best choice.

This advice applies no matter which side of the fence you're on: whether your dog was hurt or you're the one who shot at a dog that was threatening your prize sheep. But only when you understand your legal options are you ready to negotiate—or sue, if it comes to that.

Special Rules

If you own a dog that is injured or killed by a veterinarian or by government action, special legal rules apply.

The government. The government has special rights to seize and impound dogs. (See Chapter 2, State and Local Regulation.) And if a government entity injures or kills your animal and you want to sue, special rules govern when and how you can proceed. (See "Claims Against the Government" in this chapter.)

Veterinarians. Special legal standards apply when a veterinarian is responsible for injuring a dog. (See Chapter 5, Veterinarians.)

When Killing a Dog Is Justified

Sometimes, killing a dog is legally justified, and the person who does it isn't financially liable to the dog's owner. For example, if someone kills a dog because it is threatening to injure a person or livestock, the action is justified by law. This section discusses the common situations in which a dog owner whose dog has been hurt or killed is not entitled to compensation.

Dogs Attacking People or Livestock

Generally, it's perfectly legal to do anything necessary to stop a dog caught in the act of attacking a person or livestock. A dog's owner is not legally entitled to any money from someone who injures or kills the dog while protecting a person or farm animal from attack. Nor is the person guilty of a criminal offense; many animal cruelty laws specifically exempt the act of injuring or killing a dog in these circumstances.

Court decisions in such cases always depend on the unique circumstances. For example, was it self-defense for a retired deputy sheriff to shoot at two stray dogs? (She missed the dogs but hit a parked car.) Some of the facts: The retired deputy was walking a 100-pound Rottweiler and carrying a loaded semiautomatic weapon; the strays were estimated to weigh about 25 or 30 pounds each; witnesses said the dogs never ran toward the deputy and her dog and were about 25 feet away from her; all of this occurred near a strip mall in a Los Angeles suburb. When the case went to court, the retired deputy was found guilty of negligently discharging a firearm and sentenced to probation. When she appealed, the court sent the case back, ruling that the jury should have been told that self-defense could have justified her actions.[2]

"Livestock" usually means only commercially valuable animals, not pets or wild animals. Some state laws include a list of the kinds of animals protected; others say only that a dog may be killed if it attacks a "domestic animal," which historically does not include dogs and cats. Dogs and cats may even be specifically excluded; for example, in Ohio it's legal to kill a dog that is chasing or injuring a "sheep, lamb, goat, kid, domestic fowl or domestic animal except a cat or another dog." Someone who does injure a dog that's chasing another dog, or a deer, may be liable for damages to the dog's owner—and the killer may also be guilty of cruelty to animals. (See Chapter 14, Cruelty.)

A farmer or rancher doesn't have to wait until a dog has sunk its teeth into a calf or lamb; most laws allow killing a dog that is chasing or preparing to attack livestock, or fleeing after an attack. In Kentucky, for example, any dog that is "pursuing or wounding" livestock can be killed.[3] The dog must, however, be caught in the act. As one court put it, "it is not the dog's predatory habits, nor his past transgressions, nor his reputation, however bad, but the doctrine of self-defense, whether of person or property, that gives the right to kill."[4]

Hunting down a dog after an attack has taken place is not allowed. Generally, a farmer may legally kill a dog only on the farmer's own property. An Illinois court ruled that a sheep farmer who followed a dog back to its owner's home (in a residential area, no less) and shot it there an hour after the dog had killed some of his sheep was not protected under the Illinois statute.[5] Instead, he should have sued the dog's owner for the value of the sheep killed. (See Chapter 11, Dog Bites.)

A dog is not, however, necessarily safe as soon as it leaves the farmer's property. In general, a farmer who wants retaliation is allowed to pursue a dog for a "reasonable time." What is a reasonable time under the circumstances is a question that's resolved when the lawsuit gets to court.

For example, a Kansas jury vindicated a farmer who shot and wounded a dog he found attacking his hogs. He shot at the dog, but it ran away, with the farmer in hot pursuit in his pickup. The dog ran home, where the farmer shot it twice and left it hiding, wounded, under the house. When the dog's owner came home, he rushed the dog to a veterinarian; it eventually recovered from its injury. The owner sued for almost $8,000, but the jury came back with a verdict for the farmer.[6] The Kansas statute allows a livestock owner to kill a dog that has been found injuring livestock "a reasonable time" before.

A farmer must also produce proof that a dog he injures was chasing his livestock. In an old California case, for example, the rancher's belief that his sheep were in danger from dogs was not enough, the court ruled, to absolve him of financial responsibility for shooting them.[7] Testimony indicated that the dogs were following a herd of pregnant ewes, which were agitated and frightened. The dogs' owner successfully sued for $225 (this was in 1889) for the injuries to his three highly trained dogs.

Livestock Recovery Funds

In many places, farmers or ranchers who lose livestock to dogs can apply for reimbursement from a county or state fund.

Dogs Running at Large

Most statutes do not allow a farmer to shoot dogs that are merely running loose (at large). A North Dakota rancher, who shot a neighbor's greyhound after it ran through his cattle herd without particularly disturbing the cattle, was not protected by the state statute, which allows killing a dog only if it is "worrying" livestock. The rancher had to pay $300 to the dog's owner.[8]

Some states, however, allow farmers to shoot any dog that is, in the words of the Indiana statute, "roaming over the country unattended." Under this statute, an appeals court upheld the right of a farmer to shoot dogs he said were trying to get into his chicken pen in the middle of the night.[9] The dogs, two coonhounds, had been hunting with their owner but got separated from him in a heavy rainstorm about 2 a.m. (For the uninitiated, raccoon hunting is done at night.) Under the relatively severe Indiana law, it made no difference that the dogs were bothering the chickens; their hours were numbered as soon as they got away from their master.

If you lose a dog to a trigger-happy farmer, in most instances, there is absolutely no way to prove that it wasn't doing what the farmer or rancher who shot it says it was doing. The only other witness is likely to be the dog, and it isn't talking. If you're a dog owner, you don't want to end up quarreling over whether or not a certain law applies when your dog has already been shot. From this point of view, the moral is quite simple: If you live in a rural area or close to one, NEVER let your dog run loose off your property. Farmers may shoot first and ask questions later, if at all.

Unjustified Injury to a Dog

A dog owner is usually entitled to compensation if someone injures or kills a dog intentionally or through unreasonable carelessness.

Dogs Injured Intentionally

Anyone who intentionally injures a dog is financially liable for the injury, unless there's a statute (like the ones discussed above, which let a livestock owner protect animals from attacking dogs) to the contrary.

> **EXAMPLE:** Sonia is annoyed at her neighbor Julia's dogs, Labrador retrievers that sometimes chase her cat. The next time she sees the dogs, she gets out her old heavy-duty slingshot and lets fly. She hits one dog squarely on the ear, and it yelps and runs home, badly injured. There is no law allowing Sonia to do this, so she is liable to Julia for the cost of the injury to the dog. (How to figure this amount is discussed later in the chapter.)

But Julia may also be partly at fault for letting the dog run around the neighborhood, so the amount she can recover from Sonia may be reduced correspondingly. (See "If the Dog Owner Is at Fault, Too," below.)

Here are some other examples of intentional injury to dogs, for which the dog's owner is legally entitled to compensation:

- An angry neighbor poisons a dog.
- A farmer shoots a dog, even though the dog isn't threatening livestock.
- A thief takes a dog and sells it to a research lab.

In all these instances, the person could also be charged with a criminal offense. That's what happened to a Los Angeles postal carrier who shot and killed a dog that wasn't menacing him at the time, but had bitten him earlier. He was charged with cruelty to animals; the Post Office also agreed to pay for a funeral for the dog, complete with silk-lined casket.[10] (See Chapter 14, Cruelty.)

Dogs Injured Through Carelessness

Someone who is unreasonably careless (the legal term is "negligent") and as a result injures or kills a dog is legally liable to the dog's owner.

What constitutes negligence in any given situation depends on the circumstances, and every situation is unique. It's hard to generalize about when someone will be held liable. But the basic question is always the same: did the person act reasonably, under the circumstances? If the dispute gets all the way to a lawsuit and trial, the question is given to the jurors to answer, based on the evidence they hear.

Here are some examples of negligence:

- Animal control authorities pick up a dog and impound it. Not noticing that the dog is wearing a license tag, which means its owner could have been notified, an employee destroys the dog the next day.
- An employee of a dog-walking service carelessly leaves a dog in a parked car on a hot day; the dog dies of heat prostration.
- A man accidentally leaves rat poison out in his driveway, where he knows the dog from next door often lies; the dog eats the poison and becomes ill.

Often, of course, deciding whether or not someone acted unreasonably, and so may legally be at fault, is a tough question. In one case, federal government employees, trying to kill coyotes, spread poisoned bait in a field where hunters regularly took their dogs. They had the landowner's permission and posted some warning signs. When a hunter sued after his dog was poisoned, the court ruled that the government had acted reasonably.[11]

Dogs Hurt by Other Dogs

The laws that allow livestock owners to kill attacking dogs do not usually apply when it's a dog that is being attacked. So, a dog owner who injures a dog in an attempt to protect his own dog may still have to pay for the injury, or answer a cruelty to animals charge. It will be up to a judge or jury to decide if the owner acted reasonably under the circumstances. For example, a New York man was found innocent of a cruelty charge after he shot and killed a dog that charged into a family picnic, scattering the children present, and attacked his dog.[12]

Even though the owner of a dog that is being attacked may not legally be allowed to kill or injure the other dog, he probably can sue the other dog's owner. Remember that legally, a dog is its owner's property, and the owner can sue for property damage. In a slight majority of states, dog owners are financially responsible for all property damage their dog causes, in most circumstances. In the rest of the states, the injured party must show that the dog owner knew, or should have known, that the dog was likely to cause that kind of damage. (These rules are discussed in detail in Chapter 11, Dog Bites.)

> **A REAL-LIFE EXAMPLE:** In 1919, a four-and-a-half-pound Pomeranian was being walked on the streets of San Francisco when it was attacked by an Airedale terrier. The attack was fatal; as the court put it, the little dog "crossed to that shore from which none, not even a good dog, ever returns." Its owner sued the Airedale's owner for $1,000. (This Pomeranian, according to the court, was "regarded in dog circles as possessing the bluest of blood.") The Airedale's owner was found liable.[13]

Two more recent cases:
- The exasperated owner of a purebred beagle sued his neighbor after the neighbor's dog got loose and impregnated the beagle—for the second time. Because of complications of the second pregnancy, the beagle had to have a cesarean section and later, a hysterectomy. The court ruled that the amorous dog's owner was clearly negligent and liable for the beagle's $851 veterinarian's bill.[14]
- A Yorkshire terrier was attacked by a much larger dog (a Weimaraner) that got away from its owner. The dog was seriously injured and died after surgery. The terrier's owner sued the other dog's owner and was awarded $2,000 for veterinary expenses and $200 for the value of the dog.[15]

If the Dog Owner Is at Fault, Too

If the dog's owner is partly responsible for an injury, it's only fair that the owner share financial responsibility, too. To this end, most states have adopted the doctrine of "comparative fault" or "comparative negligence," which roughly means that if you sue and win, your award is reduced in proportion to your fault. So if you're one-third at fault, for example, you get one-third less.

Contributory Negligence States

A few states still follow the old legal doctrine of "contributory negligence" instead of the comparative fault rule. Under contributory negligence, someone who sues and is the least bit at fault can collect nothing.

The contributory negligence states are:

- Alabama
- District of Columbia
- Maryland
- North Carolina
- Virginia.

EXAMPLE: Sally's dog Boo is hit by her neighbor Barry's car in the street. You can certainly argue that Sally partly caused the car accident by letting her dog roam the neighborhood. She may have even broken a law, if her town or state requires all dogs to be kept on leashes.

Sally sues Barry in small claims court for her dog's $200 veterinarian bill. The judge decides that Sally is 20% at fault and Barry is 80% at fault. The judge thus reduces the $200 verdict by 20%, and awards Sally $160.

In most comparative negligence states, if Sally were more than half at fault, she would get nothing. So if a judge or jury decided she were 49% at fault, her award would be reduced by 49%, but if she were 51% at fault, she would get nothing.

The owner's negligence affects the outcome of the case only if it contributed to the injury. An owner who carelessly lets a dog run loose, resulting in its being hit by a car, obviously contributed to the risk. But if the dog is picked up by the pound, and while there a pound employee maliciously kicks the dog and injures it, the owner probably wouldn't be considered at fault. At least in the legal sense, letting the dog run loose doesn't have anything to do with the deliberate and nasty act of the employee.

Compensating the Dog Owner

How much is a dog worth?

"Easy," says the dog owner. "My dog is priceless."

Not so fast, say the courts, which are used to dealing in terms of economic value. Most pets couldn't be sold for much, if anything, and their upkeep—food, licenses, veterinary care—costs plenty. Those facts, of course, come as no surprise to pet owners. If you want to make money, you buy pork belly futures, not a cuddly mixed-breed puppy. The benefits a pet provides—companionship, laughter, security—are noneconomic and unique.

Nevertheless, some states allow pet owners to collect only the "market value" of the dog—a wholly inadequate way to compensate a dog owner who has lost a valued companion. As one writer put it, the loss of a pet is "much more than the loss of a piece of property; ... it is often the loss of a child-surrogate, a child's playmate, a companion in old age. It is the value of this relationship that must be measured, not the replacement value of the pet in the market place."[16]

In other states, a court may let a dog owner recover damages for "sentimental value," "intentional infliction of emotional distress," or "mental suffering." Whatever they are called, these legal theories are all attempts to compensate owners for the real, but hard to quantify, emotional loss they feel when they lose a pet.

Depending on the circumstances, state law, and the disposition of the judge or jury toward dogs, a dog owner may be able to convince a court to order the person responsible to pay for:

- costs of treatment if the dog is injured
- market or replacement value of the dog
- sentimental value of the dog
- emotional distress, and
- additional money damages to punish the person responsible.

Each of these is discussed below.

Remember that if the dog owner is partially at fault for the injury, whatever amount won in a lawsuit will, in most states, be reduced according to the owner's fault. (How that works is explained in "If the Dog Owner Is at Fault, Too," above.)

Cost of Treatment

The first expense a dog owner is likely to suffer when a dog is injured is the veterinarian's bills. The person responsible for the injury can be found legally liable for those bills.

Generally, courts allow the owner to be reimbursed only for "reasonable" treatment. What's reasonable in a particular case depends on the dog's "injuries, condition and prognosis," in the words of one New York court.[17] A dog owner probably can't expect to recover $10,000 for extensive surgery of an 18-year-old dog if the veterinarian says the dog is likely to die soon anyway.

But just because a dog is advanced in years doesn't mean that expensive treatment is never justified. For example, in a Kansas case where a groomer was sued for allegedly dislocating the hip of a 13-year-old Yorkshire terrier, the court ruled that the correct measure of damages was "reasonable" veterinary expenses necessary to restore the dog to her former state of health. The owners had spent more than $1,300 on surgery and other treatment for the injured dog. The groomer argued that it should be liable only for the dog's market value, but the court ruled that the old dog simply had no market value.[18]

Similarly, a California court ruled that an owner could recover the costs of treating a cat that had allegedly been shot by a neighbor, even though the cat was an adopted stray and the cost of treatment exceeded the animal's negligible market value.[19]

If your dog is injured, keep records of all bills for treatment, medication, and hospitalization to use during negotiations or at trial. You probably won't be paid back for the time you took off from work to care for the dog or take it to the vet.

Market or Replacement Value

All dogs have a market value—that is, a price they would bring if sold on the open market. That may not be much, but whatever it is, the dog's owner is entitled to it if a dog has been killed. Some courts award the dog owner the amount it would cost to replace the dog, instead of the dog's market value. This replacement value is likely to be a larger amount.

Factors to be considered in computing market value include the dog's:
- purchase price
- age
- health
- breed
- training
- usefulness, and
- special traits or characteristics of value.

Here are a few examples of how that translates into dollars in the real world:
- In a 2012 case, owners of a Jack Russell terrier, who had died after veterinary hospital staff placed a feeding tube into the dog's trachea and lungs instead of her digestive tract, sued for malpractice. They were awarded $350 as replacement value for the dog.[20]
- A woman and her dog were both hit by a car; the woman was injured, and the dog killed. The court limited her damages to the dog's "assessed value," estimated at $100 to $150. (A dissenting judge called this decision "simply medieval," and quoted the lyrics to a country song called "Old Shep" in support of his contention that the law should permit damages for sentimental value, mental suffering, or emotional distress when a pet has been lost.)[21]
- A purebred German shepherd dog was injured by a veterinarian and as a result suffered paralyzed hind legs. Calling it an "exceptional" case, the court allowed a $5,000 award to the dog's owner, noting

that the dog was highly trained, was used for stud purposes, and had won many awards at dog shows. Such a dog was not easily available on the open market, the court noted.[22]

- An Illinois couple's show dog was run over by a visitor's car in their driveway. The dog was severely injured and had to be destroyed. In small claims court, the owners testified that the one-year-old dog had cost $200 as a pup, had appeared in four dog shows and won first prize in each, and had been sired by an international grand champion. The court, in this 1979 decision, awarded them the $500 they had requested.[23]

- The owner of an injured dog was awarded $200, in 1975, for the market value of the six-year-old pedigreed dog. The amount was based on the dog's age, purchase price ($125–$150), the relatively long life of the breed, training, and desirable (but unspecified) character traits.[24]

They Don't Get Older, They Get Better

Does the fact that a dog is getting on in years—a little unsteady on its feet, maybe, with a tendency to run into table legs and door frames—mean its loss is worth less to its owner? Not at all. Listen to a town court judge from Westchester County, New York: "A good dog's value increases rather than falls with age and training."[25] Well said, your honor.

Valuable dogs. Your average mutt may not be a high-priced item, but a pedigreed purebred of championship lineage, who can trace its ancestors many generations farther back than you can, may be worth thousands of dollars on the open market.

If you own a valuable dog but aren't familiar with the current market, talk to people who raise and show dogs of your dog's breed. They can tell you the going prices. You can find breeders' names in dog owners' magazines, or by calling a local kennel club or the American Kennel Club.

Dogs kept for breeding are essentially business assets and may be given a monetary value based on not only their market value but also the revenue they would have brought their owners. A Palo Alto, California, man who claimed his dog had been rendered sterile while in an animal shelter brought suit for $250,000, his estimate of the dog's stud value. A court may, however, stick to the replacement value theory, reasoning that the owner can simply replace the dog with one that will generate the same income—and cost less than a quarter of a million dollars.

Insured Dogs

Most unusually valuable dogs are insured. If the dog is injured or killed, the owner should make a claim to the insurance company, just as when an insured car or house is damaged. It becomes the responsibility of the insurance company, after it pays the owner for the covered loss (minus the deductible amount), to sue the person responsible for the injury.

Sentimental (Special) Value

Surely an owner's affection for and attachment to a dog—not the market value—is the greater loss when a dog is killed. Tennessee law explicitly recognizes this by allowing someone whose pet is killed by the negligence of someone else to recover up to $5,000 in damages as compensation for the loss of the pet's "society, companionship, love and affection."[26]

In the other states, it's up to the courts. And some courts simply do not allow sentimental value to be considered; they stick to market value. An Alaska court stated flatly that the owners' "subjective estimation of [their dog] Wizzard's value as a pet was not a valid basis for compensation," and allowed them to recover only the $300 market value of their dog, which had been killed by mistake in a dog pound.[27] Similarly, courts in Ohio, North Carolina, and other states have held that market value is the appropriate measure of compensation when property is negligently destroyed—even when that property is a pet.[28] Other courts give up because of the difficulty in putting a dollar amount on the loss: "It is impossible to reduce to monetary terms the bond between man and dog," said one, limiting a dog owner's recovery to the cost of veterinary treatment.[29]

Some courts, however, have been willing to give it a shot. Recognizing that "the affection of a master for his dog is a very real thing ... for which the owner should recover, irrespective of the value of the animal," the Supreme Court of Florida reversed a lower court's ruling that "sentimental value" couldn't be considered when valuing a pet.[30]

Under Texas law, sentimental value can be part of the equation when items of personal property are damaged or destroyed. So, one court concluded, given that dogs are property, it only makes sense for sentimental value to be considered if a dog is injured or killed. Otherwise, the court pointed out, "damages could be awarded for a sentimental photograph of a family and its dog, but not for the dog itself." The court concluded that "the special value of 'man's best friend' should be protected."[31]

In a veterinary malpractice case in California, a jury awarded the owner of a dog $10 for the dog's market value—and another $30,000 for its special value. California law allows such an award if an item has "peculiar value" to the owner, and the person who harmed it knew that fact.[32] In a more recent case, however, another California court ruled that an animal's "peculiar value" does not include the owner's emotional attachment. In the case, a dog died while in a veterinarian's care; the owner asked for compensation based on the dog's special value to her. The court ruled that only characteristics that enhance an animal's monetary value to the owner can be considered.[33] An Illinois court compared the loss of a dog to the loss of other unique and irreplaceable items, such as family heirlooms or photographs. Because these objects, which are not bought and sold, have no meaningful market value, the court ruled, damages are measured by their "actual value to the owner."[34]

Evidence of special value can be as simple as testimony about the importance of the dog in the owner's life. If the owner is cut off from family or friends, lives alone, or is unusually dependent on a dog, a court is more likely to figure in sentimental value.

Emotional Distress

In the eyes of the law, a dog is just another thing: something you buy, sell, and own, like a car. Anyone who has lost a beloved pet, of course, knows that the law is simply wrong. And some courts have come around, recognizing that "a pet is not just a thing but occupies a special place somewhere in between a person and a piece of personal property .... To say it is a piece of personal property and no more is a repudiation of our humaneness."[35]

This change in attitude is shown by courts' willingness to let people sue for the mental anguish they suffer when they lose a pet because of malicious or extremely reckless acts. The legal theory is similar to the one that lets people sue when a child or spouse is injured; they can sue not only for lost income, but for the emotional anguish the death triggers.

The law in this area is still developing, and its boundaries are unclear. Most states' courts do not allow claims for mental suffering caused by a pet's death. For example, a woman whose car was rear-ended by a bus sued over both her physical injuries and her emotional distress over the injury to her dog, which had been in the car with her. The car had flipped over, and the dog was apparently ejected from the car through a broken window and ran away; someone found the lost dog and took her to a veterinary clinic, where the owner's boyfriend later found her. The owner argued that the dog was especially important to her because she had multiple sclerosis and an anxiety disorder and relied on the dog to help relieve her stress and depression. Her symptoms got worse in the months after the accident; her doctor attributed the decline to her distress over what had happened to the dog. The court ruled that she could sue for emotional distress that was directly associated with her own physical injuries, but not distress caused by the dog's injuries. Virginia law, the court ruled, was clear that pets are personal property and can't be treated differently than any other property.[36]

Other states impose various limitations. In some places, to recover for mental anguish, the person must see the injury take place, or suffer physical injury, or require medical treatment. In some states, an animal owner may not be able to recover compensation if a pet is negligently injured or killed. If, however, the pet is injured or killed through intentional, willful, malicious, or reckless conduct, the owner may be able to be sue for damages for the intentional infliction of emotional distress.[37] The rules change constantly as courts refine—or, just as often, confuse—them.

Generally, people can sue for two types of mental distress: first, the shock and distress caused by seeing an accident or mistreatment, and second, the grief and long-term effect the loss has on their lives. The more outrageous the conduct of the person being sued, the larger the monetary award is likely to be. Proving mental suffering, which of course is in the mind of the sufferer, is not always easy. But the person suing can testify about how he felt at the death of the pet and how the loss disrupted his life. If the person sought medical treatment or psychological counseling, that will strengthen the claims.

The best way to get a feel for what the rules are is to look at some actual cases:

- The North Dakota Supreme Court dismissed a claim for intentional infliction of emotional distress that had been filed by a couple whose dogs had been shot and killed by policemen. The dogs, four German shepherds and a golden retriever mix, had escaped through a hole in the fence of their owners' property and were running at large. The court ruled that although there could be a dispute about whether it had been necessary for the officers to shoot the dogs, the officers' actions weren't "extreme and outrageous" enough to justify a lawsuit for emotional distress.[38]

- After her dog died after surgery at a veterinary hospital, the owner sued for malpractice and intentional infliction of emotional distress, claiming that the vets had not only been negligent in their care of her dog but had lied in an attempt to cover up their actions. A California court ruled that because the veterinarians' actions were not "extreme and outrageous" and were not done in the owner's presence or directed directly at her, there could be no successful claim for the intentional infliction of emotional distress.[39]

- A Washington state court of appeals announced that pet owners could collect compensation for emotional distress when a pet is maliciously injured. In the case, three boys had taken a cat from its owner's front porch, poured gasoline on the animal, and set it on fire. The cat suffered serious burns and had to be euthanized.[40]

- The Supreme Court of Vermont ruled that dog owners could sue for compensation for the emotional distress that resulted from the intentional shooting of their dog.[41]

- A family was awarded $1,000 for the mental anguish they suffered when their nine-year-old dog died of heat prostration after state agency employees in Hawaii left it in an unventilated van in the sun.[42]

- A family sued and won $13,000 after their dog was seriously injured in a Florida animal hospital and subsequently had to be destroyed. The dog had been left on a heating pad for almost two days without care, and was severely burned. The court allowed the jury, when it decided on how much to award the family, to consider their mental pain and suffering.[43] A few years later, another court ruled that such a recovery was not permissible under state law, which requires a physical injury before emotional injuries can be considered.[44]

- An Oregon woman who asked a vet to humanely destroy her dog, which had been shot and was in extreme pain, was awarded $4,000 for her mental anguish when she discovered that the vet had not euthanized the dog, but had given it away. Her worry about what her children would go through when they found the dog living with someone else justified the jury verdict, an appeals court ruled.[45] She was also awarded $700 in punitive damages.

- A judge refused to allow a claim for intentional infliction of emotional distress in a case where an Alaska couple's dog was impounded and mistakenly killed. The couple went to the pound at 4:50 in the afternoon to retrieve the dog, which they could see chained in the back of the pound, but employees said the pound was closed and refused to release the dog. When the couple went back the next day, the dog had been killed. These circumstances weren't severe enough to warrant an emotional distress claim, the trial judge ruled.[46]

- The Wisconsin Supreme Court noted that "[l]abeling a dog 'property' fails to describe the value human beings place upon the companionship that they enjoy with a dog," but nevertheless refused to allow a woman whose dog had been shot and killed by police to sue for negligent infliction of emotional distress.[47]

In a more recent case, the Wisconsin Court ruled that someone who had been threatened could sue for negligent infliction of emotional distress. In this case, a four-year-old was threatened by a 13-year-old boy who also injured the little boy's dog—in front of him—so severely that it had to be euthanized.[48]

- A woman whose pet horses were sold for slaughter by the people who boarded them was allowed to sue for the intentional infliction of emotional distress in Kentucky.[49]

Punitive damages. In states that don't allow emotional distress claims, a dog owner may be able to get punitive damages (damages meant to punish the wrongdoer) if a dog was harmed intentionally or in some truly outrageous way. Punitive damages are discussed just below.

Whining at the Courthouse Door

Keep in mind that you can sue only for *your* loss—the loss of or injury to your property, the dog. A dog can't sue for its own suffering. A federal court threw out a $50,000 lawsuit brought in a dog's name against USAir, for example. The dog had been left on a conveyor belt in the Tampa, Florida, airport, after its owners' flight took off.[50]

Damages as Punishment

When a court orders someone who injured or killed a dog to pay the dog's owner, that money is intended to compensate the owner for the economic and emotional loss, not to punish the wrongdoer. If the actions were especially outrageous or deliberate, however, the judge or jury in a civil lawsuit may assess "punitive damages" against the wrongdoer. Punitive damages are like a fine, except that the money is paid to the other side in a lawsuit, not to the government. They are added on to the amount the dog owner gets as compensation for the loss of the dog.

Punitive damages are given only when someone has caused injury intentionally or recklessly. Punitive damages may, however, be especially appropriate in animal cases, where compensatory damages are likely to be low and don't make it worthwhile to sue.

Here are some examples:

- A jury awarded punitive damages against a man who hit a dog in the head with a large rock, giving the dog convulsions and a concussion. A New York appeals court ruled that the malicious act justified punitive damages.[51]

- An appellate court did not allow punitive damages against a Cedar Rapids, Iowa, animal shelter that picked up a woman's dog and mistakenly sent it to a research laboratory, where it was killed. The court ruled that the animal shelter must pay the owner $5,000 in compensatory damages, but not the extra $5,000 the jury had awarded in punishment. Why? Because, the court said, the shelter had been merely careless—it had sent the woman's dog to the lab after a day, even though it was required to keep animals for three days—but it had not acted willfully or recklessly.[52]

- Punitive damages were allowed, however, against a Minnesota animal warden who killed an impounded cat although he knew that a city ordinance required that it be kept five days. The warden killed the animal simply because the city had no facilities to take care of it—showing, in the words of the court, "a willful disregard for both the law and the property rights of private citizens." A jury awarded the cat's owner $40 in compensatory damages and $2,000 in punitive damages. The appeal court reduced the punitive damages to $500.[53]

Lawsuits against a government agency. Many states do not allow punitive damages against a city government unless a state law specifically authorizes it. Individual public officers, however, are liable for punitive damages just like other individuals are.[54]

Penalties built into state law. In Maine, the owner of a dog that kills or injures another pet may be subject, under state law, to a $100 forfeiture in addition to whatever damages the pet's owner suffered.[55]

Class Actions When Pets Are Injured

In 2007, dogs and cats across the United States and Canada suddenly, mysteriously began to get sick; many died. Ultimately, the cause was traced to pet food distributed by Menu Foods, which had been contaminated by ingredients from China that had been mixed with the industrial chemical melamine. More than 150 brands were affected. The products were recalled, but not before thousands of pets were sickened or killed.

The pet owners' lawsuits were consolidated into a class action, and almost 24,000 people filed claims. Eventually, the company agreed to create a $24 million fund to compensate pet owners.[56] But once the lawyers took their share—$7.4 million—and the payments were finally sent to pet owners in 2011, some owners ended up getting very little. One woman whose cat had died as a result of eating the tainted food reported getting a check for $58— which she planned to donate to a local animal shelter.[57]

If Your Dog Is Hurt or Killed

Your first step, if your dog has been injured, should be to write a letter setting out what happened. Even if the person you're writing to knows the facts as well as you do, it's a good way to organize your thoughts and make them clear to the other person. Include how much money you think would compensate you for your loss, explain how you arrived at that figure, and mention any state statute or case that applies directly to your situation. Give a deadline for payment—that's a good incentive for the person to act quickly. And say that if you don't work something out by then, you'll file a small claims (or other) court case. In some states, a letter to the other side demanding payment is required by law before you can file a small claims action.

Mediation

To negotiate a settlement, think about getting some help from a community mediation program. A mediator's job is to help people solve their own problems; the mediator has no power to impose a decision. (The mediation process is discussed at length in Chapter 7, Barking Dogs.)

> **EXAMPLE:** Your next-door neighbor hires a tree-trimming service to prune a tree that stands near the boundary of your properties. An employee drops a heavy branch into your yard; it lands on your unsuspecting dog below. Below is a sample letter you might send to the tree trimmer.

If you reach an agreement, be sure to put it in writing and have all the people involved sign it. You can type out your own agreement, or use a preprinted release form. The sample uses a release form from *101 Law Forms for Personal Use*, by Robin Leonard and Ralph Warner (Nolo).

Lawsuits

Sometimes the best, most conscientious efforts at settlement don't work. Your next stop: court. Which, by the way, doesn't necessarily mean a side trip to a lawyer's office.

Where and When Lawsuits Are Brought

Be sure to look at small claims court as an option. In most states, the amount you can sue for in a small claims court is limited to $5,000 or less. (A chart listing all the state limits is in Chapter 7, Barking Dogs.) These limits increase regularly; you can find out if your state's limit has gone up, and probably get some guidance in the form of a booklet, from your local small claims court clerk or the court's website.

If your dog was particularly valuable, or the conduct of the other person particularly shocking, you may not be able to squeeze your case

Sample Demand Letter

May 14, 20xx

Mr. Anthony Tucker
Tucker Tree Trimming
2144 Lilac Lane
Littleton, IL 61433

Dear Mr. Tucker:

Three weeks ago, on April 21, your employee Hannah Boardman dropped a large tree limb into my yard while trimming a tree on my neighbor's property. It hit my dog Buster and seriously injured his hind leg. For two weeks he had to take pain-killers; only now is he able to walk almost normally again.

As a result of your employee's carelessness, I incurred a veterinary bill of $425 for Buster's examinations, X-rays, and medication. (Copies of my receipts are enclosed.) I also suffered severe shock and distress, because I was sitting on my patio when the limb fell, and I saw it hit Buster. I thought he might be severely injured or killed.

I am willing to give up any claim I might have for my own emotional distress, but I think you should reimburse me for the cost of Buster's treatment. If you would like to discuss the matter further, please give me a call. Please get back to me by May 25. I would prefer to work this out between us rather than take the matter to small claims or circuit court.

Sincerely,

William LaForge
William LaForge
8855 Baltimore Ave.
Littleton, IL 61433
(309) 831-5755

into small claims court. You'll have to go to "regular" court, which may
be called superior, district, municipal, or circuit court (or some other
name) depending on the state. There, you may need the help of a lawyer,
especially if the other side is represented by one.

Wherever you decide to sue, act promptly. State law limits how long you
have to start your lawsuit; usually, you must file within a year or two of
the incident. You can find your state's rule by looking in the statute books
under "statute of limitations" or "limitations" for torts. If you are suing
the federal, state, or local government, you may have to act much more
quickly. (See "Claims Against the Government," below).

Lawyers and Fees

When you sue someone for a loss caused by careless or intentional conduct,
you're suing for a "tort." Negligence (carelessness), malpractice, and
intentional infliction of emotional distress are all torts.

A lawyer who takes a tort case usually charges what is called a
"contingency fee." That means the lawyer doesn't charge by the hour, and
instead agrees not to take anything unless you win. If you win, the lawyer gets
30% or more of the amount. Several states limit the percentage a lawyer is
allowed to take.

That may sound like a no-lose proposition. But before you agree, be sure to
do a couple of things:

- Find out who pays for "costs." Although you aren't paying lawyer's fees,
  the lawyer may expect you to advance money for fees charged by the
  court, investigation, and depositions.
- Get your fee agreement, including who pays for costs, in writing. A
  written contingency fee agreement is required by the law in several
  states (California is one); you should have one no matter where you live.
  If your lawyer isn't willing to put the agreement in writing, get another
  lawyer.

RESOURCE
Everybody's Guide to Small Claims Court, by Ralph Warner (Nolo), shows how to prepare and present a winning small claims court suit.

Represent Yourself in Court, by Paul Bergman and Sara Berman (Nolo), explains how to conduct a civil trial without an attorney.

What to Prove in Court

When you get to court, you want to prove three things to the judge:

- The person you're suing injured your dog.
- The defendant's conduct was unreasonably careless, reckless, or intentional.
- You need a certain amount of money to compensate you for your loss (to figure out how much, see "Compensating the Dog Owner," above).

You'll want to testify about what happened. To bolster your testimony, you may want to bring:

- written statements from people who can back up what you say about the extent of your loss
- bills and receipts (bill of sale for the dog, veterinary bills, burial expenses) that show your financial loss
- witnesses who can testify about the incident or your financial loss or emotional distress
- evidence of your attachment to the dog and the effect its loss had on your life, if your dog was killed and you are asking for damages for your emotional distress
- evidence of the outrageousness of the other person's behavior, if you are asking for punitive damages.

(For more on how small claims court works, see Chapter 7, Barking Dogs.)

Claims Against the Government

Individuals may lawfully injure or kill a dog only in the very limited circumstances discussed earlier in this chapter. The government has far broader powers to pick up, impound, and destroy dogs. But it must respect owners' constitutional ("due process") rights and, in most cases, give an owner notice and a hearing before taking action. (This is discussed in Chapter 2, State and Local Regulation.) If the government abuses its authority and wrongfully injures or kills your dog, you can sue. There are special rules, however, for suing the government. They vary from state to state, but you usually have less time to file a claim than you would have if you were suing a private person.

Typically, if you want to sue a city, county, or state government, you must first file a claim with it, within a very short time after the incident—in many places, just 90 or 100 days. You can get a claim form from the city or county clerk or the state attorney general. The city or county attorney, or the state attorney general, will review the claim and make a recommendation. Most claims are denied. Only after your claim is denied may you sue. If you go to small claims court, take the letter denying your claim with you.

If you want to sue a federal agency, you're going to need a lawyer. Suits against the federal government must usually be brought in federal district court, which has no small claims procedures of its own. The federal government cannot be sued in local small claims court without its consent.

Once you get to court, the issues and procedures are much the same as when you sue an individual: you must put a dollar value on your loss, and prove that the government is responsible for it.

Punitive damages. You may not be able to get punitive damages against the government. See the discussion of punitive damages in "Compensating the Dog Owner," above.

One Lawyer's Strategy

This book wouldn't be complete without one of the most famous speeches about dogs ever made, which was delivered by a 19th century lawyer during the trial of a lawsuit over a dog killed by a neighbor. The lawyer who made the speech, George Vest, later became a United States senator from Missouri. The jury returned a verdict of $500—more than twice the amount asked for—and would have sent the defendant to prison had the law allowed it. Judges still quote Vest. And through all the overblown, melodramatic oratory, you can see why; it is a genuinely moving statement.

Gentlemen of the jury: The best friend a man has in this world may turn against him and become his enemy. His son and daughter that he has reared with loving care may become ungrateful. Those who are nearest and dearest to us, those whom we trust with our happiness and our good name, may become traitors to their faith. The money that a man has he may lose. It flies away from him when he may need it most. Man's reputation may be sacrificed in a moment of ill considered action. The people who are prone to fall on their knees and do us honor when success is with us may be the first to throw the stone of malice when failure settles its cloud upon our head. The only absolutely unselfish friend a man may have in this selfish world, the one that never deserts him, the one that never proves ungrateful or treacherous is his dog.

A man's dog stands by him in prosperity and poverty, in health and sickness. He will sleep on the cold ground, when the wintery winds blow and the snow drives fiercely, if only he can be near his master's side. He will kiss the hand that has no food to offer, he will lick the wounds and sores that come in encounter with the roughness of the world. He guards the sleep of a pauper as if he were a prince.

When all other friends desert, he remains. When riches take wings and reputation falls to pieces, he is as constant in his love as the sun in its journey through the heavens. If fortune drives the master forth an outcast into the cold, friendless and homeless, the faithful dog asks no higher privilege than that of accompanying him to guard him against danger, to fight against his enemies, and when the last scene of all comes, and death takes his master in its embrace and his body is laid away in the cold ground, no matter if all other friends pursue their way, there by his graveside will the noble dog be found, his head between his paws and his eyes sad, but open in alert watchfulness, faithful and true even to death.

Endnotes

[1] *Drake v. Dean*, 15 Cal. App. 4th 915, 19 Cal. Rptr. 2d 325 (1993).

[2] *People v. Lee,* 32 Cal. Rptr. 3d 745 (Cal. App. 2005).

[3] Ky. Rev. Stat. § 258.235.

[4] *State v. Smith*, 156 N.C. 628, 72 S.E. 321 (1911).

[5] *People v. Pope*, 22 Ill. Dec. 802, 66 Ill. App. 3d 303, 383 N.E.2d 278 (1978).

[6] *McDonald v. Bauman*, 199 Kan. 628, 433 P.2d 437 (1967).

[7] *Johnson v. McConnell*, 80 Cal. 545 (1889).

[8] *Trautman v. Day*, 273 N.W.2d 712 (N.D. 1979).

[9] *Puckett v. Miller*, 381 N.E.2d 1087 (Ind. App. 1978).

[10] "Post Office Plans to Pay for Slain Dog's Funeral," *San Francisco Chronicle*, Dec. 29, 1989.

[11] *Molohon v. United States*, 206 F. Supp. 388 (Mont. 1962).

[12] *People v. Wicker*, 78 Misc. 811, 357 N.Y.S.2d 597 (Town Ct. 1974).

[13] *Roos v. Loeser*, 41 Cal. App. 783 (1919).

[14] *Kurash v. Layton*, 251 N.J. Super. 412, 598 A.2d 535 (1991).

[15] *Saratte v. Schroeder,* 2009 WL 685272 (Ohio App. 2009).

[16] "How Much Will You Receive in Damages From the Negligent or Intentional Killing of Your Pet Dog or Cat?" by Peter Barton and Frances Hill, 34 N.Y.L.Sch. L.Rev. 411 (1989), quoting Note, "Veterinarians at Fault: Rare Breed of Malpractitioners," 7 U.C. Davis L. Rev. 400 (1974).

[17] *Zager v. Dimilia*, 524 N.Y.S.2d 968 (Vill. Ct. 1988).

[18] *Burgess v. Shampooch Pet Industries, Inc.,* 131 P.3d 1248 (Kan. App. 2006).

[19] *Kimes v. Grosser*, 126 Cal. Rptr. 3d 581 (Cal. App. 2011).

[20] *Shera v. State University Veterinary Teaching Hospital,* 723 S.E.2d 352 (N.C. App. 2012).

[21] *Carbasho v. Musulin*, 618 S.E.2d 368 (W.Va. Sup. Ct. App. 2005).

[22] *McDonald v. Ohio State University Veterinary Hospital*, 644 N.E.2d 750 (Ohio Ct. Claims 1994).

[23] *Demeo v. Manville*, 68 Ill. App. 3d 843, 25 Ill. Dec. 443, 386 N.E.2d 917 (1979).

[24] *Stettner v. Graubard*, 82 Misc. 2d 132, 368 N.Y.S.2d 683 (1975).

[25] *Stettner v. Graubard*, 82 Misc. 2d 132, 368 N.Y.S.2d 683 (1975).

[26] Tenn. Code Ann. § 44-17-403.

[27] *Richardson v. Fairbanks North Star Borough*, 705 P.2d 454 (Alaska 1985).

[28] *Shera v. State University Veterinary Teaching Hospital,* 723 S.E.2d 352 (N.C. App. 2012); *Sokolovic v. Hamilton*, 960 N.E.2d 510 (Ohio App. 2011).

[29] *Zager v. Dimilia*, 524 N.Y.S.2d 968 (Vill. Ct. 1988).

[30] *La Porte v. Associated Independents, Inc.*, 163 So. 2d 267 (Fla. 1964).

[31] *Medlen v. Strickland*, 353 S.W.3d 576 (Tex. App. 2011).

[32] "California dog owner awarded $39,000 in veterinary malpractice suit," *American Veterinary Medical Association News* (April 15, 2004).

[33] *McMahon v. Craig*, 97 Cal. Rptr. 3d 555 (Cal. App. 2009).

[34] *Jankoski v. Preiser Animal Hospital, Ltd.*, 157 Ill. App. 3d 818, 110 Ill. Dec. 53, 510 N.E. 2d 1084 (1987).

[35] *Corso v. Crawford Dog and Cat Hospital, Inc.*, 415 N.Y.S.2d 182, 97 Misc. 2d 530 (1979).

[36] *Kondaurov v. Kerdasha*, 629 S.E.2d 181 (Va. 2006).

[37] *Harvey v. Navajo County*, 2012 WL 1605854 (D. Ariz. 2012).

[38] *Kautzman v. McDonald*, 621 N.W.2d 871 (N.D. 2001).

[39] *McMahon v. Craig*, 97 Cal. Rptr. 3d 555 (Cal. App. 2009).

[40] *Womack v. Von Rardon*, 135 P.3d 542 (Wash. App. 2006).

[41] *Scheele v. Dustin*, 998 A.2d 697 (Vt. 2010).

[42] *Campbell v. Animal Quarantine Station*, 632 P.2d 1066 (Hawaii 1981).

[43] *Knowles Animal Hospital, Inc. v. Wills*, 360 So. 2d 37 (Fla. App. 1978).

[44] *Kennedy v. Byas*, 867 So. 2d 1195 (Fla. App. 2004).

[45] *Fredeen v. Stride*, 525 P.2d 166 (Or. 1974).

[46] *Richardson v. Fairbanks North Star Borough*, 705 P.2d 454 (Alaska 1985).

[47] *Rabideau v. City of Racine*, 627 N.W.2d 795 (Wis. 2001).

[48] *Camp ex. Rel. Peterson v. Anderson*, 721 N.W.2d 146 (Wis. 2006).

[49] *Burgess v. Taylor*, 44 S.W.3d 806 (Ky. App. 2001).

[50] *Los Angeles Daily Journal*, Jan. 7, 1987, p. 1.

[51] *Rimbaud v. Beiermeister*, 168 A.D. 596, 154 N.Y.S. 333 (1915).

[52] *Schade v. Cedar Rapids Animal Shelter*, 409 N.W.2d 716 (Iowa App. 1987).

[53] *Wilson v. City of Eagan*, 297 N.W.2d 146 (Minn. 1980); see also *Molenaar v. United Cattle Company*, 553 N.W.2d 424 (Minn. App. 1996).

[54] *Smith v. Wade*, 461 U.S. 30 (1983).

[55] Me. Rev. Stat., Ann., tit. 7, § 3962-A.

[56] www.petfoodsettlement.com.

[57] "Tainted Pet Food Settlement Shortchanges Owners, Say Some," www.nbclosangeles.com/news/local/Tainted-Pet-Food-Settlement-131013283.html.

Providing for Pets

Most pet owners, who go to such lengths to care for their animals, want to make sure that when they die, their pets will still be well taken care of. For people who are elderly or seriously ill, this can be an immediate concern. And it's a real problem— some animal welfare groups estimate that 10% of animals dropped off at shelters are there because their owners have died. That totals 500,000 pets every year, according to the organization 2d Chance 4 Pets.

Some people make informal arrangements; there is an "understanding" that a friend, neighbor, or relative will care for a dog if the owner can't. Often that's enough, but not always. What if, for example, the person you've asked to provide care doesn't have much money to spare, and might be burdened by food and veterinary bills? Or isn't able to care for the dog when needed?

Emergency Care for Your Dog When You're Unavailable

While you're making arrangements for your dog's care after your death, also think about what would happen to your dog in an emergency, if you became sick or disabled and couldn't care for it for an extended period. Obviously, it makes sense to have a fallback caretaker. Arrange with someone to take care of the dog, and write down any needed instructions. Think about what food the dog eats, what medication it needs, who your veterinarian is, who takes care of grooming—and make sure the designated temporary caretaker has, or can easily get to, a copy of your instructions.

It's a good idea to carry a card in your wallet stating that you have animals that need to be cared for, and the name, address, and phone number of the person who has agreed to take over.

Usually, it is better to make more formal provisions for your dog's care. Before we get into specifics about what you can do, here are a few legal and practical rules to keep in mind:

- Don't leave money or other property to your dog through a will.
- Instead, plan to leave your dog, and some money for expenses, to someone you trust to look out for it.

- If you don't feel comfortable just leaving your dog and a cash gift to a trusted person, in most states you can set up a more formal arrangement: a trust. This lets you leave money in trust and appoint a trustee, who has a legal duty to use the trust fund for the dog's benefit.

Why You Can't Leave Money to a Dog— And What Happens If You Try

A dog, for all its admirable and unique qualities, is not a human being and is not treated in the law as such.

—Texas Court of Civil Appeals[1]

You cannot leave money or other kinds of property to your dog. And it's not just because he can't see over the bank counter to open an account. The law says animals are property, and one piece of property simply can't own another piece. (In this, as in many areas, the law lags behind the people. A 2006 survey found that 69% of the people asked considered family pets family members, not property.[2])

Because a dog can't own property, it can't be a beneficiary (someone who receives property) in a will. If you do name your dog as a beneficiary, whatever property you tried to leave it will probably go instead to the alternate beneficiary or, if there's no alternate, to the person you named as your "residuary" beneficiary (who gets everything not specifically left to other beneficiaries named in the will). If there's no residuary beneficiary, the property will be distributed to your closest relatives under the "intestate succession" laws of your state, which control what happens to property if there is no will or trust to dispose of it. The point is that in all likelihood the dog will get nothing, and the result may be not at all what you intended. (It's possible, however, that a court would construe the will as creating a trust for the pet; see the discussion of trusts, below.)

Take the case of Thelma Russell, who left "everything I own ... to Chester H. Quinn and Roxy Russell." Chester was a close friend; Roxy was a dog. Russell's niece challenged the will. The California Supreme Court agreed that the gift to Roxy was void, which left the question of what to do with half of the property. Should it go to Chester, or to the niece, who was Russell's only heir under California law? Despite a note that Russell had left, urging Chester not to let her nieces get their hands on her property no matter what it took to stop them, the court gave half the estate to the niece.[3] There's no record of what happened to Roxy, but it would be nice to think that she settled down happily for the rest of a long life with Chester, blissfully unaware of all the human squabbling.

Strategies for Taking Care of Pets

> *Animals have these advantages over man: they have no theologians to instruct them, their funerals cost them nothing, and no one starts lawsuits over their wills.*
>
> —Voltaire

Although you can't leave money directly to your dog, there are lots of things you can do to make sure it is well provided for when you can no longer take care of it.

Choose a New Owner for Your Dog

When you sit down to think about what you want done with your earthly possessions after your death, make specific plans for what you want to happen to your dog. Remember, legally your dog is an item of property, and when you die, it will have a new owner. Choosing that new owner is the most important thing you can do to make sure your pet is well taken care of after your death.

Make your decision legally binding by including it in your will. Simply include a provision like this one: "I leave my dog Taffy to my friend Lola Marquez." (Variations on this simple clause are outlined below.)

If you decide to use a revocable living trust (a document that serves the same purpose as a will, but avoids probate after your death) to transfer ownership of your property at your death, you can include a similar clause in the document that creates the trust.

Finding a Loving Home for Your Dog

It's often tough to find someone both willing and able to take care of a dog. Responding to that need, a few programs have sprung up across the country to help people be assured that their pets will have a loving home when they can no longer care for them.

After the San Francisco SPCA fought, successfully, to save a dog that was to be put to death after the death of its owner, the SPCA began a special service (called the Sido Service, after the dog that was saved) to find loving homes for the pets of deceased San Francisco SPCA members. The new owners are also entitled to free lifetime veterinary care for the pets at the SPCA's hospital.

For more information, contact the San Francisco SPCA, 415-554-3000, www.sfspca.org.

Some other organizations take a different tack. They themselves will care for your pet for its lifetime, provided you make a large (commonly, around $10,000 to $25,000) payment or gift.

Here are a few of these programs:

Kansas State University College of Veterinary Medicine, Perpetual Pet Care Program, Manhattan, KS 66506, 785-532-4013, www.vet.k-state.edu/depts/develpment/perpet

Washington Animal Rescue League, Guardian Angels program, 71 Oglethorpe Street, NW, Washington, DC 20011, 202-726-2556, www.warl.org/pages/guardian-angels

Stevenson Companion Animal Life-Care Center, College of Veterinary Medicine, Texas A&M University, College Station, TX 77843, 409-845-5051, www.cvm.tamu.edu.

Whatever method you use, don't make the gift of your dog a surprise. Talk to the people you want to take the dog, and make sure they are really willing and able to do it. They may adore your dog, but if their children are allergic to it or they live in a high-rise building, they simply may not be in a position to take it.

Because circumstances change—your first choice for someone to take your dog could take a job that requires lots of travel or move into a small apartment—it's always a good idea to line up a second choice. You should name this person as an alternate beneficiary in your will or trust, too.

If you don't name a new owner in your will or trust, one of two generally undesirable consequences will result:

- Your dog will go to the residuary beneficiary of your will (the beneficiary who inherits everything that's not taken care of by the rest of the will); or
- If you don't have a will, the dog will go to your next of kin, as determined by state law.

This means that, absent a lucky coincidence, the person who will legally inherit your dog probably won't be the person you would choose.

RESOURCE

Quicken WillMaker Plus (Nolo) is software that lets you write your own valid will and other estate planning documents on your computer.

Plan Your Estate, by Denis Clifford (Nolo), provides in-depth information on wills, trusts, taxes, and charitable giving.

Leave Money to the New Owner

It's a big responsibility to take care of a dog. So when you name a new owner for your dog in your will, consider also leaving that person some money, to go toward the costs of caring for the dog. It's usually a good idea, even if you think the new owner can easily afford to pay for the dog's upkeep. A dog who arrives with a full dinner dish is likely to be more welcome than one who is on the dole.

Here's a sample will clause that leaves both dog and money:

> If my dog, Taffy, is alive at my death, I leave her and $3,000 to be used for her care to Brian Smith. If Brian is unable to care for Taffy, I leave her and the $3,000 to be used for her care to Susan McDermott.

You should know that although the provision leaving the $3,000 to Brian is legal and enforceable, the part about using the money to take care of Taffy probably isn't. Your friend Brian could lose the whole stash in junk bond investments, and there wouldn't be a thing anybody could do about it. But this shouldn't be a big worry. You should leave your dog, and money to care for it, to someone you trust.

If Taffy isn't alive when you die, Brian won't get the $3,000. That money, along with any other property that the will doesn't specifically give away, will go to the person named in the will to receive the "residuary" of your estate.

Helping Other Animals

When you make your will or trust, remember that humane societies, rescue groups, assistance dog training centers, and other nonprofit organizations depend on donations. A gift in your will can help many animals. If you need help on wording your gift or have other questions, the organization will be more than happy to help you.

Putting conditions on the gift. It is possible, but complicated and usually impractical, to make the gift of the dog conditional on certain acts of the new owner. For example, you could put a clause like this in your will:

> If my dog, Taffy, is alive at my death, I leave her and $3,000 to Brian Smith, on the condition that Brian care for Taffy until her death, but for no more than 21 years. Should Brian stop providing necessary care for Taffy, Taffy and the $3,000 shall go to the McDonough County, Wyoming Society for the Prevention of Cruelty to Animals.[4]

Who will enforce the condition? The executor of your estate (the person you name in the will to carry out your wishes) has the responsibility as long as the estate is still before the probate court. In most states, it takes about six months to a year to get probate wrapped up and all the property distributed. After that, it's up to the alternate beneficiary—in this example, the McDonough County SPCA. Either way, it's a lot of trouble, and conditional bequests are usually a bad idea. Once again the central truth appears: don't rely on legal niceties to protect your pets. Arrange for them to be taken care of by people who know that a dog is more than another piece of property.

Leave the Dog to One Person, Money to Another

In unusual circumstances, you may want to consider leaving a dog to one person and money for the dog's care to someone else. It may be important to consider a plan like this if the person who will care for your dog receives some kind of public assistance—Social Security disability (SSI), for example. If that person receives several thousand dollars from you in a lump sum, it might mean the grant would be cut off until the money is spent—a situation that, obviously, benefits neither your friend nor your dog.

Or perhaps you don't quite trust the dog's new owner to use the money in the way you have in mind. Let's say, for example, that your friend Brian is great with dogs and has a place in the country, but his love of animals extends to the ponies—that is, he can't stay away from the track when he's got some extra cash in his pocket. You could leave your dog to Brian and $3,000 to Brian's sister Karen, with instructions to give it to Brian in chunks that he won't find quite so tempting.

Here are some sample clauses:

> I leave my dog, Taffy, if she is alive at my death, to Brian Smith.
>
> If my dog Taffy is alive at my death, I leave $3,000 for her care to Karen Smith. I desire that she give her brother, Brian Smith, as long as he has custody of Taffy, $30 a month for Taffy's care. I also desire that, in addition, she use the money to pay Taffy's veterinary bills or reimburse Brian for veterinary bills he pays.

Again, remember that legally, the $3,000 goes to Karen outright if Taffy is alive when you die. The instructions about how to use it aren't legally enforceable—but they make your wishes clear, which should be enough if you choose the right people.

More Ideas for Your Will

If you want to look at more sample will clauses and suggestions, look at *Providing for Your Pets*, published by the Association of the Bar of the City of New York. It's available from the association's Office of Communications, 42 West 44th St., New York, NY 10036-6690, 212-382-6695 or at www.nycbar.org (look under "Media & Publications").

Set Up a Pet Trust

With a pet trust, you can leave property for the benefit of your dog. You put someone, called a trustee, in charge of managing and spending it. The trustee follows a written set of instructions that you provide.

Sounds like just the ticket for making sure your dog has enough rawhide chews for life, but until recently, most states didn't allow trusts for animals. Now, most states allow you to create trusts for pets, with no human beneficiary. Only Kentucky, Louisiana, Minnesota, and Mississippi do not allow trusts for pets. Several states let you appoint someone, in the document that creates the trust, to make sure that the trustee carries out your wishes.[5]

If you try to create a pet trust in a state where such trusts are not valid, it's hard to know what will happen. Courts have sometimes shown both sensitivity and creativity when faced with legally lacking trusts that well-meaning owners had created for their pets. For example, a court might deem the trust an "honorary trust," making it a valid trust, but one that wouldn't be enforced by the court.

Most trusts for pets are written so that they take effect when the owner dies. In the document that creates the trust, there are several issues to address:

Which animals are covered. In most states, you can create a trust to provide for the care of one or more animals that are alive during your lifetime. The trust ends when the last surviving animal dies. You can't set up a pet trust to continue indefinitely—for example, for descendants of your current pet or others that the caretaker might acquire.

Someone to take care of the animal. Whether or not you use a trust, choosing a caretaker is always the most important decision you have to make. This is the person who will have custody of your pet and will responsible for day-to-day care. Don't assume the person you want to name—even if it's your spouse or best friend—is willing to take on this responsibility. Always ask. Name an alternate as well, in case your first choice can't take the pet when the time comes.

An amount of money to be used for the animal's care. Do the best you can to estimate how much the caretaker will need to take care of your dog. The appropriate amount varies widely depending on the pet's age and condition. Be aware that if you set aside an amount that's unreasonably high, family members could challenge it in court, and a judge will likely reduce it. For example, a Pennsylvania woman set up a trust that in 1974 made $40,000 to $50,000 a year available for the care of four horses and six dogs. The court ruled that as long as the animals were well taken care of, the trustee was free to give the surplus money to the alternate beneficiaries named in the will.[6] And we all heard about Leona Helmsley's dog Trouble, who came into a $12-million trust fund after Helmsley's death. In 2008, a judge reduced it to $2 million and ruled that the rest should go to Helmsley's charitable foundation.

Caretaking instructions. Pet trusts tend to be very detailed when it comes to instructions for the caregiver. It makes sense, given that animals can't tell the caregiver what they need or like. Owners often specify everything from favorite food and toys to sleeping arrangements.

Someone to go to court and enforce the terms of the trust if necessary. This is the person who makes sure the trust money is being spent appropriately on the animal, and not for any other reason.

What should be done with any money that's left over when the animal dies. If you leave more money than is necessary, where do you want the rest to go? It could go to family, a charity—it's your choice.

What happens if you can't take care of your pet before your death. One feature of a pet trust is that it can take effect before your death, if you were to become incapacitated and unable to care for your dog. The caregiver you named could immediately take custody and control of your pets if necessary. The provisions in a will, by contrast, don't have any legal effect until your death.

Keep Your Will or Trust Up to Date

What if your dog dies before you do, but your will still leaves someone money for the dog's care? If the beneficiaries fight about it in court, the money you intended to be used for the dog's care will probably still go to the person you named. For example, look at the following will clause, which was the subject of a lawsuit:

> FOURTH: Should my husband predecease me, or should we die as the result of a common disaster, I hereby give $5,000.00 to IRENE MORRISON, should she survive me, for the proper care of my dog Dutchess.

Dutchess died before her owner did, but a Colorado court ruled that Morrison should get the $5,000 anyway.[7] Other courts faced with similar situations have ruled the same way.[8] The theory is that the obligation to care for the dog doesn't arise until after the gift of the money is made. And because it's not the beneficiary's fault that she can't carry out the condition, she's entitled to keep the gift.

If you want to prevent a similar result, it's quite easy. When you write your will, all you need to do is word the clause so that the money is given only if your dog is still alive. Here's a clause written so that the beneficiary gets the money only if the dog is still living at the time of your death:

> If my dog Taffy is living at my death, I leave her and $3,000 to be used for her care to Brian Smith. If Brian is unable to care for Taffy, I leave her and the $3,000 to be used for her care to Susan McDermott.

Arranging for Veterinary Care

Veterinary care is likely to be the biggest expense incurred by the new owner of your dog. If you want to make sure the dog will get all the care it needs, you may want to arrange in advance for the dog's veterinary care for life. There are several ways to approach this problem.

One way is to leave money to the new owner, with instructions to buy animal health insurance (see Chapter 5, Veterinarians) for your pet. You must rely on the new owner to spend the money that way; you won't be around to verify it.

Another possibility is to leave money, in your will, to the vet. The amount, and what is expected of the vet, should of course be worked out with the vet in advance. Any money left when the dog dies could go to a relative, a charity, or to the vet in appreciation of services rendered—whatever you want. Again, you will be trusting the veterinarian to follow through.

A third approach is to write out a contract with a vet, and pay or leave the vet a certain amount, as a credit toward expected services. You'll also need to agree on what is to be done with any excess that's left when the dog dies.

A sample contract is shown below. If you want to explore this option with your dog's veterinarian, you can use it as a starting point for discussion.

Contract (Credit Toward Services)

Jacques Buckley, D.V.M., and Petra Campbell agree that:

1. Dr. Buckley will provide veterinary care for Ms. Campbell's dog Charlemagne from the time of Ms. Campbell's death until Charlemagne's death.

2. The veterinary care provided will include all necessary vaccinations, diagnoses and medications, reasonable treatment of diseases or injury, and euthanasia.

3. If Dr. Buckley determines that Charlemagne has a terminal condition and that further treatment is unlikely to significantly prolong the dog's life, or that prolonging his life with treatment would mean that the dog would suffer unduly, he may decline to continue treatment.

4. Ms. Campbell has paid Dr. Buckley $3,000 as a credit toward Dr. Buckley's veterinary care of Charlemagne.

5. This $3,000 will count as a credit for veterinary services for Charlemagne's new owner. Dr. Buckley will provide the new owner with statements, specifying services provided, their cost, and the amount of credit remaining.

6. If at Charlemagne's death, any of the original $3,000 payment has not been used up, Dr. Buckley will donate it to the Phoenix, Arizona, Society for the Prevention of Cruelty to Animals.

7. If the $3,000 in services is used up, Dr. Buckley may charge Charlemagne's owner for any further services.

8. If Dr. Buckley moves away from the area or ceases to practice veterinary medicine, he will either:

   a. arrange with another veterinarian, subject to the approval of Charlemagne's owner, for continued care of the dog under the terms of this agreement, so that the new veterinarian extends the same credit for services as remained when Dr. Buckley quit providing services; or

   b. refund whatever of the original $3,000 credit remains to Charlemagne's owner.

_____   _____
Jacques Buckley, D.V.M.   Date

_____   _____
Petra Campbell   Date

Will Provisions That Order Animals Destroyed

Heaven goes by favor. If it went by merit, you would stay out and your dog would go in.

—Mark Twain

While you're alive, your dog is, legally, your property. Aside from the restrictions of cruelty laws, you can do almost anything you want with an animal you own: sell it, give it away, or have it humanely destroyed.

What about when you die? If your will directs the executor of your estate to have your dog humanely destroyed, and the executor or a local humane society doesn't object—quickly—the dog will be destroyed soon after your death.

If someone does object, the probate court, which oversees the administration of your estate, will rule on the validity of the will provision. Almost always, these provisions are found to be invalid, and the court may forbid the executor from carrying out your instructions. Courts have always frowned on wills that order the destruction of any kind of property, on the ground that it goes against public policy to needlessly destroy valuable property. (This prerogative, of course, isn't exercised logically or consistently: if it were, a court could intervene whenever an owner wanted a healthy pet killed, not just when the owner tries to do so from beyond the grave.)

Generally, the court's rationale is something like this: Someone leaves instructions in a will to destroy a dog because of the worry that the dog will not be cared for properly or will end up in a pound or somewhere worse. The owner wishes to prevent pain and suffering. So, if the dog is old and ill, or so attached to the owner that it couldn't adjust to a new home, the owner's request that it be humanely destroyed may make perfect sense. But if an executor has found a good home for a young, healthy animal, and the animal seems well adjusted and well taken care of, a court may decide that the previous owner's wishes are best fulfilled by *not* carrying out the will's order.

For example, a court faced with a will provision ordering the humane destruction of two healthy Irish setters concluded that the owner wouldn't really want them killed, because the dogs were happy and well cared for in a country home: "There is no lack of care. There is no reason for carrying out the literal provision of the will. That decedent [the deceased owner] would rather see her pets happy and healthy and alive than destroyed there can be no doubt."[9]

Similarly, an 11-year-old cat that was to be put down was saved from that fate, thanks to the people at its late owner's bank who were handling her estate. The woman had drawn up her will, which directed that any animals she owned at her death be euthanized, before acquiring the cat. She had left her $1.3 million estate to animal-related charities. After the bank alerted the probate court, the court ruled that it was against public policy to euthanize a healthy cat when a good home could be found.[10]

One state legislature, moved to action by the public outcry over the impending death of Sido, a little mixed-breed dog that was being temporarily protected by the San Francisco SPCA, used the same rationale to pass a special law to save the dog's life. The legislature found that the dog's deceased owner, "having the best interests of her pet dog in mind, would not wish her instructions for the destruction of the pet dog carried out" if she knew how happy the dog was now.[11] On the same day, a judge ruled that wills could not be used to destroy property.[12]

Although courts rarely mention it, there is also overwhelming public opposition to carrying out such a will provision. It's hard to imagine a judge who wants to become famous for ordering the death of a happy, healthy pet that hundreds of families have offered to take in.

Endnotes

[1] *Arrington v. Arrington*, 613 S.W.2d 565 (Tex. Ct. Civ. App. 1981).

[2] *USA Today*, March 31, 2006.

[3] *In re Estate of Russell*, 70 Cal. Rptr. 561, 69 Cal. 2d 200, 444 P.2d 353 (1968).

[4] The 21-year provision is to avoid invalidating the gift—see endnote 6.

[5] Alaska Stat. § 13.12.907; Ariz. Rev. Stat. § 14-2907; Cal. Probate Code § 15212; Colo. Rev. Stat. § 15-11-901; Mich. Comp. Laws § 700.2722; Mo. Rev. Stat. § 456.055; Mont. Code Ann. § 72-2-1017; N.M. Stat. Ann. § 45-2-907; N.C. Gen. Stat. § 36A-147; N.Y. Est. Powers & Trusts Law § 7-6.1; Tenn. Code Ann. § 35-50-118.

[6] *Lyon Estate*, 67 Pa. D. & C.2d 474 (1974).

[7] *In the Matter of the Estate of Erl*, 491 P.2d 108 (Colo. App. 1971).

8   For example, see *In re Andrews' Will*, 34 Misc. 2d 432, 228 N.Y.S.2d 591 (Surrogate's Ct. 1962).

9   *Capers Estate*, 34 Pa. D. & C. 2d 121 (1964).

10 "Though there was a will, Fifth Third found a way to save Boots," *Chicago Tribune*, Apr. 4, 2012.

11 California S.B. 2509, signed June 16, 1980.

12 *Smith v. Avanzino,* No. 225698 (Super. Ct., San Francisco County, June 17, 1980).

Dog Bites

f you go to a hospital emergency room to observe, it probably won't be long before you see someone come in with a dog bite injury. Every year, more than 4.7 million people are bitten by dogs in this country. Almost 800,000 bites a year require some kind of medical attention.[1]

The dogs' owners are in most cases responsible for footing the bill, because they have a legal responsibility to prevent their pets from injuring people or damaging property. If a dog hurts someone, the owner will probably have to reimburse the victim for medical expenses, time lost from work, and pain and suffering. The owner's homeowner's or renter's insurance policy, however, may cover the cost, even if the injury happens off the owner's property.

The owner may also be required to take measures to prevent another incident—in the most serious cases, by destroying the dog. An owner who acts recklessly or deliberately—by letting an aggressive dog run loose around children, for example—may face a fine or even a jail sentence. (Criminal penalties are discussed in Chapter 12, Dangerous Dogs.)

Liability in a Nutshell

A dog owner is liable for injury the dog causes if:
- the owner knew the dog had a tendency to cause that kind of injury, OR
- state law makes the owner liable, whether or not the owner knew the dog had a tendency to cause that kind of injury, OR
- the dog owner was unreasonably careless, and that's what caused the injury.

Preventing Dog Bites

- **Train and socialize your dog.** Exposure to lots of people and situations at a young age is crucial. For some good tips, contact the Humane Society of the United States at www.hsus.org or the American Dog Trainers Network at www.canine.org.
- **Never let a dog run at large.** In some states, you're automatically liable for any injury your dog causes while at large.
- **Spay or neuter your dog.** According to the Humane Society of the United States, dogs are much more likely to bite when they haven't been spayed or neutered. No responsible pet owner keeps an unaltered pet—if you do, you increase the risk of injury to others, not to mention the risk of yet more unwanted dogs.
- **Watch your dog around children.** Almost half of all reported dog bites are to children under 12 years old.[2] Young children, who may unknowingly provoke a dog, are especially likely to be bitten—even by dogs they're familiar with. Never leave a dog alone with a toddler or infant. Make sure the gate to your yard is child-proof.
- **Keep your dog's vaccinations current.** If your dog bites someone, the authorities, not to mention the victim, will view it a lot more seriously if the dog doesn't have a current rabies vaccination.
- **Keep the dog out of strangers' paths.** Lots of people—mail carriers, salespeople, poll-takers, Girl Scouts—routinely come to your front door; keep the dog away from it. A fenced front yard isn't good enough; most people will open a gate and walk on up to the door.
- **Post warning signs.** If you have any reason to think that your dog might injure someone coming onto your property, post "Beware of Dog" or "Dog in Yard" signs prominently. Stay away from creative variations on the traditional signs; someone could reasonably assume that a cartoon-like "Trespassers Will Be Eaten" sign is a joke, not a serious warning.

For Dog Owners: How to Prevent Injuries

If you pick up a starving dog and make him prosperous, he will not bite you. This is the principal difference between a dog and a man.

—Mark Twain

Any dog can hurt someone. The majority of dog bites, in fact, are inflicted by dogs that belong to the victim's family or friends. Don't think that because your dog is gentle, old, or small, it can't cause an injury. Even normally docile dogs will bite when they are frightened or when they are protecting their puppies, owners, or food—not necessarily in that order. A dog can easily hurt someone accidentally, by frightening or tripping them. You may not be scared when your Pekingese comes tearing around the corner of the house barking, but someone walking by on the sidewalk might be. If that timid passer-by falls, you could be liable for any hospital bills.

The best way to avoid liability is, obviously, to prevent your dog from causing injury or damage in the first place. A few simple rules, set out in the checklist above, will help you avert incidents and, if your dog bites someone, keep your liability as low as it fairly should be.

If You're Hurt by a Dog

If you're attacked by a dog or see someone else attacked, you can, of course, fight back. The laws of nearly every state authorize anyone to take whatever action is necessary, including killing, to stop a dog caught in the act of attacking a person. (This is discussed in more detail in Chapter 9, If a Dog Is Injured or Killed.) Dogs rarely, however, engage in a sustained attack on a person. Most dogs that bite do so quickly, out of fright, nervousness, or misdirected protectiveness.

You'll want to check local animal control department records for prior attacks by the dog. That could help you negotiate with the owner or win a case in court if it goes that far. If the dog has been officially labeled "dangerous" (as some cities and states designate dogs who have bitten people), the owner may be fined, and a judge may order the dog to be destroyed. (See Chapter 12, Dangerous Dogs.)

What to Do First

- **Get the names and phone numbers of the dog's owner and witnesses.**
  Even if you don't think you'll be asking for any money, get the dog owner's
  name and address. You may change your mind the next day, when you
  discover that jumping out of the way of that lunging dog has given you
  a swollen ankle. The same goes for any witnesses. You may need them to
  back up your version of what happened if you and the dog's owner later
  disagree.

  If you don't know who owns the dog, get the witnesses' names. Animal
  control authorities may be able to find the dog from your description and
  then find its owner.

- **Get medical attention if you need it.** If your injury is serious enough to
  require medical attention, get it quickly. Keep records of doctor's office
  or hospital visits and copies of bills. You won't have much of a chance of
  getting reimbursed for your medical expenses unless you can document
  what you paid.

- **Report the incident to animal control authorities.** This is especially
  important if the dog wasn't wearing a license tag and you don't know
  who owns it. City or county authorities will try to pick it up so it can be
  quarantined. Many cities and some states require that a dog that bites
  someone be quarantined, to see if the dog is rabid, for seven to 20 days,
  either at the owner's home or in the dog pound. Confinement may not be
  required if the dog has a current rabies vaccination.

Dog Owner Liability

In most instances, dog owners are financially liable for any personal injury
or property damage their pets cause. Three kinds of laws impose liability
on owners:

- **Strict liability laws.** Many states have laws that make a dog owner
  legally liable for any injury or property damage the dog causes.
  Although commonly called "dog-bite statutes," most of these laws

cover all kinds of dog-inflicted injuries, not just bites. The dog owner is automatically liable if the statute applies.

> **EXAMPLE:** Barbara lives in Minneapolis with her spaniel-mix dog, Ray, who has always been gentle with people. But one day, while on a leash, Ray unexpectedly bites a child in a park. Barbara wasn't being careless, but under her state's law, she's financially liable because her dog, without provocation, bit someone who was "acting peaceably" in a place he had a right to be.

Strict liability may also be imposed by a court. In 2012, the Maryland Supreme Court ruled that all pit bull terriers and pit bull mixes are "vicious and inherently dangerous," making their owners strictly liable for any injury the dogs cause.[3]

> **EXAMPLE:** Kiran lives in Maryland with a dog he and his family adopted from a local shelter as a puppy; he thinks the dog looks like a cross between a Labrador retriever and a pit-bull-type dog, but he has no way of knowing. Under Maryland law, it appears likely that he would be held strictly liable for any injuries his dog causes.

- **The one-bite rule.** This misleadingly named rule makes an owner legally responsible for an injury caused by a dog if the owner knew the dog was likely to cause that type of injury—for example, that the dog would bite. The victim must prove the owner knew the dog was dangerous.

> **EXAMPLE:** A New Jersey man was scratched by a dog. He sued and won, based on the one-bite theory, because he proved that the dog's owner knew of the dog's tendency to jump up and scratch people.[4]

- **Negligence laws.** If the injury occurred because the dog owner was unreasonably careless (negligent) in controlling the dog, the owner is liable.

> **EXAMPLE:** Lucy puts her new dog, Zippy, in the backyard but forgets to close the gate. The dog runs out into her front yard

and bites the mail carrier. Lucy didn't know the dog would bite. But because her negligence—leaving the gate open—caused the injury, she is liable.

The rest of this section discusses each of these theories in more detail.

Strict Liability Laws

More than half the states have statutes that make dog owners liable if their dogs cause injury. Although commonly called dog-bite statutes, many of these laws cover all kinds of dog-inflicted injuries, not just bites. They are called "strict liability" statutes because they impose liability without fault—that is, an injured person does not have to prove that the dog owner did anything wrong. (The only exception is Hawaii, where an injured person must still prove the dog's owner was unreasonably careless.)

As mentioned, courts can also create a strict liability rule. When the Maryland Supreme Court made the owners of all pit bulls strictly liable for their dogs, the court acknowledged that it was changing the old common law rule that required the owner to know about a particular dog's tendencies. Unlike dog-bite statutes that apply to all dogs, the Maryland strict liability rule will likely prove hard to apply; as the three dissenting justices pointed out, the court did not give any guidance about how to determine whether or not a dog is a pit bull (which is not a breed but rather a type of dog) or a "cross-bred pit bull mix."

The theory behind these rules is that anyone who has a dog should be responsible for any damage it causes, period. It doesn't matter that the owner was careful with the dog, or didn't know it would hurt anyone, or conscientiously tried to keep it from injuring anyone.

For example, the Minnesota dog-bite statute says:

> If a dog, without provocation, attacks or injures any person who is acting peaceably in any place where the person may lawfully be, the owner of the dog is liable in damages to the person so attacked or injured to the full amount of the injury sustained.

The victim doesn't have to show that the dog owner did anything wrong. To win a lawsuit under this statute, an injured person must, however, prove four things:

1. The injured person was attacked or injured by a dog. This doesn't necessarily require physical contact; if a dog runs at and frightens someone, causing him to injure himself, the statute still applies.[5] Generally, courts require that the injury must be the direct and immediate result of a dog's conduct.[6]
2. The person being sued (the defendant) is the owner of the dog.
3. The victim didn't provoke the dog to bite.
4. The victim was acting peaceably somewhere he or she had the right to be.

Dogs on Duty

Many states exempt the police or military from liability if their trained dogs bite someone while they're working. So someone who is injured by an on-duty police dog may not be able to sue the police or city government successfully. Several states (Arizona and California, for example) limit this immunity from lawsuits to situations in which the government agency in charge of the dog has a written policy on proper use of its dogs.[7]

An Illinois court, however, held a city liable when a dog owned by the police bit a bystander. The court found liability because the city was the dog's owner, and the state dog-bite statute makes owner strictly liable of a dog attacks and injures someone who is on private property where he or she has the right to be.[8]

Some police departments are averting these issues by training their dogs to bark, not bite. This tactical shift has been spurred by lawsuits brought by the ACLU and other organizations, claiming that training dogs to "find and bite" suspects is an excessive use of force.

In 1995, the Los Angeles Police Department settled such a suit out of court for $13.7 million. It no longer trains its dogs to bite when they track down a fleeing suspect.

An award that large is very rare. In 2000, a federal jury in Massachusetts found that the Yarmouth police had used excessive force when a man who fled after being stopped for driving without a license or insurance was chased and bitten by a 90-pound police dog. But the jury gave him just $1 in damages. (He did, however, get $50,000 to pay his lawyer's fees.)

Strict Liability Dog-Bite Statutes		
State	**Bites Only?**	**Other Provisions**
Alabama	no	Applies only if injury on owner's property.
Arizona (two statutes)	(1) yes	
	(2) no	Applies only if dog at large.
California	yes	
Colorado	yes	Injury must be severe.
Connecticut	no	Injured person must prove not committing tort.
Delaware	no	
District of Columbia	no	Must prove negligence, but ignorance of dog's viciousness not absolute defense. Only applies if dog at large.
Florida (two statutes)	(1) no	
	(2) yes	Owner not liable (except to children under 6, or if owner was negligent) if displayed sign including words "Bad Dog."
Hawaii	no	Injured person must prove owner was negligent unless animal is known to be dangerous.
Illinois	no	Injured person must prove lack of provocation or trespassing.
Indiana	yes	
Iowa	no	Injured person must prove not doing unlawful act that contributed to the injury.
Kentucky	no	
Louisiana	no	
Maine	no	Injured person must prove not at fault.
Massachusetts	no	Injured person must prove not trespassing or committing tort (unless less than 7 years old).

Strict Liability Dog-Bite Statutes		
State	**Bites Only?**	**Other Provisions**
Michigan	yes	
Minnesota	no	Owner "primarily liable."
Missouri	yes	If injured party was partly at fault, damages reduced proportionately.
Montana	yes	Applies only in city or town.
Nebraska	no	Injured person must prove not trespasser. Applies only if dog chases, bites, kills, or wounds.
New Hampshire	no	Injured person must prove not trespassing or committing tort.
New Jersey	yes	
Ohio	no	Injured person must prove not trespassing or teasing, tormenting, or abusing dog on owner's property.
Oklahoma	no	
Pennsylvania	yes	Owner must pay injured person's medical bills.
Rhode Island	no	Only applies if dog out of enclosure. On second occurrence, double damages and court can order dog killed.
South Carolina	no	Applies only if dog bites or attacks.
Utah	no	Possible criminal liability.
Washington	yes	
West Virginia	no	Only applies if dog at large.
Wisconsin	no	After owner has notice that dog has caused injury, double damages and penalties.

Note: If you want to look up your state's dog-bite statute, you can find its citation in the appendix of this book.

The dog's owner may still be able to escape liability by proving what is called an "affirmative defense." (See "A Dog Owner's Legal Defenses," below.)

Now here's a different type of statute, this time from Arizona:

24-521 Liability for dog bites
The owner of a dog which bites a person when the person is in or on a public place or lawfully in or on a private place, including the property of the owner of the dog, is liable for damages suffered by the person bitten, regardless of the former viciousness of the dog or the owner's knowledge of its viciousness.

24-523 Provocation as defense
Proof of provocation of the attack by the person injured shall be a defense to the action for damages.

To win under this statute, the injured person must prove three things:
1. The victim was bitten (other injuries aren't covered by the statute) by a dog.
2. The person being sued (the defendant) is the owner of the dog.
3. The victim was in a public place or lawfully on private property when bitten.

Because many dog-bite statutes, like this one, are limited to injuries from bites, they don't apply when the injury is caused by a dog acting playfully. For example, take the case of a German shepherd puppy that sat down in front of a three-wheeled recreational vehicle being driven by a teenage girl. She swerved to avoid the dog and hit a barbed-wire fence. The Nebraska Supreme Court ruled that the state's dog-bite statute did not make the dog's owner liable for the injury, because the statute covers only injuries caused when a dog bites, kills, wounds, worries, or chases a person.[9] (A dissenting justice wrote that it was impossible for a juror or judge to know whether a dog's conduct was malicious or playful: "We could, with equal reliability, predict the future from the examination of a goat's entrails," he wrote scornfully.) In another case based on Nebraska law, a court ruled that dog owners were liable for injuries caused when their dog chased a motorcycle, causing an accident.[10] But after the legislature amended the law to add liability for a dog that "injures" someone, the court ruled that owners are not liable for injuries caused by the playful and mischievous acts of their dogs.[11]

In almost all states, dog-bite statutes don't affect the other rules of liability. That means someone who is injured by a dog and sues the owner has a choice of suing under the statute, if it applies to the situation, under a common law theory (and having to prove the owner knew the dog was dangerous), or on a negligence theory. For example, in a Minnesota case, a dog, distracting the driver of a car, caused an accident that killed a young boy. The dog had not "attacked or injured" the boy, the state supreme court ruled, so the state's dog-bite statute did not apply. The boy's family could, however, sue under a negligence theory, and try to prove that the dog's owner had not taken reasonable care in controlling the dog.[12]

The Postman Always Sues

More than 5,500 employees of the U.S. Postal Service were hurt by dogs in 2011, according to the USPS. (Los Angeles saw the most attacks, with 83.) The USPS warns that mail carriers who fear for their safety because of a loose dog can stop delivery and ask the dog's owner to pick up mail at the post office until the dog is restrained. If the letter carrier doesn't know where the dog belongs, delivery to a whole neighborhood could be stopped.

The Common Law "One-Bite" Rule

Under the common law rule, a dog's owner or keeper is liable for injuries the dog causes only if the owner knew or had reason to know that the dog was likely to cause that kind of injury. So if your dog tries to bite someone, from that moment on you're on notice that the dog is dangerous, and you will be liable if the dog later bites someone.

The common law rule comes into play only if the state has no strict liability dog-bite statute or if the statute doesn't apply—for example, if the statute covers only bites, and the dog caused the injury by knocking the person down.

A dog owner may be able to escape liability by proving that the injured person provoked the injury, or voluntarily and knowingly risked being injured by the dog. (See "A Dog's Owner's Legal Defenses," below.)

One-Bite Rule Only			
Alaska	Maryland	North Carolina*	Texas
Arkansas	Mississippi	North Dakota	Vermont
Georgia[13]	Nevada	Oregon	Virginia
Idaho	New Mexico	South Dakota	Wyoming
Kansas	New York	Tennessee	

*But see the section on Negligence, below.

The logic of this legal doctrine is straightforward, if not unquestionable. This rule allows a person who owns a dog to assume, until there is some concrete indication to the contrary, that the dog isn't dangerous. But an owner who knows a dog poses a particular kind of risk to people must take action to prevent the foreseeable injury—or be prepared to pay for it.

The common law rule is often called the "one-bite" rule, which is a bit of a misnomer. It implies that every dog gets one "free" bite (free for its owner), and from then on the owner is on notice that the dog is dangerous. It's true that if a dog bites someone, its owner is definitely on notice that the dog is dangerous; but less serious behavior is also enough, legally, to give the owner the knowledge the law looks for. For example, if a dog growls or snaps at people, the owner knows (or should know) that the dog may cause injury. If the dog does hurt someone, the owner will be liable, even for the first bite.

The test for liability is the same no matter how the injury was caused: Did the owner know of the dog's dangerous tendency? For example, if a dog jumps up and knocks someone down, the question is: Did the owner know of the dog's tendency to knock people down? If so, he's liable for it.

If the owner denies responsibility and the dispute ends up in court (most don't), the judge or jury will have to decide whether or not the owner should have known the dog was likely to hurt someone. Here are some factors that courts take into account when deciding:

- **Previous bites.** This one is pretty easy. If a dog bites once, even if the bite isn't serious enough to require medical treatment, the owner will forevermore be on notice that the dog is dangerous.[14] But even this is not as straightforward as it may appear; for example, at least one court has ruled that if a puppy nips someone, its owners are not necessarily on notice that the dog is dangerous.[15]

- **Barking at strangers.** If a dog, usually kept in the house or a fenced yard, barks when the doorbell rings but has never threatened a person, its owners will probably not be liable if it bites someone.[16]

- **Threatening people.** A dog that often growls and snaps at people who come near it when out in public, but hasn't ever actually bitten someone, is a different case entirely. The dog's actions should put its owner on notice that the dog might bite someone. If the dog does bite, the owner will be liable.[17]

- **Jumping on people.** The owner of a friendly, playful, and large dog, which is in the habit of jumping on house guests, will be liable if the exuberant dog knocks over someone who comes to the door one day. The owner knew that the dog behaved this way and might injure someone because of its size.[18]

- **Frightening people.** If a dog likes to run along the fence that separates his yard from the sidewalk barking furiously, or chases pedestrians or bicyclists, the owner may be liable if the dog causes an injury.[19] At least one court, however, has ruled that an owner wasn't responsible for foreseeing that a barking dog could frighten someone so much she would run into the street.[20]

- **Fighting with other dogs.** If a dog that is affectionate and gentle with people has a history of fights with other dogs, that's probably not enough to put the owner on notice that the dog might bite a person. Courts usually recognize that canine society has its own rules, and the way a dog behaves under them isn't a reliable predictor of how it will act toward humans. (As one court put it, the "question was the dog's propensity to attack a human. The canine code duello is something else. That involves the question of what constitutes a just cause for battle in the dog world, or what justifies a resort to arms, or rather to teeth, for redress."[21])

- **Fight training.** If a dog has been trained to fight, a court will almost certainly conclude that the owner should have known that the dog is dangerous. (This conclusion is disputed by at least some people familiar with breeds commonly used for fighting, who maintain that there is no connection between a dog's drive to fight other dogs and its aggression toward people. However, a dog that has been agitated and abused by someone who wants the dog to fight may well be dangerous.)

- **Complaints about the dog.** If neighbors or others complain to the owner that a dog has threatened or bitten someone, the owner would certainly be on notice that the dog is dangerous. But in one Alabama case, where a dog's owner had been scolded by a neighbor for having a dog that was a "nuisance," the court ruled that the owner did not have any knowledge that his dog was dangerous.[22]

- **The dog's breed.** Generally, courts don't consider dogs of certain breeds to be inherently dangerous. So if you have a German shepherd or chow chow, a court probably won't conclude that you should have known, just because of the dog's breed, that it might injure someone.[23] But in some places, pit bulls, rottweilers, and a few other breeds have been defined by law as dangerous dogs. (See Chapter 12, Dangerous Dogs.) Even without such a rule, if a dispute goes to court, the result will depend on the facts of the case and the judge or jury's attitude. Large dogs popularly believed to be dangerous, such as Dobermans, German shepherds, and pit bulls, may be judged more severely than dogs of cuddlier breeds.

- **Warning signs.** Don't worry that putting up a "Beware of Dog" sign is tantamount to admitting that your dog is a menace, landing you in bigger trouble if the dog does ever hurt someone. First of all, the sign will help avoid bites—which is far preferable than winning a legal battle over a bite later. Second, if you think your dog might hurt someone, there's almost certainly already more evidence of the dog's dangerousness than the fact that you put up a warning sign.

Terminology Note

Judges often say that, to be liable under the common law rule, an owner must have known the dog was "vicious" or had a "vicious propensity." The term, as it's used in this context, simply means dangerous—likely to hurt someone, even if by being overly friendly. It has nothing to do with a dog's temperament.

The Dog Owner's Negligence

Negligence is the third legal doctrine under which a dog owner may be found liable for injuries caused by a dog. A dog owner who is unreasonably careless (negligent) in handling a dog may be legally responsible if somebody is hurt as a foreseeable result.

When it comes to defining negligence, broad rules are of little help. Whether or not someone acted negligently is a question that must be resolved based on the facts of a given situation. It comes down to this question: Did the dog's owner act reasonably, under the circumstances? If so, the owner wasn't legally negligent.

Here are a few examples of how courts have come down on the negligence issue in specific cases:

- A dog is chained in the unfenced front yard, so that it can't reach the sidewalk, and a "Beware of Dog" sign is posted. Someone walks up to the dog and gets bitten. Ruled: The owner was not negligent. Confining the dog inside the owner's property and posting a sign are reasonable precautions against someone being injured.[24]

- A house guest, searching for the bathroom, is frightened when she hears the hosts' dog growl, and falls down a flight of stairs. The dog was behind a gate in the laundry room, across the hall from the bathroom. Ruled: The owners were not negligent; they took reasonable precautions and were not liable for the injury.[25]

- A dog owner lets his dog loose in his yard, and the dog runs at a bicyclist riding by. Trying to avoid the dog, the cyclist is thrown from his bicycle and suffers permanent hearing loss. Jury verdict: The dog's owner was negligent.[26]

- A dog owner lets his dog loose in his yard, and the dog runs into the street and hits a motorcycle, seriously injuring the riders. Ruled: Because the dog did not have a history of chasing vehicles, the dog owner was not negligent.[27]

It's also possible that a dog owner will be found negligent for not taking special precautions to prevent a dog of a certain breed from causing injury. In at least one case, a court ruled that dog owners were responsible for an attack by their rottweiler, even though they had no knowledge that the dog would be dangerous. (The case was in North Carolina, which has no dog-bite statute and generally follows the one-bite rule.) The court ruled that the owners were negligent because they should have known the "general propensities" of rottweilers, which an expert witness at trial had described as very strong, aggressive, and unpredictable.[28]

If a dog owner violates a law, and the violation leads to an injury, the owner may be negligent as a matter of law. In such cases, the injured person can win a lawsuit by proving only that the dog owner violated the law. The most common scenario is when a dog owner violates a local leash law by letting a dog run at large, and the dog bites someone or causes an accident.[29]

> **EXAMPLE:** A California man let his dog roam, in violation of a local leash law. The dog ran into the road, and a pickup truck crashed trying to avoid it. Two men riding in the back of the truck were thrown out; they suffered serious permanent injuries.[30] A judge ruled that the dog owner's violation of the leash law was negligence, and awarded the injured men $2.6 million. (The dog owner's insurance company ended up paying the whole amount, even though the owner's policy limit was $100,000. See "Liability Insurance," below.)

Violation of a law does not always mean instant liability for any injury that occurs as a result. For example, the owner of a Los Angeles hardware store violated a local ordinance requiring property owners to keep their sidewalks clean. As a result, a 70-year-old woman slipped on some dog droppings on the sidewalk and seriously injured herself. She sued the store owner. A jury found the owner 85% responsible for the accident and ordered him to pay $402,050. On appeal, a court ruled that the store owner's violation of the ordinance did not necessarily mean he was negligent. The ordinance was not intended to make property owners keep sidewalks safe for passers-by, the court ruled; it was intended only to transfer to property owners the city's responsibility to keep public sidewalks clean.[31]

Not all states allow someone injured by a dog to sue on a negligence claim. In New York, the only thing that makes a dog owner liable for injuries is knowledge that the dog might be dangerous (the one-bite rule); negligence is not a basis for imposing liability.

For example, a New York mail carrier sued for an injury she received while trying to jump into her car through the window to get away from a dog she was afraid would hurt her. The dog, which had been lying in its owner's front yard while landscapers worked, had run toward her but stopped about six feet away. It apparently did not bark or threaten her. The court ruled that although the owner had been in violation of a leash law that required dogs to be leashed in spaces adjacent to public areas, that was irrelevant because it was only evidence of negligence. What mattered was whether or not the owner knew of the dog's propensities to cause injury. In this case, the court ruled, there was no evidence that the owners had any knowledge that their dog might be dangerous, and that in fact the dog did not do anything vicious.[32]

A Dog Owner's Legal Defenses

So far, we've talked about the legal rights and options of someone who's injured by a dog. But the dog owner is entitled to fight back with another set of legal theories.

The owner may be able to avoid liability if the injured person:
- provoked the injury from the dog
- knowingly took the risk of being injured by the dog
- was trespassing
- was breaking the law, or
- was unreasonably careless, and that carelessness contributed to the injury.

This section discusses each of these defenses. It's important to keep in mind three things about them:
- Not all defenses can be used in all states.
- Sometimes, the defenses that can be used depend on what the dog owner is being sued for. For example, some defenses may be available if the dog owner's liability is based on a common law theory, but not under a dog-bite statute.
- Some dog-bite statutes make the victim prove that he or she *wasn't* at fault—the dog owner doesn't have to prove the victim was at fault. (See "Dog-Bite Statutes," above.)

Was the Dog Provoked?

A dog owner may be able to successfully defend a lawsuit by showing that the injured person provoked the dog.

Some acts—for example, hitting or teasing a dog—clearly are the kind of provocation that will get the dog and its owner off the hook.[33] But just as the motivation of the dog is unimportant for legal purposes—it doesn't matter that the dog that knocked you down a flight of stairs was just trying to be friendly—the motivation of the injured person is irrelevant, too. A person may innocently and unintentionally provoke a dog. If, for example, you accidentally step on a dog's tail, that's provocation.[34] Or if a toddler tries to hug a strange dog, and the dog turns and bites the child, the dog's owner will probably not be liable for the injury, regardless of the dog's prior behavior.[35]

A woman who chased two large dogs, kicked them, and stuck her fingers in their eyes was held not to have provoked the dogs to bite her— because she took these actions only after the dogs entered her property and began attacking her two cats, killing one and injuring the other. The trial court ruled that the woman had provoked the dogs into attacking her, and thus was responsible for the serious injuries she received. On appeal, however, this ruling was reversed; the appellate court ruled that the dogs were already in a state of attack and that her reaction to the attacks on her cats did not constitute provocation. The court noted that she had also been bitten while running away from the dogs.[36]

A general word of warning: Unique circumstances may always affect the legal outcome. If, for example, a dog were known to have a hair trigger around children, the legal result could be different.

There are many ways a person, especially one unfamiliar with dogs, can unknowingly provoke a dog. Petting even an otherwise friendly dog when it's eating, going near its special territory, or intervening in a dog fight can provoke a hostile response. And dogs in strange surroundings are often nervous and may bite out of fear if approached.

Some dog-bite statutes require the injured person to prove that the dog wasn't provoked. (See the summary of state laws in "Dog-Bite Statutes," above.) In two states (Massachusetts and Connecticut), if the injured person is a child less than seven years old, the law presumes the child didn't provoke the dog. In those states, an owner who wants to assert provocation as a defense bears the burden of proving it. The Ohio statute requires proof that the dog wasn't teased, tormented, or abused.

Did the Injured Person Take the Risk of Injury?

Since I am a dog, beware my fangs.

—The Merchant of Venice, Act III

A dog owner may also avoid liability by proving that the injured person knew there was a risk of injury from the dog, but voluntarily took that risk. The theory is that someone who knowingly took the risk and was injured can't later hold the dog's owner responsible for such foolhardiness.

> **EXAMPLE:** You warn a visitor that your dog, which is in the back yard, might bite a stranger who entered the yard. The visitor goes in the yard anyway and gets bitten. If sued, you would have a good argument that the visitor knew of and took the risk of injury.

In a real-life example, a jury decided that a house guest, severely bitten by a 95-pound Akita, had put himself at risk. The man, who had taken care of the dog several times over the years, had gone into a room where the dog was closed off from the rest of the house. He sued the dog's owner for negligence (the incident took place in Tennessee, which has no dog-bite statute), but the jury decided that the owner hadn't done anything wrong and rejected his $375,000 claim.[37]

The same goes for warning signs. Someone who ignores a clear, prominently posted "Beware of Dog" sign is probably not going to be able to blame the dog's owner for any injuries. For example, a Maryland delivery man ignored a "Guard Dog on Duty" sign at a warehouse and was severely bitten by a German shepherd that most definitely was on duty. He sued but lost. A court concluded that he "voluntarily left his place of safety" and knowingly took the risk of injury.[38]

People who make a living working with dogs—as groomers, pet sitters, veterinarians, or kennel operators, for example—are generally presumed to voluntarily take the risk of a dog bite. (Chapter 5, Veterinarians, discusses the liability of owners to veterinarians and their employees.) For example, the owners of a dog that bit a Georgia kennel attendant were not held liable. The court ruled that the attendant knew the risk—especially in light of the fact that the owners had told the kennel that the dog might bite, and a sign on the dog's cage said "will bite."[39] Similarly, a California kennel worker injured by a dog wasn't allowed to sue the dog's owner after being hurt.[40] (Another reason that professionals cannot sue owners is that they accept responsibility for controlling a dog. A Minnesota court ruled that a groomer had control over a dog and so was a "keeper" under the state's dog-bite law—and unable to collect for damages.)[41]

Similarly, someone who has agreed to look after a dog for the owner may not be able to sue if injured by the dog. For example, a Connecticut man, who was taking care of a friend's dog for a week, sued after the dog bit him. The court ruled that the man had assumed responsibility for and control over the dog, and was not entitled to sue the owner. The state's dog-bite statute, the court said, was intended to protect people who are *not* in a position to control a dog.[42]

This rule applies only if the worker has taken control over the dog and can presumably take measures to reduce the risk of injury. In a California case, for example, a dog bit a groomer before the groomer had decided whether or not to accept custody of the dog (which was growling at her). The court ruled that the groomer had not yet taken the risk of injury.[43]

In some states that have dog-bite statutes, this defense can't be used (Ohio, for example);[44] in other words, the owner is liable for injuries even if the injured person knowingly risked the injury. For example, in an Iowa case, the owners of a dog that bit a groomer were not allowed to argue that the groomer had taken the risk of injury upon herself. The Iowa Supreme Court ruled that under the dog-bite statute, the only defense available to a dog owner is that the injured person was "doing an unlawful act" when injured.[45] The South Carolina Supreme Court issued a similar ruling, allowing an injured veterinary assistant to sue under the state's dog-bite statute.[46]

Similarly, an Oklahoma appeals court ruled that the owners of a dog could be liable, under the state's dog-bite law, for the injury the dog caused to an animal clinic employee who was bitten by the dog while walking it. In its discussion, the court did not mention the injured person's assumption of the risk; a dissenting judge opined that this defense should have applied.[47]

Some other states (California and Illinois, for example)[48] do allow this defense in lawsuits based on the state's dog-bite statute. Some state courts have yet to consider the question.

Was the Injured Person Trespassing?

In most states, dog owners aren't liable to trespassers who are injured by a dog. But the rules are convoluted and vary significantly from state to state.

In general, a trespasser is someone who wasn't invited on the property. Unless you warn people off your property with signs or locked gates, you may be considered to have given an "implied invitation" to members of the public to approach your front door on common errands—for example, to speak with you, try to sell you something, or ask directions.

Without at least some such implied invitation, someone who ventures onto private property is a trespasser. In one case from Nebraska, a child visiting relatives stuck her hand through a fence to pet the neighbor's dog; she was found to be a trespasser.[49] Similarly, a court ruled that a ten-year-old who climbed over a fence to retrieve a ball and was bitten by a dog was a trespasser, and could not sue the dog's owners for his injury.[50]

A general rule is that a dog owner who could reasonably expect someone to be on the property is probably going to be liable for any injury that person suffers. This rule is particularly important when it comes to children. Even a dog owner who does not explicitly invite a neighborhood child onto the property will probably be held liable if it's reasonable to know the child is likely to wander in—and dogs are a big attraction to children. In other words, there is a legal responsibility either to prevent the child from coming on the property or to keep the dog from injuring the child.

Specific legal rules that determine whether or not a dog owner is liable to an injured trespasser vary from state to state. Here are the basics.

Dog-bite statutes. Most dog-bite statutes do not allow trespassers to sue for an injury. The owner is liable only if the person injured by a dog was in a public place or "lawfully in a private place." That means that the injured person must have a good reason for being where he was. Mail carriers, for example, are always covered. Police officers performing their official duties are not considered trespassers, either.[51] Neither is anyone else who has an invitation, express or implied, to be on the dog owner's property.

> **EXAMPLE 1:** A woman going door to door to take a survey was let into a house, where she was knocked down and bitten by a dog. The front yard of the house wasn't fenced, although a cartoon-like "Trespassers Will Be Eaten" sign was displayed in the window. An Arizona appeals court ruled that the survey-taker entered the property with the implied consent of the residents, so she could sue under Arizona's dog-bite statute, which applies only if the person injured is "lawfully" in a private place.[52]

> **EXAMPLE 2:** A man who drove up a farmer's driveway without an invitation—he had bought hay from a previous owner of the farm years before and thought he might be able to buy more—was deemed to be a trespasser. As a result, Michigan's dog-bite statute did not apply, and the man could not sue under it for injuries he sustained when he got out of his truck and was bitten by the farmer's dog, which had been barking at him.[53]

Common law rule. If the state follows the common law rule—which imposes liability on a dog owner who knew a dog was dangerous—technically, the fact that the injured person was trespassing doesn't matter. So if the common law rule were applied strictly, if you know your dog is dangerous, and it bites a burglar who breaks into your house, you're liable. In practice, however, courts and juries are reluctant to hold a dog owner liable to a trespasser. Many courts have softened the rule to avoid unjust results. Some have modified the rule to say that a dog owner, even one who knows a dog is dangerous, isn't liable if the dog hurts a trespasser.[54] Some say that the common law rule doesn't apply to trespassers if the dog is a guard dog.[55]

Another way courts get around an unfair result is by allowing the dog owner to charge that the victim, by trespassing, either was partly to blame (see "Was the Injured Person Careless?" below) or knowingly took the risk of injury (see discussion above). If the dog owner can prove either of those circumstances, liability may be reduced or eliminated altogether.

Negligence. The states don't agree on whether or not an injured trespasser who sues a dog owner for negligence (unreasonable carelessness) can win.

In some states, an injured trespasser can sue and win if the dog owner acted unreasonably under the circumstances.

Other states still use an old legal rule that landowners are liable to injured trespassers only if the landowner, after knowing the trespasser was on the land, intentionally harmed the trespasser or failed to warn of the danger. There is an important exception to this rule: generally, a landowner has a duty to protect trespassing children, who don't have the judgment to avoid dangerous situations.[56]

Reminder. Injured people can and do sue on more than one legal theory. So someone might raise two claims in a lawsuit, one under a state's dog-bite statute and one based on the common law theory.

Was the Injured Person Breaking the Law?

Some dog-bite statutes apply only if the victim can prove he wasn't at fault. The victim may have to show he was "peaceably conducting himself," for example (that language is from the Illinois statute). Iowa's law applies only if the injured person can show he or she wasn't doing something illegal that contributed to the injury. The dog owner doesn't have to prove that the injured person *was* doing something illegal.

Was the Injured Person Careless?

In most states, a victim whose own carelessness contributed to the injury is entitled to less money from the dog owner. The amount is reduced in proportion to the victim's fault. So a victim who is 20% at fault receives 20% less than if the dog owner were completely responsible for the injury. This doctrine is called "comparative fault."

> **EXAMPLE:** Phyllis decides to visit her new neighbors down the street. When she gets to their yard, she sees a big "Beware of Dog" sign on the picket fence around the front yard, but she opens the gate and goes in anyway. The neighbors' dog rushes out and bites her ankle, and Phyllis has to pay $300 in medical bills to treat it. When Phyllis

sues the dog's owners in small claims court, the judge gives her only $150, ruling that Phyllis, by ignoring the sign, was careless and half at fault for the injury. The judge decides that the owners were half at fault, too, because they kept an aggressive dog in an unlocked yard where visitors might be expected to enter.

Exceptions to the rule. In a few states, a victim who contributed to the injury even the least bit may recover nothing from the dog owner. These "contributory negligence" states are discussed in Chapter 9, If a Dog Is Injured or Killed.

Who Is Liable: Owners and Keepers

Usually, a dog's owner is legally responsible for damage or injury the dog causes. And usually, it's clear who the dog's owner is—but not always. Someone who isn't the registered owner of a dog may still be considered, legally, an owner. For example, a New Jersey court ruled that both members of a couple who "shared the burdens and benefits of Zeus as a family pet and held themselves out to the world as his owners" were the dog's owners for purposes of the state dog-bite statute. This was true even though only one of them had bought the dog and registered him.[57]

Someone else may also be liable, if any of the following is true:
- Someone besides the owner was taking care of and had control over the dog.
- The dog's owner is less than 18 years old.
- The owner's landlord knew the dog was dangerous but didn't do anything about it.
- The dog was on someone else's property, and that person was negligent in not removing the dog.

Keepers and Harborers

Under the common law (discussed above), someone who harbors or keeps a dog is just as liable as the legal owner of a dog if the dog causes injury. Many state dog-bite laws also make the "owner or keeper" of a dog liable for damage or injury the dog causes.

A "keeper" is someone with care, custody, and control of a dog.[58] A Minnesota court put it this way:

> Harboring or keeping a dog means something more than a meal of mercy to a stray dog or the casual presence of a dog on someone's premises. Harboring means to afford lodging, to shelter or to give refuge to a dog. Keeping a dog … implies more than the mere harboring of the dog for a limited purpose or time. One becomes the keeper of a dog only when he either with or without the owner's permission undertakes to manage, control or care for it as dog owners in general are accustomed to do.[59]

Some courts, however, consider someone who has custody only for a very limited time to be a keeper.

Here are some examples of how courts have ruled on the question of keeping or harboring a dog:

- An employee of a dog kennel is bitten while at work. Ruled: She is a "keeper" under Wisconsin law.[60]
- At the groomer's, a dog bites an employee who's giving the dog a bath. Ruled: The employee is a "keeper" of the dog and can't sue the owner.[61]
- A man lets a woman and her dog stay in his house while he's on vacation. The dog bites someone. Ruled: He is an "owner" under Minnesota law.[62]
- A dog escapes from an Illinois animal shelter and runs onto a highway, causing a motorcyclist to have an accident. Ruled: Under state law, the shelter is the "owner" for purposes of liability.[63]
- As a favor to her employer, a woman takes his two dogs for a walk. They pull her; she falls. Ruled: Because she had "care and custody" of the dogs, she was their owner under Illinois law, and can't sue.[64]
- While a woman is visiting her son, his dog injures someone. Ruled: The fact that while she was there, she gave the dog commands and let it in and out doesn't make her a keeper under New York law.[65]
- A couple's adult son brought his dog to their house; while the son was holding the dog on a leash, it bit a neighbor. The court ruled that the owner's parents were not keepers of the dog for liability purposes. There was no evidence that they ever "fed, watered,

exercised, groomed, gave shelter to, or otherwise controlled and/or cared for" the dog.[66]

- A woman lets a friend and his two dogs move into her house. When the dogs' owner lets them out of the front door one day, one of the dogs bites a passer-by. Ruled: The homeowner is an "owner" under the Wisconsin statute, because she had "harbored" the dogs.[67]

- A Minnesota landlord lets a tenant have a dog in his apartment. The dog bites another tenant in her apartment. Ruled: The landlord isn't an owner.[68] (Landlord liability is discussed in detail in Chapter 4, Landlords and Dogs.)

- The owners of a restaurant rent out part of the building to a woman who works in the restaurant and has three bulldogs. The dogs occasionally wander into the restaurant for handouts from customers, and the restaurant owners pet the dogs and sometimes take them for rides in their car. One day the dogs bite a woman coming out of the restaurant. Ruled: Because they do not give the dogs shelter, protection, or food, or exercise control over them, the restaurant owners are not keepers.[69]

Some state dog-bite statutes limit liability to the owner of the dog. Under Washington law, for example, "mere keepers or possessors of a dog" aren't liable under the state statute, which limits liability to owners.[70] But be careful not to take these statutes at face value. Sometimes another section of the statute, or a court interpreting it, defines "owner" as anyone who cares for or harbors the dog. For example, the Illinois statute says that if a dog injures a person, "the owner of such dog" is liable for the full amount of the injury. But another Illinois statute defines "owner" as anyone who keeps or harbors a dog.[71]

Local ordinances may define "owner" more broadly than state laws. Under the Oklahoma statute, for example, "owner" is given a limited meaning. A Tulsa ordinance, however, defines owner as anyone "having the care or custody of or harboring, keeping or maintaining" a dog. Tulsa residents are subject to the broader local meaning, the Oklahoma Supreme Court has ruled.[72]

A dog may have more than one owner, and so more than one person may be liable if the dog injures someone. For example, if you leave your dog with a friend for six months, and the dog bites someone, the friend may be liable as a "keeper." But you're still the owner, so you may be liable, too, either because of a dog-bite statute or, if you knew the dog was dangerous, the common law rule.

Children

If the dog is owned or cared for by someone younger than 18 years old, that minor's parents are probably legally liable in place of the minor. The dog-bite laws of Connecticut, Massachusetts, and Maine say that explicitly. Some other states have laws that make parents responsible, to a limited extent, for damage their minor children cause. In other states, courts are likely to rule that the child's parents, who allow the dog on the premises and give it food and shelter, are liable because they are "keepers" of the dog.

Family Members

In most circumstances, parents can't be sued by children who are injured as a result of parental negligence. The reason is the "parental immunity" doctrine, which is based on the theory that family harmony would be disrupted if children could sue parents for failing to supervise and protect them adequately. But this immunity is not absolute. In at least one instance, a court allowed a lawsuit brought on behalf of a toddler after the family dog bit her severely. An Arizona court ruled that because the parents had a duty, as dog owners, to keep their dog from injuring anyone—including their own child—they were not immune from a lawsuit filed on behalf of their daughter.[73]

It's a complicated area. Some states have allowed children to sue if the lawsuit isn't based on negligence, but instead on a dog-bite statute that imposes strict liability on dog owners.[74] Others have not.[75]

Property Owners

Anyone who lets a dog stay on his property may be liable for injury the dog causes if it's unreasonably careless to let the dog stay. For example, a New Jersey store was sued after a dog, tied outside the store by a shopper, bit a girl on her way inside. The court said that if a jury decided the store should have foreseen that the dog might bite someone, it would be liable for the injury.[76] Similarly, a California court ruled that a landowner has a duty to others who may come on the property to protect them from dogs he had allowed to roam freely in the yard. The homeowner was having remodeling work done and had given permission for an employee to bring two dogs to the property. A contractor's employee was bitten by one of the dogs when he entered the yard. The court ruled that the homeowner owed a duty to workers who he knew might be entering the property, whether or not he was aware that the dogs were dangerous.[77]

The Alabama Supreme Court, however, ruled that a woman whose son lived in a mobile home on her property was not liable when the son's dog attacked a gas delivery man. The Alabama statute says "owners" are liable; if the legislature had meant "owners or keepers," it should have said so, the court reasoned.[78]

In some circumstances, landlords may be held financially responsible for injury or damage caused by a tenant's dog. (The special situation of landlords whose tenants have dogs is discussed in Chapter 4, Landlords and Dogs.)

Injuries on the Job

If you're hurt at work by a dog, your legal options may be limited. A Massachusetts woman, bitten by her employer's dog, was not allowed to sue her employer; her only recourse was to file a worker's compensation claim.[79]

What the Dog Owner Must Pay For

A dog owner who is legally responsible for an injury to a person or property may be responsible for reimbursing the injured person for:

- medical bills
- lost income
- pain and suffering, and
- property damage.

If the dog has injured someone before, or the owner's conduct was particularly outrageous (letting a dog known to be dangerous run loose, for example), the owner may also be liable for:

- double or triple damages (in some states), or
- punitive damages (damages meant to punish the dog's owner for misconduct).

This section discusses each of these.

RESOURCE

How to Win Your Personal Injury Claim, by Joseph Matthews (Nolo), explains how to calculate what a personal injury claim is worth.

Medical Bills

The most obvious expenses of dog-inflicted injuries are medical bills. They include all costs that are a result of the injury, which can include bills for doctors (including specialists such as plastic surgeons) and hospital services, medication, physical therapy, and, in some cases, visits to a counselor or psychiatrist.

If the injury aggravates a victim's preexisting medical condition, the final tab may be much more than would be expected from the dog-inflicted injury alone. The common legal rule is that if you hurt someone, you are responsible for all injuries that flow from your action, even if those injuries are made worse by some condition the victim already had.

> **EXAMPLE:** Muffy the Lhasa Apso trips Leonard, an elderly visitor to her owner's house. The fall wouldn't be serious for a healthier person, but Leonard's back has been in bad shape for years, and the fall puts him in the hospital. That means some big medical bills for Muffy's owner, who can't get away with paying only for what the injury would have cost a normally healthy victim.

Lost Income

If someone injured by a dog must take time off from work, for medical diagnosis, treatment, or recuperation, the dog's owner must reimburse the injured person for any lost income. If the injury will impair the injured person's ability to work in the future, that loss in earning capacity must also be compensated.

Pain and Suffering

The pain that an injured person suffers is very real—but it's very hard to put a dollar value on it. Jurors do it, and so do lawyers who are trying to settle a lawsuit before it gets to the jury, but the amounts injured people receive vary tremendously. Some states have limited the amounts that can be awarded for pain and suffering, but the limits are too high to affect most dog-bite cases.

Here are some factors that may affect how much a victim receives, either from a settlement with an insurance company or at trial:

- A common way to get a figure for pain and suffering is to multiply the amount of actual medical damages by two to four.
- A child may suffer more from a dog bite than an adult. The child may, for example, become terrified of dogs or have recurring nightmares.
- If a dog wasn't vaccinated for rabies, the person it bit will spend at least a few anxious days wondering if the dog (which is probably quarantined) is going to start showing symptoms of the fatal disease. A jury may compensate the person for that suffering.
- If the injury was caused by a completely unprovoked attack, a sympathetic jury is likely to award more money to the victim. The same goes for injuries caused by breeds commonly viewed as unpredictable, such as Dobermans or pit bulls.

Loss of Services

A few states allow spouses or close relatives of an injured person to sue for loss of the person's services. It's hard to pin down what these services are, but they don't necessarily have to be economic; they may refer to companionship. For example, a New York woman whose nine-year-old son was bitten by a dog sued for the loss of his services, and was awarded $4,500.[80]

Multiple Damages

Some dog-bite statutes (Wisconsin's, for example) allow an injured person to collect double or triple damages if the dog has bitten someone before. And if a dog has been officially labeled "dangerous" under local or state law because of its prior behavior, the victim is probably entitled to multiple damages. (See Chapter 12, Dangerous Dogs.)

Punitive Damages

An owner whose conduct was truly outrageous—for example, repeatedly letting a dog known to be dangerous run loose—may be punished by having to pay an extra amount, over and above the amount needed to compensate the victim. A jury is free to base these "punitive damages" on the wealth of the person being punished. For example, to make a big company feel some pain, it must be stung with a bigger verdict than would be assessed against the average person.

If, however, a jury gives an injured person an unrealistically huge amount of money, a judge (in the trial court, or an appellate court if the verdict is appealed) may reduce the amount. For example, a New York woman who had been bitten on the arm by a dog received a $240,000 verdict from a jury. Her husband also got $70,000 for loss of his wife's services. The dog owner appealed the decision, and an appeals court ruled that the damage awards were excessive. After all, the court said, the injury consisted of only a bite that healed quickly and left a faint scar. The court discounted testimony that the woman had developed a dog phobia after the bite, and ordered a new trial on the amount of money she should get.[81]

Liability Insurance

It should by now be crystal clear that if a dog hurts someone or damages property, the dog's owner can be on the hook for a very large bill. In many cases, however, insurance may take some of the sting out of paying. In 2011, more than a third of the amount insurance companies paid out for homeowners' liability claims went to dog-bite cases. The average cost per claim was more than $29,000—an increase of 53% since 2003.[82]

Homeowner's Insurance

Both those who own dogs and those who are bitten by them will be glad to know that if the owner has homeowner's or renter's insurance, it usually covers damage from dog bites. A standard homeowner's policy covers any legal liability the owner incurs as a result of negligence. Usually, a homeowner's policy provides from $100,000 to $300,000 worth of liability coverage.

That's the good news. The bad news is that insurance companies typically have their own "one-bite rule." That is, a company will pay for the first occurrence, but will then either cancel the insurance or add a "canine exclusion." The next time the dog bites, the owner must pick up the tab. It follows that if an insurance company knows a homeowner has a dangerous dog—something that may be rudely discovered during a routine preinsurance inspection of the home—it may refuse to issue a policy in the first place.

Some companies refuse to cover certain breeds—pit bulls, Dobermans, rottweilers, chows—that show up on lists of breeds responsible for a disproportionate number of injuries. A few states, however, do not allow insurers to prohibit any particular breeds.[83]

The "business pursuits" exclusion. All insurance policies contain exclusions, clauses that say specific kinds of incidents aren't covered. Because homeowner's insurance is supposed to insure homes, not businesses, many homeowner's policies have a "business pursuits" exclusion. Such policies don't cover claims that arise from a homeowner's business activities. The exclusion may apply when an accident happens in the home even if the business conducted there is only a part-time activity.

> **EXAMPLE:** An Oklahoma man found his homeowner's insurance didn't cover him when a potential buyer was bitten while looking at a litter of St. Bernard puppies, which he kept at his home. The business pursuits exclusion applied, a court ruled, even though the man's primary occupation was as a salesman. The business activities in this case went beyond the infrequent sale of a litter of pups: the man had renovated his barn to use it as a kennel, and advertised dogs for sale in the newspaper and on a large sign.[84]

The business doesn't have to involve dogs for the business exclusion to apply. For example, a Kentucky couple who ran a day care operation in their home were not covered by their homeowner's insurance when their dog attacked a child in their care. The child's parents argued that the liability arose from the homeowners' status as dog owners, not as business owners, and that insurance should cover the incident. But the court concluded that the incident was associated with the business because the child would not have been at the house if the owners hadn't been operating a day care business.[85]

Incidents off the property. Homeowner's policies don't usually restrict coverage to incidents that take place on the policyholder's property. Many homeowner's policies insure against any legal liabilities the policyholder incurs. For example, a homeowner's policy covered the owners of a dog that bit a child on a farm. The dog's owners owned the farm, but didn't live there; the policy insured their residence.[86]

Insurance may, however, contain an "owned property" exclusion, which means that any incidents on property owned by someone else aren't covered. For example, dog owners who had renters' insurance took their dog to the house of one of the tenant's parents. While the parents were dog-sitting, the dog bit a postal carrier. The parents' insurance company settled the mail carrier's claim for $100,000, the policy limit. It then sued the dog owners' insurance company, arguing that the dog owner's renters' insurance should cover the claim. The court said no, because the rental insurance policy contained a clause that excluded any claims arising from acts that occur on premises owned by someone else and not on the insured premises.[87]

Some policies, however, do not cover injuries connected with vehicles. So, although the policyholder might be covered if the dog bites someone in the park, the homeowner's policy might not provide coverage if the dog leans out of the car window and bites someone on the way there. Car insurance, however, might provide some coverage. (See "Car Insurance," below.)

If circumstances change. Your policy probably requires you to notify the insurance company of significant changes in your circumstances. That means that if your dog bites someone or is declared dangerous under a local law, and you don't tell the company, the policy may not cover subsequent injuries caused by the dog. Of course, if you do notify the company that your dog has bitten someone, it may well cancel your policy or exclude coverage for the dog.

If you're not sure what your homeowner's or renter's insurance policy covers, take a deep breath and read the liability section. Then read it again. If it still doesn't make sense (this is a distinct possibility, and it's not your fault), call your insurance broker. Ask if you're covered for damage your dog causes, and how cooperative the company is about coughing up money in such cases.

Car Insurance

Bites that occur in cars—or more likely, when a dog is in the back of an open pickup truck—may be covered by homeowner's insurance or by vehicle insurance. Often the two insurance companies end up duking it out in court, each trying to escape an obligation to pay.

The courts, trying to referee these fights, have come down on both sides. Most look for a connection between the vehicle and the injury; if they find one they consider significant enough, they require the car insurer to pay. For example, a New Jersey court found that when a dog, being transported in the open rear deck of a pickup truck, bit a man, the bite "was facilitated by the height and open design of the deck." In the court's opinion, the injury "was a natural and foreseeable consequence of the use of the vehicle," and so the vehicle insurance covered the incident.[88]

Other courts, presented with fairly similar facts, have reached different conclusions. A Washington court, for example, ruled that there was no connection between the vehicle and an injury caused when a dog bit a child in the back of a pickup truck, even though the dog was often kept in the truck to protect it.[89] A federal court, relying on California law, made a similar ruling in a case that arose after a dog, sitting in the back of a parked pickup truck, bit a boy who leaned in the truck bed and made a noise. The truck was simply the location of the incident, the court concluded; the injury did not arise out of the use of the truck.[90]

Separate Liability Insurance for a Dog

If you really need liability insurance for your dog, but your homeowner's or renter's policy doesn't cover you, you may be in for a tough time. The reason is that if you feel a pressing need for insurance, you're probably in one of these predicaments:

- the dog has bitten someone
- the dog has been declared "dangerous" by a judge or animal control department, meaning you must furnish proof of liability coverage, or
- local law requires owners of certain breeds to have insurance.

Any of those circumstances is a red flag to an insurance company, which is in the business of taking as few risks as possible. You'll probably have to go to a specialty insurance company, which will charge you $1,000 to $1,500 a year for a policy that will provide $100,000 of liability coverage.

The Insurance Company's Duty to Pay

It's notoriously hard for a policyholder who has a claim to squeeze money out of some insurance companies. But if a company unreasonably refuses to settle with an injured person suing the policyholder, the company may have to pay the whole amount for which the policyholder is eventually found liable.

> **EXAMPLE:** A California man whose dog caused a serious traffic accident was sued by men permanently injured in the accident. He had $100,000 of liability insurance from his homeowner's policy, but the insurance company refused to settle the lawsuit for that amount. Instead, the lawsuit went to trial, and the dog owner lost big—he was found liable for $2.6 million. But the policy owner charged that the insurance company had not acted in good faith when it refused to pay the policy limit, and the insurance company ended up paying the whole amount.

Multiple and Punitive Damages

Many insurance policies require the company to pay all sums that a policyholder becomes legally obligated to pay because of bodily injury or property damage. Whether or not that includes extra damages, which are imposed to punish the homeowner for misconduct, depends on what state you're in. Courts don't agree.

Multiple damages. A few statutes provide that in certain circumstances, the amount of damages awarded by a court or jury in a dog-bite case is doubled or tripled. The goal is to punish the owners for their conduct. Wisconsin law, for example, triples an award if the dog has bitten someone before and its owner knew about the previous incident. After one couple whose dog bit a child for the second time was sued, the tripled damages came to more than $30,000. The company that insured them tried to argue that it was liable only for the basic award, not the tripled amount. The Wisconsin Supreme Court ruled that "all sums" means all sums, and the company did have to pay.[91]

Punitive damages. Punitive damages are also intended to punish, but they differ from the extra damages mandated by statutes in several ways. First, whether or not to give them, and how much, is left up to the jury. The jury's decision is disturbed only if a judge thinks the jury is being completely outrageous. It's also proper for the jury to take into account the wealth of the person who has to pay the punitive damages, because an amount that might be a severe hardship on one person might barely be noticed by a richer person.

State courts are split over whether or not insurance policies cover punitive damages, but a slight majority seems to say that standard insurance policies do cover punitive damages. There are good arguments that insurance shouldn't cover punitive damages: after all, it's the wrongdoer, not the insurance company, who is supposed to be punished. On the other hand, if the person who bought the policy quite reasonably thinks it covers all such damages, it's not fair to change the rules in the middle of the game. And, obviously, an insurance company is free to put unambiguous language in its policies so that there would be no doubt about what's covered.

Negotiating With the Owner or Insurance Company

Most dog-bite disputes never get to court; they're settled by negotiations between the injured person and the dog owner or insurance company. You don't want to get embroiled in a lawsuit if you can help it; the time and expense are mind-boggling. In many large cities, lawsuits routinely take two years or more to get to trial. Most attorneys charge $150 to $350 an hour or, if they work on a "contingency fee" basis, keep one-third or more of what you finally collect from a lawsuit.

If you've been injured by a dog, contact the dog's owner. Write a letter setting out what happened—even though the owner may know the facts as well as you do. Include an itemized list of your expenses, and mention any local or state dog-bite laws. Give a deadline for payment—that's a good incentive for the owner. And stress that if you don't work something out by then, you'll file a small claims (or other) court case. It's also a good idea to mention that homeowner's insurance may cover the cost; many dog owners may not realize that. A sample letter is shown below, in the section on a sample small claims case.

If you do work out an agreement, put it in writing. The agreement you sign is called a release, because the injured person releases the dog owner from all legal claims arising out of the incident. A sample release is included in the section on small claims court, below.

RESOURCE

How to Win Your Personal Injury Claim, by Joseph Matthews (Nolo), explains how to negotiate successfully with an insurance company.

Bringing a Lawsuit

If attempts at settlement fail, a lawsuit may be your last resort. Choose small claims court if you can; it's the best our legal system has to offer when it comes to disputes that don't involve too much money. It's relatively fast—you'll wait a few weeks or months, instead of years—procedures are simple and designed for laypeople, and (in many states) lawyers aren't allowed.

The most you can sue for in small claims court is around $5,000 to $10,000 in most states. (A list of every state's small claims court limit is in Chapter 7, Barking Dogs.) But don't automatically give up on small claims court just because your claim is over the limit. Because of the higher cost of proceeding in regular court, you may still come out ahead by reducing your claim so it fits in small claims court.

> **EXAMPLE:** Natalie lives in Iowa, where the small claims court limit is $5,000. She is injured when a dog runs in front of her as she rides her new 15-speed bicycle down the street. The bike is totaled, and Natalie runs up more than $4,000 in medical bills. All together, she's out about $5,300. Should she abandon small claims court and get a lawyer? You probably already know the answer. By the time Natalie pays a lawyer, and the higher filing fees of regular court, she'll pay at least the $300 that she must give up if she files in small claims court.

Before you start a small claims court case, check on other limits peculiar to small claims court in your state. For example, some states do not allow people to sue for pain and suffering. Most states have free publications that explain the rules for filing a small claims court case: what papers to file, when to file them, how to schedule a hearing, and other procedures.

If you have much in the way of medical bills or time off work, small claims court may not be any help, and you may need to go to "regular" court. If that's the case, you may want to see an experienced lawyer, at least to get some advice on whether or not you have a good case.

 RESOURCE

Everybody's Guide to Small Claims Court, by Ralph Warner (Nolo), provides valuable guidance on preparing a small claims court case.

Represent Yourself in Court: How to Prepare and Try a Winning Case, by Paul Bergman and Sara Berman (Nolo), explains how to handle a civil trial from start to finish.

> **Somehow You Knew You'd End Up in Court**
>
> "As a general rule dogs in a dream are a good omen and symbolize friends. To hear a dog bark happily signifies pleasing social recognition, but if it barked fiercely, you are being warned of possible legal troubles."[92]

A Small Claims Court Case

The best way to show how small claims court works is to follow a hypothetical case from beginning to end. Here is how a typical case might unfold:

One Sunday morning, Jake was jogging along a dirt trail when he met two women and a dog. The dog, Jake thought, looked like a cross between a large Doberman and a medium-sized wolf. Because the women and the dog took up most of the center of the road, Jake moved to the far right edge. Then, noticing that the beast was on a long leash, he moved off the path into the ditch.

As it turned out, Jake didn't go quite far enough. The dog lunged for him, fangs first. Jake tried to bound into the brush at the side of the ditch (poison oak looking like the lesser of two evils at the moment), but he wasn't quick enough. The dog bit Jake's ankle before the woman holding the leash could restrain him.

Jake yelled in pain, the woman hauled the dog back to the other side of the road, and her friend went to see how bad the bite was. Before Jake hobbled off to see a doctor—his ankle was bleeding from a good-sized gash—he got the name and phone number of the dog's owner, Allison Finley, and of her friend, Kathleen Huxley.

Because it was Sunday morning, Jake had to go to a hospital emergency room to see a doctor. After he sat an hour in a crowded waiting room, a doctor stitched up the bite and gave him some painkillers and orders to stay off the leg for a few days. Jake spent the rest of the day restless and uncomfortable. He didn't sleep well that night, and decided not to try to go to work on Monday. Tuesday morning, he saw his regular doctor, who pronounced the wound "healing nicely." That afternoon he limped back to work.

Meanwhile, Jake contacted officials at the county animal control department, notifying them of the incident and confirming that the dog was properly licensed and vaccinated for rabies. Jake consoled himself with the thought that at least he wouldn't start foaming at the mouth. After a few weeks, he could jog again without pain, although his fear of encountering the beast again prompted him to choose a new route. Jake decided it was time to add up his costs and demand payment from Allison Finley.

Looking Up the Law

First, however, he decided to check on California law to see just what he was entitled to. Looking up "Dogs" in the California code (the state statutes) gave him a long list of laws. The most promising was under "Bite, liability of owner." Jake turned to the statute.

It read, in part: "The owner of any dog is liable for the damages suffered by any person who is bitten by the dog while in a public place … regardless of the former viciousness of the dog or the owner's knowledge of such viciousness."

Reading the statute closely told Jake he had to prove:
- Allison Finley owned the dog
- the dog bit him
- he was in a public place when bitten, and
- he suffered damages as a result.

Piece of cake, Jake thought. Allison couldn't even argue about anything but the amount of the damages. And as far as Jake could tell, she didn't have any defenses to make—nobody could say, Jake was sure, that by jogging along minding his own business he had provoked the dog into biting him.

Adding Up Damages

Jake's out-of-pocket costs looked like this:

Hospital emergency room	$260
2 doctor visits	200
1½ days off work	300
Torn sock	3
Medication	40
Total	$803

Choosing a Strategy

If your state doesn't have a dog-bite statute, or if it doesn't apply in your situation, you may be able to sue under the common law rule or a negligence theory, discussed above.

To win under a common law theory, you must prove that the owner knew (or should have known) that the dog was likely to cause the kind of injury suffered.

The third option, trying to prove a dog owner was negligent, is usually desirable only if there's no dog-bite statute to sue under, and it doesn't look possible to prove, on a common law theory, that the dog's owner knew the dog was dangerous.

In some states, time limits on filing lawsuits may differ depending on the theory of the lawsuit. For example, in Arizona, lawsuits under the dog-bite statute must be filed within one year of the incident. But an injured person who sues under a common law theory has two years to file a case.[93]

But what about his pain and suffering? Jake had spent two very uncomfortable days, and another ten unable to do a lot of the things he enjoyed, such as running and playing tennis. His pleasure in jogging on his formerly favorite running trail had also been displaced, in part, by anxiety about being attacked again. Puzzling over a monetary amount for this, Jake decided he didn't want to ask for a ridiculously large amount and feel as irresponsible as the dog's owner, but he did feel wronged. Finally he decided to ask for a total of $2,000.

Negotiating

Jake's next step was to call Allison Finley, who told him she considered the whole incident at least half his fault. Her theory was that when Jake leaped into the ditch, it sent a signal to Fred, her dog, that Jake was afraid and fleeing. It's a well-known fact, she went on, that dogs naturally go for cowards. Eventually, she offered to pay Jake's medical bills but nothing else, claiming Jake could have gone to work if he had wanted to.

Jake, his blood pressure rising, hung up and went for a walk. When he'd calmed down, he wrote a letter. In California, such a demand letter is required before a small claims suit may be brought. In any state, it's a good idea.

A few days later, Jake got a reply from Allison. She said she didn't have any insurance and offered to pay $600 in six monthly installments. He filed his small claims court suit the next day.

Settlement

Let's interrupt this story and give it an alternate ending: Allison suffered a change of heart and called Jake back, offering to pay $1,400 if he wouldn't take her to court. Jake, rather than go through the hassle of small claims court, where he is not guaranteed to get anything, accepted her offer. Jake and Allison get together to put their agreement in writing, using a personal injury release form such as the one shown below, taken from *101 Law Forms for Personal Use,* by Robin Leonard and Ralph Warner (Nolo).

Preparing for Court

To prepare for his court appearance, Jake first gathered all his emergency room, doctor, and pharmacy bills and made photocopies of them. He also got a statement from his boss, documenting the time lost from work.

He then called the only witness to the incident, Allison's jogging companion, Kathleen Huxley. She obviously felt bad about what had happened, but didn't want to testify against her friend. Finally, she agreed to write a four-sentence note confirming that Jake had not provoked the dog and had tried to avoid it, and that the dog had lunged at and bitten him. (This kind of letter is generally allowed in small claims court, but not in regular court.) Jake could have had Kathleen served with a subpoena—an order to show up and testify in court—but he decided against it, for the sensible reason that it wouldn't be wise to force an unwilling witness to come to court.

Thinking about what other evidence would be convincing to a small claims court judge, Jake decided a picture of ferocious-looking Fred the dog would definitely help. To get it, Jake sent a neighborhood teenager who was an avid amateur photographer to Allison's house, where Fred was in a fenced yard and easily visible from the street.

The only witness Jake decided to call at his hearing was a friend who had brought him homemade chicken soup when he was laid up the day after the incident. She would testify to Jake's obvious suffering.

In court, everything went just about as Jake had expected. He presented all his evidence and even did a Lyndon Johnson routine, showing the judge the scar on his ankle. Allison testified that Fred was really a sweet animal. She reminded the judge that several women had been attacked while jogging in the area, and said she needed the dog for protection. She brought along a couple of witnesses who said nice, but irrelevant, things about Fred's good disposition. (Whatever impression that testimony made, Jake thought to himself, was dispelled by the snapshot of Fred.)

What did the judge say? We gave this hypothetical to four experts: two small claims court judges and two small claims court advisers (court employees who help people going to small claims court prepare their cases). Their verdicts:

Judge #1:	$ 2,000
Judge #2:	$ 1,300
Adviser #1:	$ 900
Adviser #2:	$ 860

There's no better way to show you the inherent unpredictability of taking a dispute to court, even when a jury isn't involved.

Sample Demand Letter

December 17, 20xx

Allison Finley
1143 Rose Street
Oakland, CA 94616

Dear Ms. Finley:

As you will recall, on Sunday, November 24, 20xx, your dog Fred bit me on the leg for no apparent reason at about 10 a.m. on the Strawberry Canyon trail in Berkeley. I went immediately to the emergency room at General Hospital in Berkeley, where I received six stitches and medication for the pain.

During the next two days, I experienced a great deal of pain and discomfort, so much that I missed work on Monday, November 25, and half a day on Tuesday, November 26. I had to see Dr. Elizabeth Goldthwait twice (November 26 and December 2). On her orders, I was not able to exercise until December 4. I am normally an active person, and this forced idleness was frustrating and unhealthy.

My out-of-pocket expenses are as follows:

Hospital emergency room	$ 260
2 doctor visits	200
1½ days off work	300
Torn sock	3
Medication	40
TOTAL	$ 803

In addition, I believe that my very real pain and discomfort, which have significantly disrupted my life, should be compensated, for a total of $2,000.

Please promptly compensate me for my losses or have the matter taken care of by your insurance company. If I don't hear from you by January 1, 20xx, I will file a lawsuit in small claims court. If you wish to discuss the matter, you can reach me at 398-9987.

Sincerely,

Jake Kurtz

Jake Kurtz
Encl: copies of all bills and receipts

Sample Release for Personal Injury

1. _____ Jake Kurtz _____ , Releasor, voluntarily and knowingly executes this release with the express intention of eliminating the Releasee's liabilities and obligations as described below.

2. Releasor hereby releases _____ Allison Finley _____ , Releasee, from all liability for claims, known and unknown, arising from injuries, mental and physical, sustained by Releasor as described below:

   ___ Leg injuries from bite by Releasee's dog on Nov. 24, 20xx ___

   _____

   _____ .

3. Releasor has been examined by a licensed physician or other health care professional competent to diagnose (choose one or more):

   ☑ physical injuries and disabilities   ☐ mental and emotional injuries and disabilities.

   Releasor has been informed by this physician or health care professional that the injury described in Clause 2 has mended without causing permanent damage.

4. By executing this release Releasor does not give up any claim that he/she may now or hereafter have against any person, firm or corporation other than Releasee.

5. Releasor understands that Releasee does not, by providing the consideration described below, admit any liability or responsibility for the above described injury or its consequences.

6. Releasor has received good and adequate consideration for this release in the form of ___ $1,400.00 ___ .

7. In executing this release Releasor additionally intends to bind his spouse, heirs, legal representatives, assigns, and anyone else claiming under him. Releasor has not assigned any claim arising from the events described in Clause 2 to any other party. This release applies to Releasee's heirs, legal representatives, insurers, assigns, and successors as well to Releasee.

8. This release was executed on _____ December 24 _____ , 20 _XX_ at
_____ Oakland, California _____ .

Jake Kurtz _____
Releasor's Signature

2514 Gleneden Ave. _____
Address

Oakland, CA 94618 _____

_____
Releasor's Spouse's Signature

Allison Finley _____
Releasee's Signature

1143 Rose St. _____
Address

Oakland, CA 94616 _____

Witnesses:

Bernard Rubble _____
Name

Dave McFarland _____
Name

1530 Stone Way, Albany, CA _____
Address

636 65th St., Oakland, CA _____
Address

Injury to Livestock

In the eyes of the law, injuring economically valuable livestock is traditionally a more serious matter than injuring a person. Strict liability statutes (which make an owner liable just because he owns a dog, not because he is at fault in any way) are relatively new when it comes to personal injury caused by dogs, but for years dog owners have been strictly liable for damage to livestock. Many states that still don't impose strict liability for injury to persons do impose strict liability if the dog injures livestock. In at least one state, Minnesota, a dog owner is even guilty of a minor criminal offense—a petty misdemeanor—if the dog kills or pursues domestic livestock.[94]

The two cardinal rules, which apply almost everywhere, are:

1. A livestock owner is free to kill a dog that is killing, wounding, chasing, worrying, harassing, or attacking livestock. (This is discussed in more detail in Chapter 9, If a Dog Is Killed or Injured.)

2. A dog's owner or keeper is financially liable for any livestock damage the dog causes.

In some states, the dog's owner may be liable for double the amount of actual damages. In California, for example, the owner of livestock injured or killed by a dog may sue the dog's owner for twice the amount of the financial loss.[95]

Several states have funds to reimburse farmers or ranchers who lose livestock to dogs. The animal owner must file a claim with the state, following procedures set out in the statute. To seek reimbursement from the Illinois Animal Control Fund, for example, an owner must:

- be an Illinois resident
- report the loss to the state within 24 hours, and
- appear before the County Board and make a sworn statement setting out how many animals were killed, their value, and the owner of the dog, if known.[96]

The Board investigates and files a written report with the county treasurer, who makes payments once a year. Unless the county sets the amount to be paid at the reasonable market value, maximum amounts per injured or killed animal are set by state law.

The livestock owner may still sue the owner of the dog responsible for the damage. An amount equal to what the livestock owner has received from the Animal Control Fund is simply deducted from what is awarded in court, if anything, and paid back to the fund.

Endnotes

[1] Estimate of the Centers for Disease Conrol and Prevention in Atlanta.

[2] *A community approach to dog bite prevention*, J. Am. Vet. Med. Ass'n, Vol. 218, No. 11 (2001).

[3] *Tracey v. Solesky*, WL 1432263 (Md. 2012).

[4] *Jannuzzelli v. Wilkens*, 158 N.J. Super. 36, 385 A.2d 322 (1978).

[5] *Morris v. Weatherly*, 488 N.W.2d 508 (Minn. App. 1992).

[6] *Anderson v. Christopherson*, 802 N.W.2d 832 (Minn. App. 2011), rev. granted 2011.

[7] Cal. Civ. Code § 3342; Ariz. Rev. Stat. § 11-1020 (D).

[8] *Wilson v. City of Decatur*, 389 Ill. App. 3d 555 (2009).

[9] *Holden ex rel. Holden v. Schwer*, 242 Neb. 389, 495 N.W.2d 269 (1993).

[10] *Johnson v. Lindley*, 41 F. Supp. 2d 1021 (D. Neb. 1999).

[11] *Underhill v. Hobelman*, 776 N.W.2d 786 (Neb. 2009).

[12] *Lewellin v. Huber*, 465 N.W.2d 62 (Minn. 1991).

[13] Georgia has a dog-bite statute, but instead of imposing strict liability (liability without fault) as other statutes do, it merely puts the common law rule in a statute.

[14] *Bailey v. Veitch*, 814 N.Y.S.2d 459 (A.D. 2006).

[15] *Tessiero v. Conrad*, 588 N.Y.S.2d 200 (App. Div. 1992).

[16] See, for example, *Slack v. Villari*, 59 Md. App. 462, 476 A.2d 227, *cert. denied*, 301 Md. 177, 482 A.2d 502 (1984), and *Collier v. Zambito,* 1 N.Y.3d 444 (2004).

[17] See, for example, *Fontecchio v. Esposito*, 108 A.D.2d 780, 485 N.Y.S.2d 113 (1985).

[18] For example, see *Drake v. Dean*, 19 Cal. Rptr. 2d 325 (1993).

[19] See, for example, *Henkel v. Jordan*, 644 P.2d 1348, 7 Kan. App. 2d 561 (1982). (Dog ran after bicyclists, who fell and were injured. The owners, who knew of the dog's habits, were held liable.)

[20] *Nava v. McMillan*, 176 Cal. Rptr. 473, 123 Cal. App. 3d 262 (1981).

[21] *Fowler v. Helck,* 278 Ky. 361 (1939).

[22] *Rucker v. Goldstein*, 497 So. 2d 491 (Ala. 1986).

[23] See, for example, *Roupp v. Conrad,* 287 A.D.2d 937, 731 N.Y.S.2d 545 (2001), *Earl v. Piowaty,* 839 N.Y.S.2d 861 (A.D. 2007).

[24] *Alfano v. Stutsman,* 471 N.E.2d 1143 (Ind. App. 1984).

[25] *Partipilo v. DiMaria,* 211 Ill. App. 3d 813, 156 Ill. Dec. 207, 570 N.E.2d 683 (1991).

[26] *Laylon v. Shaver,* 590 N.Y.S.2d 615 (App. Div. 1992).

[27] *Williams v. Hill,* 658 So. 2d 381 (Ala. 1995).

[28] *Hill v. Williams,* 144 N.C. App. 45, 547 S.E.2d 472, *rev. denied* 354 N.C. 217, 557 S.E.2d 531 (2001).

[29] For example, see *Delfino v. Sloan,* 20 Cal. App. 4th 1429, 25 Cal. Rptr. 2d 265 (1993), *petition for review denied* (1994), and *Silva v. Micelli,* 178 A.D.2d 521, 577 N.Y.S.2d 444 (1991).

[30] *Los Angeles Daily Journal,* Jan. 26, 1987.

[31] *Selger v. Steven Brothers, Inc.,* 222 Cal. App. 3d 1585, 272 Cal. Rptr. 544 (1990).

[32] *Petrone v. Fernandez,* 12 N.Y.3d 546 (Ct. App. 2009).

[33] *Von Behren v. Bradley,* 266 Ill. App. 3d 446, 640 N.E.2d 664, 203 Ill. Dec. 744 (1994), *petition for leave to appeal denied* (1995).

[34] *Brans v. Extrom,* 266 Mich. App. 216 (2005).

[35] See, for example, *Kizer v. O'Neal,* 51 Conn. L. Rptr. 180 (Conn. Super. 2010) (boy who lunged at a dog in a confined space to hug it provoked the dog to bite); *Reed v. Bowen,* 503 So.2d 1265 (Fla. App. 1986); *Toney v. Bouthillier,* 129 Ariz. 402, 631 P.2d 557 (1981).

[36] *Koivisto v. Davis,* 277 Mich. App. 492 (2008).

[37] "Retired doctor not at fault for dog's attack, jury says," *Memphis Commercial Appeal,* Dec. 7, 1990.

[38] *Benton v. Aquarium, Inc.,* 62 Md. App. 373, 489 A.2d 549 (1985).

[39] *Lundy v. Stuhr,* 185 Ga. App. 72, 363 S.E.2d 343 (1987).

[40] *Priebe v. Nelson,* 39 Cal. 4th 1112, 47 Cal. Rptr. 3d 553, 140 P.3d 848 (2006).

[41] *Carlson v. Friday,* 694 N.W.2d 828 (Minn. App. 2005).

[42] *Murphy v. Buonato,* 241 Conn. 319, 696 A.2d 320 (1997).

[43] *Prays v. Perryman,* 213 Cal. App. 3d 1133, 262 Cal. Rptr. 180 (1989).

[44] *Pulley v. Malek,* 25 Ohio 3d 95, 495 N.E.2d 402 (1986).

[45] *Collins v. Kenealy,* 492 N.W.2d 679 (Iowa 1992).

[46] *Harris v. Anderson County Sheriff's Office,* 673 S.E.2d 423 (S.C. 2009).

[47] *Hass v. Money,* 849 P.2d 1106 (Okla. Civ. App. 1993).

[48] *Nelson v. Hall,* 165 Cal. App. 3d 709, 211 Cal. Rptr. 668 (1985); *Vanderlei v. Heideman,* 83 Ill. App. 3d 158, 38 Ill. Dec. 525, 403 N.E.2d 756 (1980).

[49] *Kenney v. Barna*, 215 Neb. 863, 341 N.W.2d 901 (1983).

[50] *Alvin v. Simpson*, 195 Mich. App. 418, 491 N.W.2d 604 (1992).

[51] See, for example, *Wroniak v. Ayala*, 14 Conn. L. Rptr. 328 (1995) (officer bitten while investigating a burglary in the dog owner's home could sue under state dog-bite statute).

[52] *Jones v. Manhart*, 120 Ariz. 338, 585 P.2d 1250 (1978).

[53] *Tieman v. Grinsteiner*, 2011 WL 5108506 (Mich. App. 2011).

[54] Restatement (Second) of Torts § 514 (1977).

[55] *Mech v. Hearst Corp.*, 64 Md. App. 422, 496 A.2d 1099 (1985).

[56] *DeRobertis v. Randazzo*, 94 N.J. 144, 462 A.2d 1260 (1983).

[57] *Pippin v. Fink*, 794 A.2d 893 (N.J. Super. 2002).

[58] *Mitchell v. Chase*, 87 Me. 172, 32 A. 867 (1895).

[59] *Verrett v. Silver*, 244 N.W.2d 147 (Minn. 1976).

[60] *Armstrong v. Milwaukee Mutual Ins. Co.*, 191 Wis. 2d 562, 530 N.W.2d 12 (1995).

[61] *Lewis v. Chovan*, WL 1681400 (Ohio App. 2006).

[62] *Verrett v. Silver*, 244 N.W.2d 147 (Minn. 1976).

[63] *Kirchgessner v. County of Tazewell*, 162 Ill. App. 3d 510, 114 Ill. Dec. 224, 516 N.E.2d 379 (1987).

[64] *Hassell v. Wenglinski*, 243 Ill. App. 3d 398, 183 Ill. Dec. 807, 612 N.E.2d 64 (1993), *petition for leave to appeal denied* (1993).

[65] *Zwinge v. Love*, 37 A.D.2d 874, 325 N.Y.S.2d 107 (1971).

[66] *Jacobson v. DiBernardi*, WL 1375274 (Conn. Super. 2010).

[67] *Pawlowski v. American Family. Mut. Ins. Co.*, 777 N.W.2d 67 (Wis. 2009).

[68] *Gilbert v. Christiansen*, 259 N.W.2d 896 (Minn. 1977).

[69] *Hagenau v. Millard*, 195 N.W. 718 (Wis. 1923).

[70] *Guerrero v. Capron*, 121 Wash. App. 1063 (2004).

[71] 510 Ill. Comp. Stat., §§ 5/2.16, 5/16.

[72] *Hampton ex rel. Hampton v. Hammons*, 743 P.2d 1053 (Okla. 1987).

[73] *Schleier ex rel. Alter v. Alter*, 767 P.2d 1187 (Ariz. App. 1989). The Arizona Supreme Court abolished the doctrine of parental immunity in *Broadbent v. Broadbent*, 184 Ariz. 74 (1995).

[74] *Thelen v. Thelen*, 174 Mich. App. 380, 435 N.W.2d 495 (1989) (child allowed to sue father and stepmother for bite by father's dog).

[75] See, for example, *Squeglia v. Squeglia*, 234 Conn. 259 (1995) (four-year-old child couldn't sue father, under state strict liability statute, for dog bite).

[76] *Nakhla v. Singer-Shoprite, Inc.*, 500 A.2d 411 (N.J. Super. A.D. 1985).

[77] *Salinas v. Martin*, 82 Cal. Rptr. 3d 735 (Cal. App. 2008).

[78] *Humphries v. Rice*, 600 So. 2d 975 (Ala. 1992).

[79] *Barrett v. Rodgers*, 408 Mass. 614, 562 N.E.2d 480 (1990).

[80] *Graham ex rel. Graham v. Murphy*, 135 A.D.2d 326, 525 N.Y.S.2d 414 (1988).

[81] *Fontecchio v. Esposito*, 108 A.D.2d 780, 485 N.Y.S.2d 113 (1985).

[82] Insurance Information Institute, *Prevent Dog Bites—And a Lawsuit: Average Cost of Dog Bite Claims Is on the Rise* (press release, May 17, 2012).

[83] 3 Pa. Cons. Stat. Ann. § 459-507-A; Mich. Comp. Laws Ann. § 500.2103; and Michigan Dept. of Licensing and Regulatory Affairs Bulletin No. 2003-07-INS.

[84] *Wiley v. Travelers Ins. Co.*, 534 P.2d 1293 (Okla. 1974).

[85] *Holzknecht v. Kentucky Farm Bureau Mut. Ins. Co.*, 320 S.W.2d 115 (Ky. App. 2010).

[86] *Lititz Mutual Ins. Co. v. Branch*, 561 S.W.2d 371 (Mo. App. 1977).

[87] *California Casualty Ins. Co. v. American Family Mut. Ins. Co.*, 94 P.3d 616 (Ariz. App. 2004).

[88] *Diehl v. Cumberland Mutual Fire Ins. Co.*, 296 N.J. Super. 231, 686 A.2d 785 (1997).

[89] *Heringlake v. State Farm Fire & Casualty Co.*, 74 Wash. App. 179, 872 P.2d 539 (Wash. Ct. App. 1994).

[90] *Oregon Mut. Ins. Co. v. National General Ins. Co.*, 2010 WL 1343529 (E.D. Cal. 2010).

[91] *Cieslewicz v. Mutual Service Casualty Ins. Co.*, 84 Wis. 2d 91, 267 N.W.2d 595 (1978).

[92] *The Dreamer's Dictionary*, by Robinson and Corbett (Taplinger Pub. Co., 1974).

[93] *Murdock v. Balle*, 144 Ariz. 136, 696 P.2d 230 (1981).

[94] Minn. Stat. § 347.01(b).

[95] Cal. Food & Agric. Code § 31501.

[96] 510 Ill. Comp. Stat., § 5/19.

Dangerous Dogs

Most dogs, even those that bite someone, aren't career criminals: they bite from fear or nervousness or overprotectiveness. They may bite just once in their lives. But once a dog has bitten or displayed dangerous tendencies, it makes sense to require its owner to take measures to prevent further injuries.

Many cities, and an increasing number of states, are adopting "dangerous dog" or "vicious dog" laws. These laws seek to identify dangerous dogs and prevent injuries by making their owners take specific precautions, such as confining the dogs securely or muzzling them when in public. They may also require owners to buy liability insurance to cover any injuries the dog does cause. Owners who have deliberately created dangerous dogs by mistreating them may be subject to criminal fines and even jail sentences.

Some laws automatically classify "pit bulls" as dangerous, and ban them from the city or impose strict regulations on their owners. Not surprisingly, these controversial laws have been tested in courts across the country—with mixed results.

Dangerous Dog Laws

"Vicious dog" or "dangerous dog" laws impose special restrictions on dogs that are officially labeled dangerous or potentially dangerous. These laws, which emphasize prevention, have much to commend them. By focusing on dogs known to pose a danger to people, they can protect the public, crack down on irresponsible dog owners, and lessen the temptation to over-regulate (as in the case of breed-specific bans, discussed below). Unfortunately, many of the laws are so vague that they invite arbitrary enforcement.

Most dangerous dog laws are local, but more and more states are passing such laws. The state laws follow the same general pattern, although they differ significantly from state to state.

Generally, the process of having a dog declared dangerous is set in motion by a formal complaint from an animal control officer or someone who has been threatened or injured by the dog. A hearing follows, at which a judge or public health official hears evidence and determines whether or not the accused dog is actually dangerous under the terms of the law.

If a dog is found to be dangerous, the judge will order the owner to take certain measures to prevent the dog from injuring anyone. At the least, the owner will have to keep the dog securely confined. If the judge determines that the danger can't be kept within an acceptable level, the owner may be ordered to have the dog destroyed or remove it from the city. An owner who violates the court's order will probably be fined and possibly be jailed, especially if the dog seriously injures someone. The dog will be impounded and probably killed.

States With Dangerous Dog Laws		
Arizona	Maryland	Ohio
California	Massachusetts	Oklahoma
Colorado	Michigan	Oregon
Delaware	Minnesota	Pennsylvania
District of Columbia	Montana*	Rhode Island
Florida	Nebraska	South Carolina
Georgia	Nevada	South Dakota
Hawaii	New Hampshire	Tennessee
Idaho	New Jersey	Texas
Illinois	New Mexico	Vermont
Kentucky	New York	Virginia
Louisiana	North Carolina	Washington
Maine	North Dakota	West Virginia

*Cities or counties can enact dangerous dog laws that comply with state requirements.

Many other states have laws on the books that make it illegal to keep vicious dogs or dogs that are a "public nuisance," but don't provide a procedure for having a judge determine what dogs are vicious. In South Dakota, for example, it is illegal to keep a vicious dog, which is defined as a dog that attacks people unprovoked.[1] These laws aren't much help when it comes to preventing injuries; they serve primarily to increase penalties on owners after a dog injures someone.

The next sections discuss the procedures for having a dog declared dangerous.

The Complaint

If a dog has threatened or attacked someone, the frightened or injured person may file a formal complaint with the agency or court in charge of implementing the dangerous dog law. In many places, a local court receives complaints, but sometimes they are handled by the local sheriff, health department, or animal control department.

Who may make such a complaint depends on the law. Most laws allow anyone to complain, but in some states, only a person who has been attacked may lodge a formal complaint. In Vermont, it takes three residents of a town to file a written complaint with the town legislature (selectmen, aldermen, or trustees), and they may do so only if they know that a dog has bitten someone while off the premises of its owner or keeper.[2] Under most laws, law enforcement and animal control officers may also file a complaint.

After a complaint is made, a dog that has seriously hurt someone may be seized and held until the hearing is held. New York law, for example, allows a judge to order a dog impounded before the hearing if there is "probable cause" to believe the dog is dangerous.[3] Similar rules apply in most places. As a practical matter, by the time a hearing has been scheduled to determine the viciousness of a dog, the dog will probably have been impounded.

The Hearing

Under most dangerous dog laws, after a dog owner has been notified of a complaint, a hearing is held to determine if the dog is dangerous, as that term is defined in the law.

In some states, however, a hearing is held only if the dog owner requests one, after an animal control officer has investigated a complaint and decided to classify the dog as dangerous. The owner is mailed a notice of the decision and gets a chance to argue only by requesting a hearing.

To meet constitutional due process requirements, the law must give dog owners some kind of opportunity for a hearing. The Ohio Supreme

Court overturned that state's vicious dog law because it didn't give owners a meaningful opportunity to be heard and declared all "pit bulls" vicious, requiring their owners to take drastic precautions (muzzling, locked enclosures, and more) regardless of the individual dog's actual behavior.[4] The Court later ruled that a city ordinance regulating vicious dogs was constitutional, because the dog's owner had a chance to be heard before any restrictions were placed on his dogs.[5]

Basically, the hearing is a shorter, less formal version of a trial. The dog owner, the person who complained, and members of the public can attend and present evidence about the dog's behavior or disposition. Expert witnesses may testify about the likelihood that the dog will cause more problems.

Most often, judges in local courts preside over these hearings. Local health or animal authorities, however, may sometimes hold hearings and make dangerous dog determinations.

Ultimately, the judge's decision must be based on the statute or ordinance, which will define the term "dangerous dog." These definitions range from vague to extremely detailed. Rhode Island officials, for example, have a detailed definition to help them make their decisions. According to the state statute, a vicious dog is one that:

- threatens someone, unprovoked, in a public place
- has a known tendency to attack unprovoked or otherwise endanger people or domestic animals
- bites, injures, or attacks a person or domestic animal without provocation, on public or private property, or
- is trained or kept for dog-fighting.

The Rhode Island law states that a dog cannot, however, be declared vicious if it injured someone who was deliberately trespassing on the dog owner's property, teasing or abusing the dog, assaulting another person, or committing a crime.

This statute is more detailed than most. But the factors it sets out are the things any judge would consider when determining whether or not a dog is dangerous.

In Rhode Island, the hearing to determine whether or not a dog is vicious is conducted by the chief of police, executive director of the SPCA, and a third person chosen by the first two. A dog owner who wants to appeal a vicious dog determination has five days to petition the district court for a new hearing. The court then conducts its own hearing and decides whether the dog is vicious according to the law's definition.[6]

Restrictions on Dangerous Dogs

Usually, a judge who pronounces a dog dangerous has fairly free rein to impose penalties or restrictions on the dog's owner. At a minimum, laws require that the dog be kept enclosed on the owner's property at all times unless it's leashed and, in some places, muzzled as well. The judge may also order the dog to be sterilized. Again, the Rhode Island statute spells out in great detail the conditions under which a vicious dog is allowed off its owner's property. There, it is unlawful for an owner to let a vicious dog outside the owner's dwelling or a locked enclosure

> unless it is necessary ... to obtain veterinary care ... or to sell or give away the vicious dog or to comply with commands or directions of the dog officer.... In such event, the vicious dog shall be securely muzzled and restrained with a chain having a minimum tensile strength of three hundred (300) pounds and not exceeding three feet (3') in length, and shall be under the direct control and supervision of the owner or keeper of the vicious dog.

Depending on the specific city or state law and the danger posed by the dog, its owner may also be required to:

- Post "Beware of Dog" signs prominently. Some states require a sign that contains a warning symbol, not just words, to alert young children.
- Keep the dog in a locked enclosure, or one that meets certain specifications for height, strength, and other features.
- Buy a certain amount of liability insurance (at least $100,000) that covers damage or injury caused by the dog.
- Post a bond with the city or county to cover any damage or injury caused by the dog.
- Obtain a special "vicious dog" license from the city or county. These licenses are much more expensive than the standard license; for example, in New Jersey, they cost $150 to $700 annually.

- Have the dog permanently identified with a tattoo or microchip.
- Have the dog wear a distinctive bright fluorescent collar when outside.
- Have the dog neutered.
- Muzzle the dog when it's off the owner's property.
- Notify animal control officials if the dog is sold or given away, and notify the new owner in writing that the dog has injured someone.

A judge who decides that a dog poses a great risk of serious harm may order that the dog be seized and humanely killed by animal control authorities. This penalty, of course, is reserved for dogs considered incorrigible: dogs that have repeatedly bitten people, severely injured or killed someone, or have been trained and used for fighting.

A few states, however, don't give the judge any choice. In Michigan, if a dog is found to be dangerous and has caused serious injury or death to a person—or to another dog—the court must order the dog to be destroyed.[7] The same is true in North Dakota; if a dog is found to be a public nuisance that "habitually molests persons traveling peaceably on the public road," the judge must order a peace officer to kill the dog.[8]

Injuries Caused by Dangerous Dogs

Once a dog has been declared legally vicious but allowed to live, it's unlikely to get a second chance if its owner doesn't follow the judge's restrictions scrupulously. The laws of Kentucky, for example, authorize peace officers to kill any dog that has been found to be vicious if it is running at large.[9]

At the least, a dog officially labeled vicious will be impounded if it later injures someone. Owners may also have to pay double or triple damages to the injured person. In Maine, for example, an owner who doesn't comply with a judge's order to confine or muzzle a dog is liable for three times the amount of damage the dog causes.[10] In Rhode Island, if a vicious dog injures someone, the owner must pay a fine to the government and triple damages to the injured person.

The owner of a vicious dog who doesn't comply with the law's conditions on keeping the dog securely confined and away from people may be guilty of a crime. (See "Criminal Penalties for Owners of Dangerous Dogs," below.)

Criminal Penalties for Owners of Dangerous Dogs

Unless a dog mauls or kills someone—a very rare event—its owner probably won't be charged with a crime. In such cases there is almost always evidence that the owner knew the dog presented a grave danger to people—usually because the owner had trained the dog to fight or knew of previous unprovoked attacks or very aggressive behavior by the dog—and failed to take precautions.

Depending on the circumstances and state law, an owner may be charged with anything from letting a vicious dog run loose to manslaughter or even murder. Here are some examples:

- In the most well-publicized case of its kind, a San Francisco woman was convicted of second-degree murder after the Presa Canario dogs she was walking attacked and killed a woman in the hall of the apartment building they both lived in. Affirming the conviction, the appeals court wrote that the dog's owner knew that the dog that attacked "was a frightening and dangerous animal: huge, untrained and bred to fight" and had endangered others by keeping it.[11]

- A California woman who ordered her Doberman pinscher to attack someone was convicted of assault with a deadly weapon.[12]

- A California court sentenced a dog owner to 90 days in jail and fined him $500 for failing to keep his dog on a leash, as ordered by the county after the dog attacked two people.[13]

- An Ohio man was convicted of failing to confine a vicious dog, a felony in that state. His dogs, an American pit bull terrier and a rottweiler, had attacked and killed a toddler. The pit bull was presumed to be a vicious dog under Ohio law then in effect.[14]

- In 1987, a Georgia man was convicted of involuntary manslaughter after his three dogs, which he had allowed to run loose, attacked and killed a four-year-old boy. He was sentenced to five years in prison and five years of probation. (One of the conditions of the probation was that he not own any dogs.)

- A California man whose chained dog mauled to death a two-year-old in 1987 was charged with murder. He was convicted of a lesser charge, involuntary manslaughter, and sentenced to three years in prison.[15]

As state and local lawmakers have become more concerned about dog attacks, they have passed specific criminal laws aimed at people who allow their dogs to seriously injure people. Florida, for example, has made it a crime to own a dog that "aggressively attacks" someone and causes severe injury or death. If the dog hasn't already been found dangerous under the Florida dangerous dog law, the crime is a misdemeanor; if the dog has been declared dangerous, it's a felony.[16] In Michigan, if a "dangerous dog" (defined as a dog that bites a person without provocation) kills someone, the owner is guilty of involuntary manslaughter.[17] In 1994, a woman whose two dogs had killed her two-year-old nephew, after she left him alone with the dogs, was sentenced to three years' probation under this law.[18]

It's unusual, but local law may make anyone whose dog bites someone guilty of a crime. A woman in Topeka, Kansas, was charged with violating a city ordinance making it a crime to permit a dog to attack someone. The woman's dog rushed from her garage and bit a mail carrier. The dog owner was found guilty, despite her testimony that the mail carrier had "jammed her arm in the dog's mouth."[19]

Breed-Specific Restrictions

Whether or not certain breeds are inherently ferocious—most animal behaviorists and observers believe they are not—some breeds do account for a disproportionate number of serious injuries to people.

Cities across the country have responded by passing ordinances specifically prohibiting possession of pit bulls, rottweilers, and a few other breeds, or imposing strict requirements on their owners. For example, some cities require owners to buy liability insurance, keep their dogs behind six-foot-high fences, and muzzle the dogs whenever they're in public. (Not all cities are free to do this; in many states, local governments are forbidden, by state law, from adopting ordinances based on the breed of the dog.[20]) Some cities have not banned the breeds, but require owners to pay large license fees for animals of certain breeds.

For years, Ohio had a state law that declared all pit bulls vicious; that law was changed in 2012. The current law defines dangerous vicious dogs without regard to breed. Dogs that injure someone or kill another dog without provocation—or are caught running loose three times—are considered dangerous. Only a dog that kills or seriously injures someone will be labeled vicious.[21]

Military Families and Dogs

Military families are used to disruption—when orders come through, they must pick up and move across the country or across the world. But dealing with pets can be an especially tough part of a move for service members and their children. An additional wrinkle is that although all branches of the service allow pets in family housing, some bases now ban dogs of certain breeds considered "dangerous."

Dogs on Deployment (dogsondeployment.org) is a nonprofit organization devoted to helping service members find temporary homes for their dogs when necessary. (Even if you can't take in an extra dog, check out the site; they can use donations, too.)

Legal Challenges to Breed-Specific Laws

Dog owners have challenged these ordinances in court, and a few have been thrown out by judges. The clear trend, however, is to uphold laws that impose special restrictions on certain breeds or ban them outright.[22] The U.S. Supreme Court has refused to disturb decisions of state supreme courts, upholding ordinances that regulate the ownership of pit bulls.[23]

These ordinances are attacked primarily on two grounds. First, opponents claim the laws are unconstitutionally vague because they don't define "pit bull" sufficiently. To be constitutional, a law must be specific enough to give dog owners fair warning about what kinds of dogs are illegal. One court ruled that a Lynn, Massachusetts, ordinance was unconstitutionally vague because it depended on "the subjective understanding of dog officers of the appearance of an ill-defined 'breed,' [and] leaves dog owners to guess at what conduct or dog 'look' is prohibited … [S]uch a law gives unleashed discretion to the dog officers charged with its enforcement … "[24]

But most courts don't require much in the way of specifics. The Colorado Supreme Court, upholding a Denver ordinance regulating pit bulls, stated that the behaviorial and physical characteristics set out in the law were enough to put a dog owner on notice. The court stressed that a law passes constitutional muster if it gives dog owners *some* standard of conduct, even if it is imprecise.[25]

The second argument is that it is arbitrary to ban one kind of dog, so the laws violate the owners' constitutional due process rights. After all, pit bulls aren't the only dogs that injure people. Fatal dog attacks have been caused by, among other breeds, such small and apparently mild-mannered creatures as cocker spaniels and dachshunds.[26] This argument has been largely unsuccessful. As the Colorado Supreme Court noted, it is generally recognized that when a legislature chooses to regulate a hazard, it is "not required to simultaneously regulate every similar hazard."

RESOURCE

For more information on breed-specific laws and litigation, check out the website of the American Dog Owners' Association, www.adoa.org.

Now We Like 'Em, Now We Don't

Pit bulls are the current villains of the dog world. Before they took center stage, German shepherds and Dobermans were characterized in the same way: vicious, unpredictable canine time-bombs.

Pit bulls, in fact, were the epitome of the all-American dog in the early part of this century. Pete the Pup, in the old "Our Gang" movies, was a pit bull. Teddy Roosevelt had a pit bull in the White House. And on a World War I poster that used dogs to symbolize the various nations, America was a pit bull—stalwart, unafraid, but not belligerent.

Should Some Breeds Be Banned?

From 1979 to 1998, pit-bull-type dogs and rottweilers accounted for more than half of the 238 fatal attacks on humans.[27] And along with huskies and Malamutes, and breeds developed for guarding and police work, including German shepherds, mastiffs, akitas, chow chows, and Dobermans, they consistently show up on the list of most-likely-to-bite breeds. Why not ban them?

First of all, bans are hard to enforce. What exactly is a pit bull? There is no one pit-bull breed and no reliable way of identifying a dog as one of the pit-bull breeds. And because "pit bull" has become synonymous with "mean," any dog that bites someone and has a passing resemblance to a bulldog is likely to be labeled a pit bull.

They may also be ineffective at solving the underlying problem of too many dangerously aggressive dogs. When one breed is banned, people who want a macho dog just get a different breed. For example, after some cities banned pit bulls, rottweilers increased in popularity.

The most basic problem with breed-specific laws, however, is that they ignore the fact that dogs are individuals. Within any breed, there are sweet dogs and aggressive ones—and even within breeds that have been bred for reactivity, most of the individual dogs are not dangerous. Any dog's temperament is influenced by its breeding, its health, its socialization, and its environment.

Banning a breed is easy—but may give "a false sense of accomplishment," according to the report of a task force of the American Veterinary Medical Association. The report advocates a far more rigorous and broad-based approach to preventing dog bites, including community education and organization, better reporting, and spaying and neutering programs (about three-quarters of reported dog bites are by intact males.)[28]

RESOURCE

Bandit: Dossier of a Dangerous Dog, by Vicki Hearne (Harper Collins), is the story of a dog branded vicious and ordered destroyed by the State of Connecticut—and how the dog became the author's valued companion. The book is a philosophical discussion of dogs, people, and the laws that try to regulate the relationship between them. It's also full of insights into dog behavior and breed traits, gained from the author's many years as a trainer.

BADRAP (Bay Area Doglovers Responsible About Pit Bulls) is an award-winning nonprofit group. Its mission is to make sure pit bull terriers keep their long-held place as cherished family dogs. To that end, it runs training classes, rescues dogs, holds community outreach events, advocates for sensible legislation, and partners with other organizations to educate the public about pit bulls. Check out its website, www.badrap.org.

Endnotes

1 S.D. Codified Laws Ann. § 40-34-14.

2 Vt. Stat. Ann., tit. 20, § 3546(a).

3 N.Y. Agric. & Mkts. Law § 123.

4 *State v. Cowan*, 103 Ohio St. 3d 144, 814 N.E.2d 846 (2004); *State v. Mallis*, 964 N.E.2d 1096 (2011).

5 *Youngstown v. Traylor*, 914 N.E.2d 1026 (2009).

6 R.I. Gen Laws § 4:13.1-2.

7 Mich. Comp. Laws Ann. § 287.322.

8 N.D. Cent. Code § 42-03-03.

9 Ky. Rev. Stat. § 258.235(7).

10 Me. Rev. Stat. Ann., tit. 7, § 3952.

11 *People v. Noel,* 128 Cal. App. 4th 1391, 28 Cal. Rptr. 3d 369 (2005).

12 *People v. Nealis,* 232 Cal. App. 3d Supp. 1, 283 Cal. Rptr. 376 (1991).

13 *San Francisco Chronicle,* June 16, 1988.

14 *State v. Ferguson,* 76 Ohio App. 3d 747, 603 N.E.2d 345 (1991).

15 "Pit Bull Owner Handed Three-Year Prison Term," *San Francisco Recorder,* Feb. 20, 1990.

16 Fla. Stat. § 767.13.

17 Mich. Comp. Laws Ann. § 287.323 (1).

18 *People v. Trotter,* 209 Mich. App. 244, 530 N.W.2d 516 (1995).

19 *City of Topeka v. Mayer,* 16 Kan. App. 2d 567, 826 P.2d 527, rev. denied (1992).

20 See, for example, 3 Pa. Cons. Stat. Ann. § 459-507-A.

21 Ohio Rev. Code Ann. § 955.11.

22 See, for example, *State v. Lee,* 257 P.3d 799 (Kan. App. 2011); *Toledo v. Tellings,* 114 Ohio St. 3d 278, 871 N.E.2d 1152 (2007); *Bess v. Bracken County Fiscal*

Court, 210 S.W.3d 177 (Ky. App. 2006); *City of Pagedale v. Murphy,* 142 S.W.3d 775 (Mo. App. 2004); *American Dog Owners Ass'n, Inc. v. City of Des Moines,* 469 N.W.2d 416 (Iowa 1991); *Vanater v. Village of South Point,* 717 F. Supp. 1236 (S.D. Ohio 1989); *State v. Peters,* 534 So. 2d 760, *rev. denied,* 542 So. 2d 1334 (Fla. App. 1988).

[23] *State v. Anderson,* 57 Ohio St. 3d 168, 566 N.E.2d 1224, *cert. denied,* 501 U.S. 1257, 111 S. Ct. 2904 (1991); *Hearn v. City of Overland Park,* 244 Kan. 638, 772 P.2d 758, *cert. denied,* 493 U.S. 976, 110 S. Ct. 500 (1989).

[24] *American Dog Owners Ass'n, Inc. v. City of Lynn,* 404 Mass. 73, 533 N.E.2d 642 (1989).

[25] *Colorado Dog Fanciers, Inc. v. City and County of Denver,* 820 P.2d 644 (Colo. 1991).

[26] "Breeds of dogs involved in fatal human attacks in the United States between 1979 and 1998," by Sacks, Sinclair, Gilchrist, Golab, and Lockwood, *Journal of the American Veterinary Medical Association,* Vol. 217, No. 6 (Sept. 15, 2000).

[27] Sacks, Sinclair, Gilchrist, Golab, and Lockwood, cited above.

[28] *A community approach to dog bite prevention,* J. Am. Vet. Med. Ass'n, Vol. 218, No. 11 (2001).

Dogs and Divorce

Given that most Americans now consider their animal companions part of the family, it's not surprising that pets are getting more attention when families are riven by divorce or violence. Some legal commentators have suggested that judges treat family pets as they do children, and make decisions based on their best interests—but legally, pets are still property. And overburdened courts are unlikely to take on the challenge of supervising how divorcing couples deal with their pets.

Ownership, Custody, and Visitation

Divorce lawyers say that disputes over pets are on the rise in divorce cases. Courts, however, do not welcome yet more arguments from divorcing couples and, given the current state of the law, often find themselves unable to come up with a satisfying resolution to these issues.

Work It Out Yourselves

If you are considering divorce, or already in the throes of the process, don't for a minute think that court is a good place to resolve your disagreements about who gets the dog. As discussed below, courts do not treat custody battles over pets like they do child custody cases; they will not consider the "best interests of the pet." Instead, they almost always simply award ownership of an animal to one spouse or the other, usually with minimal discussion.

What's Best for the Dog?

If you really want a decision based on the best interests of your pet, make the decision yourself. After all, you know your animal best—especially compared to an overworked judge who will never set eyes on your beloved pet. Step back and think about these factors:

Who does most of the caretaking now? If you're the one who's done the lion's share of walking the dog, training the dog, buying dog food and other supplies, and taking the dog to the vet, there's little reason to think the other person really wants to take on all that responsibility.

Who will be best situated to care for the dog later? After the divorce, someone needs to have the time, energy, money, space, and inclination to take care of the pet. A spouse who must travel a lot, lives in a small apartment, or works very long hours may not be able to provide a good home.

Where will the children be? If you have children who are attached to your pet, and one parent will have primary custody of them, that's a good argument for having the dog stay with that spouse. Assuming your primary consideration in your divorce is the well-being of your kids, this should be a determining factor.

If there's no clear answer after you honestly evaluate these questions, then it's probably best to simply accept that the animal will be fine with either of you. You might want to talk to a mediator—a neutral third party who can help you arrive at a decision, but has no power to impose one. Or just flip a coin to see who will keep the animal, and give the other spouse a compromise on some other issue.

Sharing Ownership or Visitation

You can consider some kind of shared arrangement, but tread carefully. Animals, like children, do best with consistent schedules and training, so shared custody isn't likely to be a good solution for most families. But if you will still live close to one another, you might consider a visitation schedule—there's nothing wrong with agreeing that one former spouse can take the dog for a romp at the dog park every weekend.

If you do come up with an agreement for shared custody or visitation, you should realize that later, if you think your ex-spouse doesn't live up to his or her side of the bargain, the court won't help you. For example, a Pennsylvania couple made an agreement declaring that their dog Barney was the wife's property but giving the husband the right to visit the dog. After the woman moved away and stopped making the dog available for visits with her former husband, he went to court seeking an order for "shared custody" of the dog. The court declined, stating that shared custody of personal property was not contemplated by state law.[1]

Getting Help From a Mediator

Many divorcing couples find that meeting with a mediator—a trained, neutral third party—can greatly facilitate communication and decision making. A divorce mediator is often a lawyer who has extensive training in helping couples reach decisions that they can live with. During mediation, each spouse gets a chance to talk, with the mediator keeping the conversation on track and civil. The mediator may suggest options the couple hasn't thought of, but has no power to impose a decision.

Many courts now require couples who have issues over child custody or support to have several sessions with a mediator. This process reduces the number of nasty fights that go to court, saving the court (and the divorcing couples) time and money. The primary benefit, however, is to the families—especially the children—because mediation, in stark contrast to litigation, tends to reduce animosity between divorcing spouses. Courts aren't equipped to address the emotional components of loaded issues like custody of a child or pet, but couples can explore those dimensions in their mediation sessions.

Mediation is also far, far less expensive than going to court. If a couple can resolve their pet issues in an hour or two with a mediator—not uncommon—the bill may be just a few hundred dollars. (Couples typically split the cost.) Hiring lawyers to argue in court will likely cost each spouse thousands.

A subspecialty in pet mediation has sprung up in recent years among divorce mediators. If you're looking for someone to help you and your spouse come to a compromise that looks out for your pet's best interests, ask divorce lawyers and mediators to recommend someone who will take your issues seriously and help you out.

RESOURCE

Nolo's Essential Guide to Divorce, by Emily Doskow (Nolo), contains lots of great information about the divorce process (including mediation) and how to keep a divorce as civil as possible. The key to avoiding anguish and expense: agreeing on the big issues, not fighting about them before a judge.

If You Can't Agree: What the Court Might Order

If you and your spouse have tried in good faith but can't come up with an agreement about your dog, you can ask the court to decide. But the court will simply award ownership; it won't try to determine what's in the pet's best interests and fashion a custody or visitation plan accordingly. Family law courts, which face huge caseloads and bitter arguments over child custody and support, are not willing to take on the added burden of deciding disputes over the best interests of pets.

Ownership

The law in most places requires that courts treat a dog as a piece of property, to be allocated to one spouse or the other in a divorce. That means the court will not be interested in which of you loves the dog more—or which of you the dog loves more.

Treating a dog like a piece of furniture creates obvious problems for the courts (not just the owners). First of all, unlike other assets that divorcing couples fight over, most dogs have very little economic value. In fact, they are likely to be a source of continuing expense. So if a court is trying to divide property based on its monetary value, how is a dog counted? And the law doesn't actually treat dogs exactly like inanimate objects—for example, there are no laws that make abusing your couch a crime.

Still, if there's a simple property-law basis for giving the dog to one spouse, the court will probably use it. For example:

- If one person owned the dog before the marriage, that person will probably keep ownership of the animal.
- If one spouse received the dog as a gift, he or she will probably be able to keep it.
- If it's obvious that one spouse won't be able to keep the dog—for example, doesn't have a stable address, is living in a no-pets building, or is about to be deployed in the military—the dog will probably be given to the other.

Sentimental value. If there isn't such a straightforward way to resolve the dispute, some courts will take into account a dog's "sentimental value." The dog is still an item of property, but the court recognizes that it's a special kind of property, like a one-of-a-kind heirloom, whose primary value is emotional. That was the reasoning of a New Jersey court, called on to resolve a couple's dispute over the dog they had acquired while they were engaged. It was appropriate, the court ruled, to consider "special subjective value when resolving a dispute between co-owners of "property that cannot be partitioned or sold without hardship or violation of public policy." The court could resolve such a dispute "based on one party's sincere affection for and attachment to" the dog.[2]

Mistreatment of the animal. If there is evidence that one person abused or neglected the dog, the other will probably be awarded ownership. For example, a Minnesota court awarded ownership of a couple's two Saint Bernards to the wife because there was evidence that the husband had mistreated the dogs. The court was careful to say that it was not applying a "best interests of the dogs" standard, however.[3] Similarly, a court awarded the wife ownership of a dog that was registered in the husband's name because of evidence of mistreatment and the husband's inability to provide it a good home.[4]

A Florida dispute between spouses illustrates why courts are so reluctant to get into matters of pets' best interests. The couple agreed on everything except who should get their dog. The trial judge held a hearing and gave the husband possession of the dog and gave the wife the right to take the dog for "visitation" every other weekend and every other Christmas. The spouses weren't satisfied with this and headed back to court; after another hearing, the court order was modified to give the wife every other month with the dog.

The husband took the matter to an appeals court, which said wearily, "Based on the history of this case, there is every reason to believe that there will be continued squabbling … concerning the dog." That court (named Judge Wolf, as it happens) sent the matter back, directing the trial court to award the animal outright to one spouse under the Florida law that requires equitable (fair) distribution of assets at divorce. "Our courts are overwhelmed with the supervision of custody, visitation, and support matters related to the protection of our children. We cannot undertake the same responsibility as to animals," concluded the court.[5]

If you're not happy with a trial court's ruling on who gets the dog, don't expect much help from an appeals court. For example, a Virginia court awarded a dog to the wife, and $750 to the husband to buy a similar dog. The husband appealed the decision, but the appeals court wouldn't change it. The court concluded that it had no reason to disturb the lower court's ruling "awarding wife possession of the dog on the ground that the dog had resided with wife since the parties acquired her. ... Wife owned the residence, she planned to continue residing there, and she provided the dog with a stable and caring environment ..."[6]

Exceptions to the Rule

A few courts have ventured into murky legal territory, issuing dog "custody" orders. For example, an Alaska trial court gave the husband "legal and physical custody" of the couple's dog Coho, and gave the wife "reasonable visitation rights" as determined by the husband. Less than a year later, the couple was back in court; the wife argued that her ex-husband didn't give her enough time with the dog, and he claimed other dogs at the ex-wife's home threatened the dog's life. Each asked for a restraining order against the other. The court changed the order, giving the ex-husband sole custody and telling the ex-spouses not to have any contact with each other. On appeal, the Alaska Supreme Court let the trial court's ruling stand.[7]

A Texas court appointed the wife "managing conservator" of her dog, Bonnie Lou; the husband was to have visitation rights. He objected, in court, not because he wasn't getting to see the dog, but that he hadn't also been appointed managing conservator. The court said simply that "We are sure there is enough love in that little canine heart to 'go around.' Love is not a commodity that can be bought and sold or decreed. It should be shared and not argued about."[8]

Will the Law Change?

A few states have proposed legislation that would allow courts to issue custody orders for pets when couples divorce. Laws that were proposed—but did not pass—in Maryland, Michigan, and Wisconsin would have required divorcing couples to list their pets and state whether or not they had reached any custody agreements. Either spouse could have asked the court to determine where the pet would be placed.

Even without specific laws, as society's attitudes shift, courts may become more willing to take on issues of shared custody or ownership of companion animals. It's not unheard of for courts to order couples to share other items of property that are unique or freighted with emotional attachment—for example, season tickets or a boat.

Domestic Violence and Pets

The sad truth is that it's all too common for an estranged abusive spouse to frighten, control, and punish other family members by harming or killing their pets. In a 1997 study, 71% of women who had sought refuge in shelters reported that their abuser had threatened, harmed, or killed family pets.[9] Other women delay leaving a dangerous home environment because they fear what will happen to their pets.

Randall Lockwood of the ASPCA, who has studied the link between cruelty to animals and violence toward people for many years, conducted a study of middle-class New Jersey households where child abuse had occurred. He found that where there was domestic violence or physical abuse of children, "the incidence of animal cruelty was close to 90%." The households had more pets than other households in the same community, but generally didn't keep the animals very long. The pets died, ran away, or were discarded.[10]

Restraining Orders That Include Pets

In recent years, many states have amended their laws on domestic violence restraining orders (called personal protection or protective orders in some states) to let courts protect pets as well as people. More states are considering these measures and will doubtless follow suit.

To get a restraining order, generally you must show the local family court that the person against whom you're seeking the order has abused or seriously threatened you or someone else in the household, and that you need immediate protection. A judge can usually issue a temporary order very quickly, often on the same day you request it. The restraining order will order the potential abuser to stay away from you and, if you request it, from your household's pets. The order gives you temporary legal custody and control of the household's pets.

It's a crime to disobey a court order, and someone who violates the terms of a restraining order can be arrested.

States That Include Pets in Restraining Orders		
Arizona	Louisiana	Oklahoma
Arkansas	Maine	Oregon
California	Maryland	Tennessee
Colorado	Minnesota	Texas
Connecticut	Nevada	Vermont
District of Columbia	New Jersey	Washington
Hawaii	New York	West Virginia
Illinois	North Carolina	

Taking Pets to Shelters or Other Safe Places

If you need to get out of an abusive home but fear what might happen to your animals if you leave them behind, you may have some options. Some domestic violence shelters accept dogs. In some states, you can leave your animals at a public animal shelter for at least a few days without charge.

You may also be able to find a "safe haven" for your pet—a kennel, animal shelter, or veterinarian's office. Call around to see whether someone at a local animal shelter or domestic violence shelter knows of a facility near you that might lend a hand. Also check the "Safe Havens for Animals" directory, which lists facilities that can help. It's maintained by the Humane Society of the United States at www.humanesociety.org/issues/abuse_neglect/tips/safe_havens_directory.html.

Endnote:

1 *DeSanctis v. Pritchard*, 803 A.2d 230 (2002), appeal den., 572 Pa. 757, 818 A.2d 504 (Pa. 2003).

2 *Houseman v. Dare*, 405 N.J. Super. 538 (2009).

3 *Pratt v. Pratt*, 1988 WL 120251 (Minn. Ct. App. 1998).

4 *Vargas v. Vargas*, 1999 WL 1244248 (Conn. Super. Ct. 1999).

5 *Bennett v. Bennett*, 655 So.2d 109 (Fla. Ct. App. 1995).

6 *Whitmore v. Whitmore*, 2011 WL 588497 (Va. App. 2011).

7 *Juelfs v. Gough*, 41 P.3d 593 (Alaska 2002).

8 *Arrington v. Arrington*, 613 S.W.2d 565 (Tex. Ct. Civ. App. 1981).

9 Ascione, Weber, and Wood, *The Abuse of Animals and Domestic Violence: A National Survey of Shelters for Women Who Are Battered*, 5(3) Soc. and Animals 205-218 (1997).

10 Quoted in Charles Siebert, "The Animal-Cruelty Syndrome," *New York Times*, June 13, 2010.

Cruelty

More than one philosopher has concluded that an accurate measure of a society's morals is the way it treats animals. America's official position toward animals is admirable: cruelty is forbidden and, at least on paper, severely punished. Then there is the real world, where cruelty is an undeniable reality.

In general, the law is even more reluctant to interfere with an owner-animal relationship than it is to get involved in parent-child relations. Or, as the late animal trainer Barbara Woodhouse lamented, "there is no law that permits dogs to be taken away from stupid owners."[1]

But animal abuse cases are now taken more seriously than they used to be. Almost all states now classify some animal cruelty crimes as felonies, which is a dramatic and recent change in the law. One reason is that the link between violence against animals and violence against people has become so well documented. A high percentage of violent offenders in prison have animal cruelty offenses in their past; similarly, a high percentage of people who abuse animals will go on to be convicted of violence against other people.[2]

Criminal penalties are invoked only for what society considers the most serious forms of misconduct involving animals: cruelty, neglect, fighting, and theft. Experimenting on animals for scientific research is usually not considered cruelty punishable by law, and neither is injuring an animal to defend people or valuable property.

What to Do If You Suspect Mistreatment

Almost all of us have seen neglected animals—hungry, mistreated, left in filthy conditions without enough food or water. This section discusses when and how to help.

Where to Complain

If you know or have good reason to suspect that an animal is being mistreated—abused, neglected, used in dog fighting, or in any other way cared for improperly—talk to your city or county animal control department or local humane society officials. Authorities in many states rely on humane societies, which are private agencies, to monitor treatment of animals and to investigate complaints, especially in commercial operations such as pet shops or horse-drawn cabs. Humane society employees work with law enforcement personnel or investigate cruelty complaints on their own and then notify authorities.

Humane society staffers will have a good sense of what kinds of conduct the local police or prosecutor's office will act on. These community standards, more than the language of anticruelty laws, ultimately determine who is convicted or even who is prosecuted in the first place. And even if the behavior isn't against the law, the humane society may be able to correct it, eliminating the need for recourse to the criminal justice system.

If a humane society isn't available or helpful, talk to:

- the owner, if you think explaining your concern might have a good effect
- animal control authorities
- city police or the county sheriff
- the local prosecutor (usually called the district attorney or state's attorney)
- the closest office of the U.S. Department of Agriculture, if your concern involves conditions in a puppy mill or pet shop
- your representatives in the state legislature or Congress, if the problem should be addressed by legislation (for example, the problem of puppy mills)
- the FBI, if dogs are being taken across state lines for fighting.

If you make a written complaint to law enforcement officials, send a copy to a local or national humane society and keep a copy yourself.

What Happens to Rescued Animals

Neglected or mistreated animals are usually seized by animal control authorities when their owner is charged with cruelty. If the animals don't need to be taken immediately, however, the owner of the animals has a constitutional right to notice and a hearing before the animals can be taken away.

If the animals are taken without first notifying the owner, the owner is entitled to a hearing, usually before a judge, as soon as possible.[3] In most places, the owner is responsible for reimbursing the government for the costs of impoundment, and can't get the animals back until the bill is paid.

(For more on what can happen to impounded animals, see Chapter 2, State and Local Regulation.)

Criminal Law Terms

Infraction. A minor offense, such as a driving over the speed limit, usually punishable by a small fine. Infractions aren't considered actual crimes, and they don't give you a "criminal record."

Misdemeanor. A crime that is punishable in most states by up to a year's imprisonment in a county jail, a fine, or both. Violating anticruelty statutes is often a misdemeanor.

Felony. A serious crime. Conviction can mean a state prison sentence of a year or more, a fine, or both. Entering a dog in an organized dog fight is a felony in most states. Some states have different classes or degrees of misdemeanors and felonies; for example, Class A crimes may be the least serious, Class C crimes the most serious.

Cruelty and Neglect

Even a dog knows the difference between being tripped over and being kicked.

—Oliver Wendell Holmes

Cruelty to animals is against the law everywhere in this country, but it wasn't always so. If you were to pick up a famous old treatise called *Chitty's Criminal Law*, blow the dust from its leather-bound pages, and look inside, you would search in vain for mention of a crime called "cruelty to animals." It simply didn't exist in 1819, when Chitty was expounding. At most, someone who beat an animal could be accused of being a public nuisance. Most states didn't pass anticruelty laws for another century.

And when anticruelty statutes were written, they were often vague. A statute may, for example, forbid deliberate cruelty, inadvertent neglect, or everything in between. People prosecuted for cruelty under these statutes sometimes complain that the language is too vague to warn them of what conduct is prohibited, but this argument virtually never works. Courts say that people are perfectly capable of knowing what kinds of conduct toward animals won't be tolerated.[4]

Typical Anticruelty Laws

Anticruelty laws usually punish several different kinds of conduct, ranging from abandoning a dog to neglecting it to intentionally harming it. Some states have only one or two broadly worded statutes that simply prohibit any kind of "inhumane" or "needlessly cruel" treatment. Others have several statutes: both a catch-all ban on cruel treatment and prohibitions of specific acts—for example, abandoning an animal, leaving it in a car without proper ventilation, or cropping its ears without anesthesia.

A broadly worded statute prohibits many kinds of cruelty, even though it doesn't list them specifically. Locking a dog in a car that overheats could be illegal under a catch-all statute that forbids cruelty to animals, even if there's no specific mention of that conduct in the statute.

Here's the Texas anticruelty statute, which combines the broad and the specific to cover nearly every kind of misconduct toward animals (there is also a specific and detailed statute outlawing dog fighting):

A person commits an offense [in Texas, a misdemeanor] if the person intentionally, knowingly, or recklessly:

(1) tortures an animal or in a cruel manner kills or causes serious bodily injury to an animal;

(2) without the owner's effective consent, kills, administers poison to, or causes serious bodily injury to an animal;

(3) fails unreasonably to provide necessary food, water, care, or shelter for an animal in the person's custody;

(4) abandons unreasonably an animal in the person's custody;

(5) transports or confines an animal in a cruel manner;

(6) without the owner's effective consent, causes bodily injury to an animal;

(7) causes one animal to fight with another animal, if either animal is not a dog;

(8) uses a live animal as a lure in dog race training or in dog coursing on a racetrack; or

(9) seriously overworks an animal.[5]

If you need to investigate the anticruelty laws of your state, you may have to dig to make sure you've found all the statutes that cover mistreatment of animals. Dog-fighting statutes (discussed in the next section) are almost always separate from general anticruelty laws, and carry their own stiff penalties.

The next section discusses the general kinds of conduct that are typically prohibited by state criminal law.

Neglect

A righteous man regardeth the life of his beast.

—Proverbs 12:10

Failing to provide an animal with the necessities of life is always illegal. A Colorado statute, for example, makes it a crime not to furnish "food, drink, or protection from the weather consistent with the species, breed, and type of animal."[6] In California, those general rules apply, along with a specific prohibition on leaving an unattended animal tethered for more than three hours a day.[7] A separate statute requires that confined animals be given an adequate exercise area.[8] Some cities impose more detailed requirements. San Francisco, for example, has an ordinance requiring doghouses to be clean, dry, raised off the ground, and big enough for the dog to lie comfortably.

Whether or not a person accused of neglecting an animal will be convicted by a judge or jury depends, of course, on the circumstances and the evidence. But to convict someone of a crime, the state must prove guilt "beyond a reasonable doubt"—a tough standard to meet. For example, a District of Columbia man was arrested for failing to give his dog adequate shelter and protection from the weather. A physician had seen the dog, a German shepherd, tied by a three-foot chain on an open concrete back porch, on a January day when the temperature never got above 28 degrees. The owner was convicted, but an appeal court overturned the conviction because no one "experienced in the care of a dog of this type" had testified that the dog had been made to suffer. After all, said the court, it's common knowledge that some breeds of dogs can stay out in bitter cold with no ill effects.[9]

A New York man, however, was convicted of cruelty and failure to provide "necessary sustenance" to his cat because he didn't seek any medical attention for its many painful ailments, which included a bloody, swollen paw (the result of an untreated tumor), dehydration, emaciation, a polyp in its nasal passage that made it hard for the animal to breathe, and other chronic diseases. The owner admitted that he had never, in 15 years, taken the cat to a veterinarian and that the paw had been in its sad condition for a year. The judge concluded that although the law did not usually require pet owners to seek medical attention for their animals, neglecting the animal and letting it suffer was unjustifiable.[10]

Unless a statute requires that the neglect be malicious, it doesn't matter that someone accused of neglecting animals didn't intend to be cruel. Under most statutes, it is enough that someone knowingly neglected animals. For example, an Ohio woman who kept a dog and 25 cats in her house, in deplorable conditions, was convicted of animal neglect.[11]

In another case, two New York men were convicted of neglecting a horse by allowing it to pull a hansom cab even though they knew the horse was limping. Whether or not they had acted maliciously was irrelevant, the court said: "The question is whether they wilfully caused certain things to be done."[12]

Some neglect statutes don't even require the conduct to be knowing. Under those statutes, if an animal is neglected because of someone's actions, that person is guilty, period. For example, a North Dakota law makes it a crime to deprive an animal of necessary food, water, or shelter. The prosecution is not required to prove that the person acted knowingly or willfully.[13]

EXAMPLE: Simone goes on vacation and makes arrangements with her friend John to care for her dog, but John forgets to feed the dog. He could be prosecuted for neglect. What he intended or didn't intend doesn't matter; he had charge of the dog and neglected it.

Malicious Cruelty

Malicious (intentionally mean) cruelty is punished more severely than other cruelty to animals. California law, for example, punishes malicious cruelty to an animal with a state prison sentence, a fine of up to $20,000, or both.[14]

The most obvious and widespread kind of malicious cruelty is organized dog fighting; someone responsible for putting two animals in a ring and having them tear at each other is certainly someone who "maliciously and intentionally maims, mutilates, tortures, or wounds a living animal," in the words of the California law. Dog fighting, however, is usually prosecuted under separate, specific state and federal statutes, not generic anticruelty laws. (See "Organized Dog Fighting," below.)

Cruelty to Your Own Dog

One interesting loophole in some old animal cruelty laws is that they punished only cruelty to an animal that belonged to another person. This reflected the legal idea of the dog as property, which an owner could treat according to personal whim. Most of these laws have been changed to make cruelty a crime no matter who owns the animal.[15] It's a step toward the recognition of animal rights—rights that aren't incidental to an owner's rights, but exist separately— although it's doubtful lawmakers think of it in those terms.

Conduct may be malicious even if it isn't particularly harmful. Take, for example, the case of the North Carolina man who grew so annoyed at his neighbor's cat (it threatened bluebirds and walked over his wife's car) that he set a live trap for it. He put red paint in the trap, so that when the cat was caught it was covered with paint from neck to tail. The paint was to identify the cat, he said. He was convicted of animal cruelty and fined $40.[16] (The cat was fine after a couple of shampoos.)

Hoarding

You may have heard of cases where animal control authorities have discovered large numbers of severely neglected dogs or cats. The owner, unaccountably, seems oblivious to the appalling filth and disease and remains convinced that he or she is actually a loving caretaker.

For years, this situation has been treated as an animal control problem—but of course, it's really a people problem. People who collect an excessive number of animals (hundreds, sometimes) and don't begin to care for them are called hoarders, and hoarding is now seen as a distinct psychological problem. Hoarders see themselves as rescuers, ignoring the reality that their obsession is causing suffering and death for the animals they love so desperately.

Hoarders are commonly charged with violating animal cruelty laws, and may spend time in jail. But many of them go right back to their old habits when released unless they receive effective psychological treatment.

> **RESOURCE**
> **More on hoarding:** For more information on the pathological collecting of animals, see the website of Tufts University's Hoarding of Animals Research Consortium at www.tufts.edu/vet/cfa/hoarding.

Abandonment

Anyone who lives in the country, or even on the edge of town, knows that dog owners who have tired of their pets sometimes dump the unfortunate animals on deserted roads. In most places, that's illegal. New York law makes it a misdemeanor, with a penalty of up to one year's imprisonment, a $1,000 fine, or both.[17] In Colorado, intentionally abandoning a dog is punished as cruelty to animals.[18] Enforcing these laws, however, is extremely difficult. Just about all witnesses can do is report license plate numbers to police and try to get them to follow up.

Confining a Dog in an Unventilated Car

Some states and cities specifically forbid confining a dog in a car without adequate ventilation. A Texas man was convicted of violating such a statute after he left his dog in a car, parked in the sun on a hot day, while he and his wife went to a movie. The car windows were open about an inch and a half; the sun shone directly into the car through a tinted glass roof.[19] Remember that even without a specific statute, this could constitute cruelty under a general anticruelty law.

Leaving a Dog Hit by Your Car

The law of several states (Pennsylvania, for one) specifically provides that a driver who hits a dog and knowingly doesn't stop to help it is guilty of a crime.[20] Again, this might be a crime under more general laws as well.

Cosmetic Cruelty: Cropping Ears and Tails

It is still the fashion, among those who breed and show certain kinds of dogs, to cut off part of the ears and tails of puppies. Massachusetts is the only state that makes it illegal to exhibit a dog with cropped ears, unless a veterinarian has certified that the cropping was reasonably necessary.[21] A violation can be punished by a fine up to $250. A bill to outlaw ear cropping was introduced in California in 2005, but opposition from purebred dog breeders stopped it in committee.

Some states (Connecticut, New Hampshire, Pennsylvania, and New York, for example) at least attempt to make the process less painful for the pups. They require ear-cropping to be done by a veterinarian, while the dog is under anesthesia.[22]

Penalties range from stiff in New York to trivial across the river in Connecticut. In New York, those convicted of violating the statute are punished by a fine of $1,000, imprisoned for a year, or both. In Connecticut, the fine is $50 for the first offense; for subsequent convictions, it's another $50, 30 days in jail, or both.

It's doubtful that these laws are enforced vigorously. If you're accused of violating them, you will have to prove that your dog's ears were cropped by a veterinarian, in conformance with the law. You should have a certificate from the vet, showing the date of the operation, a description of the dog, and your name.

Pippi Longstocking Comes Out Against Hurting Puppies

It is against the law in Sweden to trim a dog's tail for cosmetic reasons. Astrid Lindgren, the creator of the Pippi Longstocking children's stories, was 80 years old when she campaigned for the law, which became effective in 1988. The law is informally known as "Lex Astrid" (Astrid's law).

Inhumane Conditions in Pet Shops and Puppy Mills

Many states have special anticruelty laws for pet shops, where animals are sometimes treated as just more merchandise. California, for example, requires pet shops to provide animals with sanitary conditions, adequate space, heating, ventilation, and humane care. Violators can be punished by a fine of up to $1,000, 90 days in jail, or both.[23]

There are also state laws aimed specifically at "puppy mills," large-scale dog breeding operations that churn out puppies for pet shops across the country. The Humane Society of the United States (HSUS) evaluated each state's laws in a 2012 report and found that Virginia had the strongest protections for puppy mill dogs (as well as for people who buy dogs from pet stores). The HSUS looked at licensing, frequency of inspections, limits on the number of dogs allowed, standards of care, and penalties for violating the rules. Other states that scored well were Pennsylvania, Oregon, New Hampshire, and Washington. The lowest ranked states were Mississippi, Kentucky, North Dakota, Idaho, South Dakota, and Alabama.[24]

These operations may also be found in violation of local or state anticruelty laws or federal laws regulating interstate transport of animals. For example, a Tennessee woman who ran a Maltese breeding business—advertising online and shipping puppies across the country for up to

$1,600 each—was convicted of animal cruelty. Local law enforcement officials searched her home and found more than 200 dogs, many in wire cages stacked on top of each other. The odor of the residence was described as overpowering; the dogs' coats were matted with urine and feces, and their eyes and ears were infected. Animal control staff worked through the night to get the dogs out.[25] (See Chapter 3, Buying and Selling Dogs.)

The HSUS helps local authorities raid puppy mills across the country. One problem with these rescue operations is that local shelters must immediately deal with a huge number of animals, many of whom are likely to be sick. For example, in 2009 the HSUS helped take almost 300 dogs from a kennel in North Carolina; in 2012, more than 80 dogs were seized from another North Carolina breeder.

An Exception to Anticruelty Laws: Self-Defense

Even if an anticruelty law doesn't say so explicitly, it may not apply if the cruelty to the animal was inflicted for what, under the law, is considered a good reason. Many anticruelty laws excuse anyone who injures or kills a dog that is attacking a person or livestock. For example, a New York court acquitted a man who shot a dog that frightened his children and attacked his own dog during a family picnic.[26]

A comparable Oklahoma statute did not, however, protect a man convicted of cruelty for shooting three hunting dogs as they chased a deer. He had left the dogs, wounded but still alive, on someone else's land. The law justified killing a dog that was chasing livestock, but not one chasing wildlife, the court ruled. The defendant "knew that he had hit the dogs and he was willing to let them drag themselves off and suffer and die," said the court. "The trial court felt that this was cruelty to animals, and we can but agree."[27]

Civil liability. Someone who injures or kills a dog while defending another person or livestock may not be liable in a civil lawsuit, if the owner sues to recover the value of the dog. (Those rules are discussed in Chapter 9, If a Dog Is Injured or Killed.)

Organized Dog Fighting

Organized dog fighting is now a felony in every state. Federal law also punishes dog fighting with up to five years in prison and hefty fines.[28] Despite the stiffening of these laws, there is a dog fight "on any weekend in any of the 50 states," according to Eric Sakach of the Humane Society of the United States.[29] And it's not just amateurs enjoying an ancient "sport," as shown by the well-publicized case of Atlanta Falcons star quarterback Michael Vick. Vick pleaded guilty to felony charges stemming from a well-financed, large dogfighting operation run from property he owned.

Putting a dog in the ring to fight is not the only conduct these laws punish. Most dog fighting laws make it illegal to watch, bet on, or train dogs for dog fights. New York's statute is typical. It makes it a felony, punishable by up to four years in prison, a fine of up to $25,000, or both, to:

- cause an animal to fight
- train an animal under circumstances showing an intent to have the dog fight
- let an animal fight, or be trained to fight, on premises under one's control, or
- own or keep an animal trained to fight on premises used for fighting.

It's a misdemeanor, punishable by a year's imprisonment and stiff fine, to own or keep a dog under circumstances showing an intent to have the dog fight. Paying an admission fee or making a bet at a dog fight is another misdemeanor.[30]

Convictions for dog fighting offenses are still infrequent. But arrests are made: 40 people at a backwoods site in Louisiana, nine at a dog fight in upper Manhattan, and so on. The organizer of the Louisiana dog fight was sentenced to the state's maximum penalty of one year in prison and a $1,000 fine, despite his lack of a criminal record.[31] A federal judge gave a Missouri man a sentence of 18 months in prison for his role in a sophisticated operation that used steroids, weight training, and medicine to get the dogs to fight long and hard. The federal sentencing guidelines set out a penalty of zero to six months of incarceration, but the judge increased the sentence because of the "extraordinary cruelty" involved in the crime. The longer sentence was upheld on appeal.[32] Almost 200 dogs had been seized from the men involved, who had routinely killed (by electrocution, in some cases) or abandoned dogs that lost fights.

Law enforcement officials depend on citizens to help them find and break up illicit dog fights. Veterinarians are also being pressed into service. Laws in Arizona and California, for example, require vets to tell local law enforcement about any dog injuries or deaths they think were inflicted in a dog fight.[33]

RESOURCE

The Lost Dogs: Michael Vick's Dogs and Their Tale of Rescue and Redemption, by Jim Gorant (Gotham), is a truly inspiring book that tells what happened to the dogs rescued from NFL star Michael Vick's appalling dog-fighting operation. Contrary to the experts' expectations, almost of the dogs were saved. Many were rehabilitated and became family pets, and a few even became certified therapy dogs.

Scientific Research

One controversial question about anticruelty laws is whether or not they apply to scientific experiments on animals. Some states (Texas, for example) exempt scientific research specifically.[34] The New York law exempts experiments in labs that have been approved by the state health commissioner; Vermont exempts research conducted by competent researchers "in a humane manner" with a minimum of suffering. In most states, however, scientists are not prosecuted because statutes prohibit only "needless pain or suffering," and pain inflicted in the name of science is not considered "needless."

The most famous case of a scientist prosecuted and convicted for cruelty to animals is that of Dr. Edward Taub, who in 1981 was in charge of animal research at the Institute for Behavioral Research in Silver Spring, Maryland. His experiments involved severing nerves in monkeys' arms and legs and then trying to teach the animals to use the limbs again. His federally funded laboratory was regularly inspected by the U.S.

Department of Agriculture, which has responsibility for laboratory animals' welfare; the USDA found no violations.[35]

An employee, however, complained about conditions, and county police took 11 monkeys from the lab and arrested Taub. Taub appealed his conviction to the Maryland Supreme Court, which reversed it. The court ruled that it didn't think the state legislature had intended the anticruelty statute to apply to federal research programs.[36] The legislature eventually amended the law to say that research was not subject to anticruelty laws, if it were conducted in accordance with protocols approved by an animal care and use committee, as required by the federal Animal Welfare Act or Health Research Extension Act.[37]

The emotional issue of whether or not scientific research should be exempt from anticruelty laws is being debated all over the country. Those who want to protect researchers emphasize the importance of animal research in discovering cures or treatment for human illnesses: cancer, AIDS, and all the other killers. Those who want to protect animals stress the thoughtless overuse of animals, the indifference to suffering that could often be avoided, and the existence of alternative research methods.

There certainly seems no good reason for giving science a blanket exemption from anticruelty laws. It encourages callous disregard for animals and closes off legitimate debate on what, as a society, we want to allow in the name of science. Merely labeling an activity "science" should not put it beyond scrutiny.

Even under existing laws, it seems obvious that much of the cruelty inflicted on animals in the name of research or education is "needless"— and thus illegal. Much of the experimentation done on animals for scientific "education" is especially egregious. Students perform experiments that countless others before them have done, learning little except, perhaps, disregard for animal life.

Making scientists justify their actions or face prosecution under anticruelty statutes might mean some abuses would be stopped. But criminal prosecutions are hit-and-miss. They depend on local politics, citizen involvement, government budgets, and a host of other unpredictable factors.

A much better approach would be to evaluate and approve or disapprove research programs involving animals before they begin. Such a system would provide both much more consistent protection of animals and needed guidelines for researchers and educators. Current federal law (the Laboratory Animal Welfare Act and the Improved Standards for Laboratory Animals Act)[38] doesn't address actual research methods; it covers only laboratory conditions such as food and housing, and enforcement of even those minimal standards is spotty. The analysis should be based on such factors as importance of the research, number of animals, availability of alternatives, and the methods to be used.

Killing Animals for Religion or Food

Our society lives easily with the large-scale slaughter of animals—after all, it's hard to go far in a typical town without passing a McDonald's. But people become squeamish when the killing is done by people with less mainstream methods and customs.

Some residents of Hialeah, Florida, developed a sudden concern about cruelty to animals when they got wind that a Santeria church planned to open in their town. The Santeria religion, a conflation of Catholicism and African religion, was developed in the 19th century by people from eastern Africa who were taken to Cuba and enslaved. Animal sacrifice is central to the practice of Santeria. Animals, including chickens, pigeons, doves, ducks, guinea pigs, goats, sheep, and turtles, are killed by cutting their carotid arteries. The animals are then cooked and eaten.

The Hialeah city council, at an emergency public session, passed several ordinances aimed at stopping church members' ritual sacrifice of animals. Among other things, the laws defined sacrifice as an "unnecessary killing," which made it fall under the state's anticruelty law. The laws exempted slaughtering animals "specifically raised for food purposes." Violators of the ordinances could be fined and put in jail for up to 60 days.

Freedom of religion is, of course, guaranteed by the U.S. Constitution. But when church members took the city to court, a federal trial court upheld the ordinances, ruling that the city had shown "compelling interests" that justified the restriction on religion. The United States Supreme Court reversed and threw out the ordinances. It was obvious, the court concluded, that suppressing Santeria worship—not promoting health and safety—was the prime object of the ordinances. Further, it ruled, the reasons the city gave to justify the burden on religion were not compelling, and even if they were, the ordinances could be tailored much more narrowly and still address these alleged concerns.[39]

Anticruelty laws have also been invoked against immigrants whose customs offend their neighbors. For example, two Cambodian refugees were charged with violating California's anticruelty law because they killed a six-month-old puppy for food. A judge dismissed the charges, ruling that to do otherwise "would subject every slaughterhouse employee or farmer to prosecution." Under California law, evidence that the dog was "maimed, wounded, tortured, mutilated or tormented" beyond what was necessary to use it for food was necessary for a conviction.[40] The California legislature responded to this case by passing a law making it a crime to kill an animal "traditionally or commonly kept as a pet" for food.[41]

Endnotes

1 *No Bad Dogs*, by Barbara Woodhouse (Summit Books, 1982).

2 Randall Lockwood, *Animal Cruelty Prosecution* (American Prosecutors Research Institute 2006).

3 See, for example, *Carrera v. Bertaini*, 63 Cal. App. 3d 721, 134 Cal. Rptr. 14 (1976); Cal. Penal Code § 597.1 (procedure for hearing after animal is seized).

4 For example, *Commonwealth v. Crawford*, 24 A.3d 396 (Pa. Super. 2011); *State v. Albee*, 118 Or. App. 212, 847 P.2d 858 (1993) (arrests made before cockfight began under law that prohibits presence at "preparations" to a cockfight); *State v. Hafle*, 52 Ohio App. 2d 9, 367 N.E.2d 1226 (1977); *People v. Allen*, 657 P.2d 447 (Colo. 1983).

5 Tex. Penal Code Ann. § 42.092.

6 Colo. Rev. Stat. § 18-9-202.

7 Cal. Health & Safety Code § 122335.

8 Cal. Penal Code § 597t.

9 *Jordan v. United States*, 269 A.2d 848 (D.C. App. 1970).

10 *People v. Walsh*, 19 Misc. 3d 1105(A) (N.Y. Crim. 2008).

11 *State v. Moriarty*, 2008 WL 2058681 (Ohio App. 2008).

12 *People v. O'Rourke*, 369 N.Y.S.2d 335 (Crim. Ct. 1975).

13 *State v. Prociv*, 417 N.W.2d 840 (N.D. 1988).

14 Cal. Penal Code § 597(a).

15 For example, Cal. Penal Code § 597 (amended in 1987).

16 *National Law Journal,* Aug. 15, 1988.

17 N.Y. Agric. & Mkts. Law § 355.

18 Colo. Rev. Stat. § 18-9-202(b).

19 *Lopez v. State,* 720 S.W.2d 201 (Tex. App. 1986).

20 See, for example, *Commonwealth v. Fabian,* 14 Pa. D. & C. 3d 551 (1980).

21 Mass. Gen. Laws Ann., ch. 272, § 80B.

22 N.Y. Agric. & Mkts. Law § 365; Conn. Gen. Stat. § 22-366; N.H. Rev. Stat. Ann. § 466:40; 18 Pa. Cons. Stat. § 5511(h).

23 Cal. Penal Code § 597L.

24 *The HSUS Ranks State Puppy Mill Laws,* press release, March 12, 2012, at www.humanesociety.org.

25 *State v. Siliski,* 283 S.W. 3d 338 (Tenn. Crim. App. 2007).

26 *People v. Wicker,* 78 Misc. 2d 811, 357 N.Y.S.2d 587 (Town Ct. 1974).

27 *Laner v. State,* 381 P.2d 905 (Okla. 1963).

28 7 U.S.C. § 2156; 18 U.S.C.A. § 49.

29 Quoted in "The Pit Bull: Friend and Killer," by E.M. Swift, *Sports Illustrated*, July 27, 1987.

30 N.Y. Agric. & Mkts. Law § 351.

31 *State v. Digilormo,* 505 So. 2d 1154 (La. App. 1987).

32 *United States v. Hackman*, 630 F.3d 1078 (8th Cir. 2011).

33 Ariz. Rev. Stat. Ann. § 32-2239; Cal. Bus. & Prof. Code § 4830.5.

34 Tex. Penal Code § 42.09 exempts persons "engaged in bona fide experimentation for scientific research."

35 *"Taub v. State:* Are State Anticruelty Statutes Sleeping Giants?" 2 Pace Envt'l L. Rev. 255 (1985).

36 *Taub v. State,* 296 Md. 439, 463 A.2d 819 (1983).

37 Md. Code [Crim. Law] § 10-603.

38 7 U.S.C. §§ 2131 and following; §§ 2143 and following.

39 *Church of the Lukumi Babalu Aye, Inc. v. City of Hialeah*, 508 U.S. 520 (1993).

40 "Refugees Who Killed, Ate Puppy Not Guilty of Animal Cruelty," *San Francisco Recorder*, Mar. 16, 1989.

41 Cal. Penal Code § 598b.

State Dog-Bite Statutes

State	Citation
Alabama	Ala. Code § 3-6-1
Arizona	Ariz. Rev. Stat. §§ 11-1020, 1025
California	Cal. Civ. Code § 3342
Colorado	Col. Rev. Stat. Ann. § 13-21-124
Connecticut	Conn. Gen. Stat. Ann. § 22-357
Delaware	Del. Code Ann., tit. 7, § 1711
District of Columbia	D.C. Code Ann. § 8-1812
Florida	Fla. Stat. Ann. §§ 767.01, 767.04
Georgia	Ga. Code Ann. § 51-2-7
Hawaii	Haw. Rev. Stat. §§ 663-9, 663-9.1
Illinois	510 Ill. Comp. Stat., § 5/16
Indiana	Ind. Code § 15-5-12-1
Iowa	Iowa Code Ann. § 351.28
Kentucky	Ky. Rev. Stat. § 258.235
Louisiana	La. Civ. Code, art. 2321
Maine	Me. Rev. Stat. Ann., tit. 7, § 3961
Massachusetts	Mass. Gen. Laws Ann., ch. 140, § 155
Michigan	Mich. Comp. Laws Ann. § 287.351
Minnesota	Minn. Stat. Ann. § 347.22

State	Citation
Missouri	Mo. Rev. Stat. § 273.036
Montana	Mont. Code Ann. § 27-1-715
Nebraska	Neb. Rev. Stat. § 54-601
New Hampshire	N.H. Rev. Stat. Ann. § 466:19
New Jersey	N.J. Stat. Ann. § 4:19-16
Ohio	Ohio Rev. Code Ann. § 955.28
Oklahoma	Okla. Stat. Ann., tit. 4, § 42.1
Pennsylvania	3 Pa. Cons. Stat. § 459-502(b)
Rhode Island	R.I. Gen. Laws § 4-13-16
South Carolina	S.C. Code Ann. § 47-3-110
Utah	Utah Code Ann. § 18-1-1
Washington	Wash. Rev. Code Ann. § 16.08.040
West Virginia	W.Va. Code § 19-20-13
Wisconsin	Wis. Stat. Ann. § 174.02

Index

 **NOLO** *Keep Up to Date*

 Go to Nolo.com/newsletters to sign up for free newsletters and discounts on Nolo products.

- **Nolo's Special Offer.** A monthly newsletter with the biggest Nolo discounts around.

- **Landlord's Quarterly.** Deals and free tips for landlords and property managers.

 Don't forget to check for updates. Find this book at **Nolo.com** and click "Legal Updates."

Let Us Hear From You

 Register your Nolo product and give us your feedback at Nolo.com/customer-support/ productregistration.

- Once you've registered, you qualify for technical support if you have any trouble with a download (though most folks don't).

- We'll send you a coupon for 15% off your next Nolo.com order!

DOG7

⚖ NOLO *Online Legal Forms*

Nolo offers a large library of legal solutions and forms, created by Nolo's in-house legal staff. These reliable documents can be prepared in minutes.

Create a Document

- **Incorporation.** Incorporate your business in any state.
- **LLC Formations.** Gain asset protection and pass-through tax status in any state.
- **Wills.** Nolo has helped people make over 2 million wills. Is it time to make or revise yours?
- **Living Trust (avoid probate).** Plan now to save your family the cost, delays, and hassle of probate.
- **Trademark.** Protect the name of your business or product.
- **Provisional Patent.** Preserve your rights under patent law and claim "patent pending" status.

Download a Legal Form

Nolo.com has hundreds of top quality legal forms available for download—bills of sale, promissory notes, nondisclosure agreements, LLC operating agreements, corporate minutes, commercial lease and sublease, motor vehicle bill of sale, consignment agreements and many more.

Review Your Documents

Many lawyers in Nolo's consumer-friendly lawyer directory will review Nolo documents for a very reasonable fee. Check their detailed profiles at **Nolo.com/lawyers**.

Nolo's Bestselling Books

Neighbor Law
Fences, Trees,
Boundaries & Noise
$29.99

**Every Tenant's
Legal Guide**
$34.99

Plan Your Estate
$34.99

**Estate Planning
Basics**
$24.99

**Nolo's Encyclopedia
of Everyday Law**
$29.99

*Every Nolo title is available in print
and for download at Nolo.com.*

 **Lawyer Directory**

Find an Attorney

Qualified lawyers • In-depth profiles

When you want help with a serious legal problem, you don't want just any lawyer—you want an expert in the field who can give you and your family up-to-the-minute advice. You need a lawyer who has the experience and knowledge to answer your questions about personal injury, wills, family law, child custody, drafting a patent application or any other specialized legal area you are concerned with.

Nolo's Lawyer Directory is unique because it provides an extensive profile of every lawyer. You'll learn about not only each lawyer's education, professional history, legal specialties, credentials and fees, but also about their philosophy of practicing law and how they like to work with clients.

www.nolo.com